The Dictionary of Standard C

REX JAESCHKE

FOR REFERENCE
Do Not Take From This Room

Many entries refer directly to other entries. For example, the above entry refers to "assignment," "associativity," "modifiable lvalue," "operator," and "pointer," among others. I deliberately chose *not* to set such references in some special font because there are so many of them; many entries would become unreadable due to the continual font changes that would be needed. The rule, then, is that every term used in an entry is either specific to C and is described in its own entry, or it is a general computing term that the reader should already know. Related entries that are *not* otherwise referenced in an entry are explicitly identified at the end of that entry, as in "*See also* assignment operator, compound."

A number of entries, as well as names in various tables, have superscripts as in `CHAR_MAX`^{C89}, `and`^{C95}, and `restrict`^{C99}. Such a superscript indicates that entry or name was introduced in the C standard or amendment produced in the corresponding year. For more information on these versions, see the entry of the same name. All entries or names not having such a superscript are deemed to have been in general use in C implementations prior to the first C standard in 1989.

Many entries describe the library functions. Ordinarily, the entry name for a library function is an identifier, such as `isupper` or `printf`. As numerous floating-point functions come in groups of three, as in `acos`, `acosf`, and `acosl`, supporting `double`, `float`, and `long double` precisions, respectively, they are described in one entry using the following format:

---

acos[**f**|**l**] A function that computes the arc cosine of its argument `x` and returns a value in the range $[0, \pi]$ radians.

```
#include <math.h>
double acos(double x);
float acosf(float x);
long double acosl(long double x);
```

If the argument is not in the range $[-1, +1]$, a domain error occurs.

The `float` and `long double` versions were an invention of C89, where they were optional; however, in C99, they are required.

Each library entry begins with a short description of that function's purpose. This is followed by the name of the header(s) to be used to gain proper access to that function, and a prototype for that function. That is followed by the details of using that function and any related information.

C99 introduced the type qualifier keyword **`restrict`** and allowed it to be used in function prototypes. It was also added to numerous existing standard library functions, for example,

---

`fgets` A function ...

```
#include <stdio.h>
char *fgets(char * restrict s, int n,
    FILE * restrict stream);
```

...

Of course, if you are using a pre-C99 implementation, this keyword will not be supported, nor will it be present in any library function declarations.

Operators, Punctuators, etc.

Token	*Dictionary Entry*
!	logical negation operator
!=	inequality operator
()	cast operator
	declarator, punctuation in
	function call operator
	parentheses punctuator
*	declarator, punctuation in
	indirection operator
	multiplication operator
*=	multiplication assignment operator
+	addition operator
	unary plus operator
++	increment operator
+=	addition assignment operator
,	comma operator
	comma punctuator
-	subtraction operator
	unary minus operator
--	decrement operator
-=	subtraction assignment operator
->	arrow operator
.	dot operator
	radix point
...	ellipsis punctuator
/	division operator
/* */	comment
//	comment
/=	division assignment operator
:	colon
:>	digraph
;	semicolon punctuator
<	less-than operator
<%	digraph
<:	digraph
<<	left-shift operator
<<=	left-shift assignment operator
<=	less-than-or-equal-to operator
=	assignment operator, simple
	equals punctuator
==	equality operator
>	greater-than operator
>=	greater-than-or-equal-to operator
>>	right-shift operator

Operators, Punctuators, etc., (cont'd)

<table>
<tr><th>Token</th><th>Dictionary Entry</th></tr>
<tr><td>>>=</td><td>right-shift assignment operator</td></tr>
<tr><td>?:</td><td>conditional operator</td></tr>
<tr><td>??x</td><td>trigraph</td></tr>
<tr><td>[ ]</td><td>declarator, punctuation in</td></tr>
<tr><td></td><td>subscript operator</td></tr>
<tr><td>#</td><td>null preprocessing directive</td></tr>
<tr><td></td><td>stringize operator</td></tr>
<tr><td>##</td><td>token pasting operator</td></tr>
<tr><td>%</td><td>conversion specifier</td></tr>
<tr><td></td><td>remainder operator</td></tr>
<tr><td>%:</td><td>digraph</td></tr>
<tr><td>%:%:</td><td>digraph</td></tr>
<tr><td>%></td><td>digraph</td></tr>
<tr><td>%=</td><td>remainder assignment operator</td></tr>
<tr><td>&</td><td>address-of operator</td></tr>
<tr><td></td><td>AND operator, bitwise</td></tr>
<tr><td>&&</td><td>AND operator, logical</td></tr>
<tr><td>&=</td><td>AND assignment operator, bitwise</td></tr>
<tr><td>\</td><td>backslash</td></tr>
<tr><td>\"</td><td>double quote escape sequence</td></tr>
<tr><td>\'</td><td>single quote escape sequence</td></tr>
<tr><td>\0</td><td>null character</td></tr>
<tr><td>\?</td><td>question mark escape sequence</td></tr>
<tr><td>\\</td><td>backslash escape sequence</td></tr>
<tr><td>\a</td><td>alert escape sequence</td></tr>
<tr><td>\b</td><td>backspace escape sequence</td></tr>
<tr><td>\ddd</td><td>octal escape sequence</td></tr>
<tr><td>\f</td><td>form-feed escape sequence</td></tr>
<tr><td>\n</td><td>new-line escape sequence</td></tr>
<tr><td>\r</td><td>carriage-return escape sequence</td></tr>
<tr><td>\t</td><td>horizontal-tab escape sequence</td></tr>
<tr><td>\U</td><td>universal character name</td></tr>
<tr><td>\u</td><td>universal character name</td></tr>
<tr><td>\v</td><td>vertical-tab escape sequence</td></tr>
<tr><td>\xhh</td><td>hexadecimal escape sequence</td></tr>
<tr><td>^</td><td>OR operator, bitwise exclusive</td></tr>
<tr><td>^=</td><td>OR assignment operator, bitwise exclusive</td></tr>
<tr><td>_</td><td>underscore</td></tr>
<tr><td>{}</td><td>braces</td></tr>
<tr><td>|</td><td>OR operator, bitwise inclusive</td></tr>
<tr><td>|=</td><td>OR assignment operator, bitwise inclusive</td></tr>
<tr><td>||</td><td>OR operator, logical</td></tr>
<tr><td>~</td><td>complement operator</td></tr>
<tr><td>op=</td><td>assignment operator, compound</td></tr>
</table>

A

`abort` A function that causes the program to terminate abnormally unless the signal `SIGABRT` is being caught and the signal handler does not return. It does not return to its caller.

```
#include <stdlib.h>
void abort(void);
```

It is implementation defined as to whether or not output streams are flushed, open streams are closed, or temporary files are removed. The exit code of the program is some implementation-defined value that represents failure. A program abort also can be generated by a call to `raise` using the argument `SIGABRT`. *See also* `assert`; `exit`.

`abs` A function that computes the absolute value of its argument `j`.

```
#include <stdlib.h>
int abs(int j);
```

The behavior is undefined if the result cannot be represented (such as `abs(x)` on a two's-complement 16-bit machine, where `x` has the value -32,768).

absolute-value functions A family of functions, each member of which computes the absolute value of its argument. The floating-point members (`fabs`, `fabsf`, and `fabsl`) are declared in math.h, the integer members (`abs`, `labs`, and `llabs`) are declared in stdlib.h, and the complex members (`cabs`, `cabsf`, and `cabsl`) are declared in complex.h.

abstract machine A theoretical system on which a language standard is modeled. In the abstract machine, optimization (and hence, the semantics of `volatile`) is irrelevant. However, this is not so in the real world, and things such as sequence points are needed so optimizers know how much flexibility they have.

access To read or modify the value of an object at run time.

`acos[f|l]` A function that computes the arc cosine of its argument `x` and returns a value in the range $[0, \pi]$ radians.

```
#include <math.h>
double acos(double x);
float acosf(float x);
long double acosl(long double x);
```

If the argument is not in the range $[-1, +1]$, a domain error occurs.

The `float` and `long double` versions were an invention of C89, where they were optional; however, in C99, they are required.

`acosh[f|l]`^C99 A function that computes the (nonnegative) arc hyperbolic cosine of its argument `x` and returns a value in the range $[0, +\infty]$.

```
#include <math.h>
double acosh(double x);
float acoshf(float x);
long double acoshl(long double x);
```

If the argument is less than 1, a domain error occurs.

active position The position on a display device at which the next character output by `fputc` will appear. In most Western cultures, screen output is produced from left to right and top to bottom. However, in other environments this is not the case. The direction used for such writing is locale specific.

addition assignment operator A binary operator, `+=`, that permits addition and assignment to be combined such that *exp1* `+=` *exp2* is equivalent to *exp1* `=` *exp1* `+` *exp2* except that in the former, *exp1* is only evaluated once. The order of evaluation of the operands is unspecified. Both operands must either have arithmetic type, or the right may have integer type if the left is a pointer to an object. The left operand must be a modifiable lvalue. The type of the result is the type of *exp1*. This operator associates right to left. *See also* assignment operator, compound.

addition operator A binary operator, `+`, that causes the values of its operands to be added together. The order of evaluation of the two operands is unspecified. Both operands must either have arithmetic type, or one may have integer type if the other is a pointer to an object. The usual arithmetic conversions are performed on the operands. This operator associates left to right.

address The memory location at which an object or function resides. Most machines are either byte- or word-addressable. That is, the level of granularity for unique addresses is a byte or word, respectively. An object or function can (and often does) occupy more than one memory location, in which case, the address of that object or function is the address of its beginning. In C, an expression designating an address is also called a pointer expression or, more simply, a pointer. *See also* address-of operator.

address-of operator A unary operator, `&`, that causes the address of its operand to be taken. The operand must be either a function designator or an lvalue that designates an object (other than a bit-field or object declared with storage class `register`). This operator associates right to left. The result has type "pointer to the type of the operand." Note that if `ary` designates an array, `&ary` is a pointer to the whole array, which is quite different from `&ary[0]`, a pointer to the first element in the array.

aggregate An array or structure object. Typically, an aggregate contains two or more elements. However, C does permit an array of one element and a structure with only one member. Nonaggregate object types are scalars and unions.

alert escape sequence[C89] An escape sequence, `\a`, which indicates an alert (such as a terminal bell).

aliasing A method of giving something an alternate name. C permits an infinite number of aliases for an object or function by using pointers. You can access an object or function either by its name or via any one of the pointers that points directly or indirectly to it. Historically, there has been no way to promise a function that has arrays passed to it as arguments, that those arguments don't overlap, or that in general two pointers point to distinct objects. As such, it was difficult to optimize certain code and impossible to vectorize or parallelize loops if overlap potentially existed. *See* type, effective.

During the deliberations for C89, the standards committee invented the `noalias` type qualifier to help resolve this long-standing and difficult issue. However, after considerable and heated debate, that keyword was removed from the working draft. After further research by the NCEG, C99 added the qualifier `restrict` to help address this issue.

alignment The process of placing objects of certain types in memory such that their storage begins on specific address boundaries. Some machines require objects to be aligned and, while other machines can manipulate objects on any boundary, it is more efficient if words are aligned on word boundaries, longwords on longword boundaries, and so on. Structures may contain holes between members (or after the last member) so padding can be provided by the compiler to honor alignment requirements. Alignment might either be forced on you by your compiler or it might be user selectable via a compiler option. Some compilers allow alignment to be specified using a pragma (called `pack`, for example).

Amendment 1[C95] *See* C95.

`and`[C95] A macro, defined in iso646.h, that expands to the token `&&`. It allows programmers using source character sets (such as ISO 646) that are missing certain characters necessary for writing C programs to enter those characters using identifiers instead. Note that in C++, this name is a keyword.

AND **assignment operator, bitwise** A binary operator, `&=`, that permits bitwise AND and assignment to be combined such that *exp1* `&=` *exp2* is equivalent to *exp1* `=` *exp1* `&` *exp2* except that in the former, *exp1* is evaluated only once. Both operands must have integer type. The order of evaluation of the operands is unspecified. The left operand must be a modifiable lvalue. The type of the result is the type of *exp1*. This operator associates right to left. *See also* assignment operator, compound.

`and_eq`[C95] A macro, defined in iso646.h, that expands to the token `&=`. It allows programmers using source character sets (such as ISO 646) that are missing certain characters necessary for writing C programs to enter those characters using identifiers instead. Note that in C++, this name is a keyword.

AND **operator, bitwise** A binary operator, `&`, that performs a bitwise AND of its operands. Both operands must have integer type. The order of evaluation of the operands is unspecified. The usual arithmetic conversions are performed on the operands. This operator associates left to right.

AND **operator, logical** A binary operator, `&&`, that performs a logical AND of its operands. Both operands must have scalar type. The result has type `int` and value 0 (if false) or 1 (if true). There is a sequence point after the evaluation of the left operand. If the left operand tests false, the right operand is not evaluated. This operator associates left to right.

ANSI The acronym for the American National Standards Institute, the U.S. national standards body responsible for most programming language standards.

ANSI C The formal definition of the C language, preprocessor, and run-time library as accepted by the American National Standards Institute (ANSI). The first version is known as C89, was produced by committee X3J11, and was officially called ANSI X3.159-1989. The second version (which is technically identical to the first) is known as C90 and was produced by the ISO C committee SC 22/WG14 and then adopted by ANSI as ANSI/ISO 9899-1990. Later, an amendment, known as C95, was published. The third version, C99, was produced by committees SC 22/WG14 and NCITS/J11; its formal designation is ANSI/ISO 9899-1999. Synonymous with Standard C.

ANSI/IEEE 754 *See* IEEE Floating-Point Arithmetic Standards.

ANSI/IEEE 854 *See* IEEE Floating-Point Arithmetic Standards.

`argc` The first argument passed to `main`. This `int` argument contains the number of arguments found on the command line when the program was invoked. Typically its value is at least one, although the actual name used on the command line to invoke the program itself might not be preserved by the task loader. Note that while the name **argc** is widely used for this argument, the name **argc** is local to that function and, in fact, can be replaced by any unreserved identifier the programmer chooses. *See also* **argv**; **envp**.

argument *See* argument, actual; argument, formal.

argument, actual The expression actually passed in a call to a function, or the token sequence actually passed in a call to a function-like macro. For example, in `f(a, b + c)`, `a` and `b + c` are the two actual arguments passed to `f`. An actual argument may contain commas, provided they are enclosed in parentheses. *See also* argument, formal.

argument, command-line One of a (possible) set of tokens specified on the command line when a program is invoked. By definition, each command-line argument is separated by horizontal white space. The number and value of command-line arguments are accessed via **argc** and **argv**, respectively.

argument, formal The object declared in a function definition that takes on a value when that function is called, or an identifier in the comma-separated list in a function-like macro definition. For example, in

```
void f(int a1, long a2) { /* ... */ }

#define Add(a, b) (a + b)
```

`a1` and `a2` are the formal arguments expected by the function `f`, and `a` and `b` are the formal arguments expected by the macro `Add`. Synonymous with parameter. *See also* argument, actual.

argument list A comma-separated list of actual or formal arguments.

argument list, variable An argument list containing at least one argument and having a trailing ellipsis. The only Standard C functions having variable argument lists are the `printf`/`wprintf` and `scanf`/`wscanf` families. *See also* stdarg.h for details of defining a function that expects a variable argument list. Prior to C99, macros could not be defined or called with variable argument lists; now they can by using `__VA_ARGS__`.

argument promotion, default *See* conversion, function arguments.

argv The second argument passed to **main**. **argv** is an array of pointers to **char**, each of which points to a string specified as a command-line argument. The number of elements in the array is **argc**+1 where **argv[argc]** is `NULL`. If the program's name is not available, **argv[0]** points to a null character. Note that different loaders/compilers may treat quoted arguments and arguments with embedded white space differently. Also, while the name **argv** is widely used for the second argument to **main**, the name **argv** is local to that function and, in fact, can be replaced by any unreserved identifier the programmer chooses. *See also* **argc**; **envp**.

arithmetic conversions, usual *See* conversion, usual arithmetic.

arithmetic type Any one of the integer or floating types.

array An aggregate type consisting of one or more elements, each of which has exactly the same attributes and occupies consecutively higher memory locations. The number of dimensions in an array is not restricted by C except that an implementation is required to support at least 12. The theoretical maximum value for the size of any dimension of an array is the maximum value of the type **size_t**. Elements in each dimension begin at subscript zero and each dimension is specified separately in both the array declaration and in subscript expressions. *See* array, variable-length.

array, storage order Row-major order. That is, arrays are stored such that the right-most subscript varies fastest.

array, variable-length[C99] An array in which the size of any dimension can be a nonconstant integer expression, provided that the array is declared with block scope and automatic storage duration, or prototype scope. The following example includes some variable-length arrays (VLAs):

```
void f(int m, int C[m][m])
{
        int v1[m];
        double v2[6][m];
        long int v3[m][4][n];
        typedef int VLA[m][m];
        /* ... */
}
```

In a function declarator that is not also the definition of that function, parameters may use the notation `[*]` to indicate variable-length array types; for example,

```
double maximum(int n, int m, double a[*][*]);
```

array, zero-sized An array containing no elements. Prior to C89, quite a few implementations allowed arrays with zero elements. Such an array was typically used as the last member of a structure. Support for this was added in C99; it is known as a flexible array member.

Standard C allows an implementation to accept an allocation request for zero bytes via `calloc` and `malloc`, thereby allowing the creation of an array with zero elements.

arrow operator A binary operator, `->`, that is used to select the right operand from the structure or union pointed to by the left operand. The order of evaluation of the operands is unspecified. The type of the left operand must be pointer to structure or union and the right operand must be the name of a member in that structure or union. This operator always produces an lvalue. A `->` expression can always be rewritten using the dot operator. For example, `p->m` is equivalent to `(*p).m`. The type of the result is the type of the named member. This operator associates left to right.

"as if" rule A characteristic of C set up in the C standard that permits implementations to take full advantage of their environment without being unduly forced to perform inefficient operations. For example, the traditional requirement that all `char` arithmetic be done in `int` precision, is no longer true from a practical viewpoint. Now, an implementation is permitted to perform optimizations and operations in any way it sees fit, provided it arrives at the same result *as if* it had followed the strict rules of the abstract machine for which the standard was defined. That is, if there is no discernable difference between doing an optimization and not doing it, the optimization is permitted.

ASCII An acronym for the American Standard Code for Information Interchange. This 7-bit code can represent 128 different characters and is in common use. Standard C is not character-set specific. *See also* EBCDIC; `iscntrl`; Unicode.

`asctime` A function that converts the broken-down time stored in the structure pointed to by `timeptr` into a string.

```
#include <time.h>
char *asctime(const struct tm *timeptr);
```

The pointer returned points to a string containing the time in the form `Day Mon dd hh:mm:ss yyyy\n\0`. This function is not locale-specific. For locale-specific times use `strftime`. (The `asc` prefix implies ASCII and is purely historic—Standard C is not character-set specific.)

`asin[f|l]` A function that computes the arc sine of its argument `x` and returns a value in the range $[-\pi/2, +\pi/2]$ radians.

```
#include <math.h>
double asin(double x);
float asinf(float x);
long double asinl(long double x);
```

If the argument is not in the range $[-1, +1]$, a domain error occurs.

The `float` and `long double` versions were an invention of C89, where they were optional; however, in C99, they are required.

asinh[f|l][C99] A function that computes the arc hyperbolic sine of its argument `x`.

```
#include <math.h>
double asinh(double x);
float asinhf(float x);
long double asinhl(long double x);
```

asm Numerous compilers permit assembler instructions to be inserted inline in C source. They typically do this using either a keyword such as **asm** or a preprocessor directive such as **#asm** possibly with a matching **#endasm**. This is not part of Standard C.

asm is also a C++ keyword. If you think you might wish to move C code to a C++ environment in the future, you should refrain from using **asm** as an identifier in new C code you write.

assert A macro, defined in assert.h, that causes a diagnostic message to be written to `stderr` and then `abort` to be called, provided the macro argument evaluates to false and the macro `NDEBUG` is not currently defined, for example,

```
#include <assert.h>
void assert(type exp);
```

Prior to C99, *type* was required to be `int`; however, C99 allows it to be any scalar type.

If the user has defined `NDEBUG` before assert.h is included, **assert** is defined as a `void` expression and all calls to **assert** become vacuous.

The format of the message output is implementation defined. However, it must contain the macro argument in its text form, with the source filename and line number of the invocation of the failing **assert**, and, in C99, the name of the enclosing function. *See also* `__FILE__`; `__func__`; `__LINE__`.

The behavior is undefined if you **#undef assert** to try to get a function version.

assert.h A header that provides a crude debugging traceback facility. It is the only standard header designed to be included multiple times such that it can behave differently each time it is included. *See also* `assert`.

assert.h contains a definition for the following identifier:

`assert` Put diagnostic assertions in code

assignment The operation of assigning the value of an expression to the memory location designated by another expression (which is typically a variable name or an expression of the form `a[i]`, `*ptr`, `p->m`, or `s.m`). The expression designating the destination must be a modifiable lvalue. Because assignment is implemented in C using operators, assignment expressions have type and value and therefore can be embedded in larger expressions. *See also* assignment operator, compound; assignment operator, simple.

assignment operator, compound The general form of a binary compound assignment operator. `x` *op*`=` `y` is equivalent to `x = x` *op* `y` except that in the former, `x` is only evaluated once. The complete set of compound assignment operators is: `+=`, `-=`, `*=`, `/=`, `%=`, `>>=`, `<<=`, `&=`, `^=`, and `|=`. *See also* assignment operator, compound, archaic; assignment operator, simple.

assignment operator, compound, archaic An archaic form (`=`*op*) for a binary compound assignment operator was long ago (pre-C89) replaced by *op*`=` and is not part of Standard C.

assignment operator, simple A binary operator, `=`, that causes the value of the right operand to be stored in the location designated by the left operand. The order of evaluation of the two operands is unspecified. This operator associates right to left. The left operand must be a modifiable lvalue. *See also* assignment operator, compound. Note that this operator *must not* be confused with the equality operator `==`. The two are easily confused and can be interchanged syntactically; however, their semantics are quite different. For example, in the following:

```
if (a = b) /* ... */
```

the value of `b` is assigned to `a`, and the value of `a` is tested for truth. In the following:

```
if (a == b) /* ... */
```

the values of `a` and `b` are compared for equality.

associativity The property that determines the relative precedence of operators when the precedence table shows them as otherwise having the same precedence. Associativity is either left to right or right to left, as the expression is written. For example, `a/b/c` is equivalent to `(a/b)/c` because the associativity of the division operator is left to right. On the other hand, `!++i` is equivalent to `(!(++i))` because these unary operators associate right to left.

`atan`[`f`|`l`] A function that computes the arc tangent of its argument `x`.

```
#include <math.h>
double atan(double x);
float atanf(float x);
long double atanl(long double x);
```

It returns a value in the range $[-\pi/2, +\pi/2]$ radians.

The `float` and `long double` versions were an invention of C89, where they were optional; however, in C99, they are required.

`atan2`[`f`|`l`] A function that computes the arc tangent of `y/x` and returns a value in the range $[-\pi, +\pi]$ radians.

```
#include <math.h>
double atan2(double y, double x);
float atan2f(float y, float x);
long double atan2l(long double y, long double x);
```

If both arguments are 0 a domain error may occur. The sign of both arguments is used to determine the quadrant of the returned value.

The `float` and `long double` versions were an invention of C89, where they were optional; however, in C99, they are required.

`atanh`[`f`|`l`][C99] A function that computes the arc hyperbolic tangent of its argument `x`.

```
#include <math.h>
double atanh(double x);
float atanhf(float x);
long double atanhl(long double x);
```

An argument outside the interval $[-1, +1]$ causes a domain error. An argument of ± 1 might cause a range error.

`atexit`[C89] A function that permits a function to be registered such that it is called automatically by the implementation during normal program termination.

```
#include <stdlib.h>
int atexit(void (*func)(void));
```

The function being registered must take no arguments and have no return value. Standard C requires that at least 32 functions can be registered. (However, to get around any limitations in this regard, you can always register just one function and have it call the others directly. This way, the other functions can also have argument lists and return values.) The same function can be registered more than once. If the registration fails, a nonzero value is returned; otherwise, zero is returned. *See also* `exit`; `_Exit`.

`atof` A function that converts the leading part of the string pointed to by `nptr`, to a `double` value.

```
#include <stdlib.h>
double atof(const char *nptr);
```

A call to `atof` is identical to

```
strtod(nptr, (char **)NULL)
```

except that `strtod` can handle errors. Note that the format of a valid floating-point value on input is locale specific. `strtod` is preferred over `atof` because the former provides more control over the conversion and error detection and handling.

`atoi` A function that converts the leading part of the string pointed to by `nptr` to an `int` value.

```
#include <stdlib.h>
int atoi(const char *nptr);
```

A call to `atoi` is identical to

```
(int) strtol(nptr, (char **)NULL, 10)
```

except that `strtol` can handle errors. `strtol` is preferred over `atoi` because the former provides more control over the conversion and error detection and handling.

`atol` A function that converts the leading part of the string pointed to by `nptr` to a `long int` value.

```
#include <stdlib.h>
long int atol(const char *nptr);
```

A call to `atol` is equivalent to

```
strtol(nptr, (char **)NULL, 10)
```

except that `strtol` can handle errors. `strtol` is preferred over `atol` because the former provides more control over the conversion and error detection and handling.

`atoll`^{C99} A function that converts the leading part of the string pointed to by `nptr` to a `long long int` value.

```
#include <stdlib.h>
long long int atoll(const char *nptr);
```

A call to `atoll` is equivalent to

```
strtoll(nptr, (char **)NULL, 10)
```

except that `strtoll` can handle errors. `strtoll` is preferred over `atoll` because the former provides more control over the conversion and error detection and handling.

`auto` A storage class keyword used in the declaration of an object inside a function definition to designate automatic storage duration. If such a declaration contains no storage class keyword, `auto` is assumed. (As such, this keyword is rarely used and is *never* needed.) Formal parameters in a function definition behave as if they were declared as `auto` (unless they are explicitly declared with `register`). However, the keyword `auto` cannot actually be present in a formal parameter declaration.

automatic storage duration *See* storage duration, automatic.

B

B A typeless language invented by Ken Thompson at Bell Labs that was an ancestor of C.

backslash The character used to introduce an escape sequence (as in `\f` for form-feed and `\n` for new-line) in string literals and character constants. *See also* backslash escape sequence; backslash/new-line sequence.

backslash escape sequence An escape sequence, `\\`, that allows the backslash character to be represented in a string literal or character constant.

backslash/new-line sequence A source line terminated with a backslash immediately followed by a new-line. This sequence deems the source line to be continued on the following source line. Traditionally, this capability was only permitted in cases where you wanted to continue long macro definitions or long string literals. However, Standard C permits this notion by allowing any token to be broken across multiple source lines. Note there must be no characters between the backslash and new-line, not even white-space or comments. For example, the following is permissible:

```
#  \
def\
in\
e MAX  \
10\
00
in\
t i;
```

and is equivalent to

```
#define MAX  1000
int i;
```

See also phases of translation.

backspace escape sequence An escape sequence, `\b`, which represents the backspace character.

base documents Documents from which substantial parts of C89 were derived. Specifically, the language section was derived from "The C Reference Manual" by Dennis M. Ritchie, a version of which was published as Appendix A of *The C Programming Language*, first edition, by Brian W. Kernighan and Dennis M. Ritchie. *See also* K&R.

The library section was based on the 1984 */usr/group Standard* by the /usr/group Standards Committee, Santa Clara, California (November 14, 1984).

benign redefinition[C89] A method in which an object-like or function-like macro can be redefined multiple times in the same translation, provided the token sequence in each definition exactly matches that in all other definitions. All white-space character sequences are treated as being equivalent. *See also* macro, redefinition of.

binary operator *See* operator, binary.

binary stream *See* stream, binary.

`bitand`[C95] A macro, defined in iso646.h, that expands to the token `&`. It allows programmers using source character sets (such as ISO 646) that are missing certain characters necessary for writing C programs to enter those characters using identifiers instead. Note that in C++, this name is a keyword.

bit-field A structure or union member whose size is specified in bits. Bit-fields may have signed or unsigned `int` types. (C99 also allows bit-fields of type `_Bool` as well as other implementation-defined types.) It is implementation defined as to whether a plain `int` bit-field is signed. You cannot take the address of a bit-field (and therefore can't have an array of bit-fields) or find its size using `sizeof`. Standard C permits a bit-field to be a member of a union. Bit-fields are packed in an implementation-defined size storage unit. The order in which bit-fields are packed, and whether or not they may span storage unit boundaries, is implementation-defined.

bit-field, plain `int` A bit-field specified as having type `int`. When an object has type `int`, it is implied that this means it is signed. However, a bit-field having type `int` without either of the modifiers `signed` or `unsigned`, is an exception; such a bit-field might or might not be signed, as the implementation chooses.

`bitor`[C95] A macro, defined in iso646.h, that expands to the token `|`. It allows programmers using source character sets (such as ISO 646) that are missing certain characters necessary for writing C programs to enter those characters using identifiers instead. Note that in C++, this name is a keyword.

bitwise operators The operators `&` (*See* AND operator, bitwise), `|` (*See* OR operator, bitwise inclusive), `^` (*See* OR operator, bitwise exclusive), `<<` (*See* left-shift operator), `>>` (*See* right-shift operator), and `~` (*See* complement operator).

blank character *See* `isblank`; `iswblank`.

block That part of a function definition delimited by a matching pair of braces (excluding those braces delimiting initializer lists, structure or union layouts, enumeration definitions, or compound literals). A block defines the scope of locally declared identifiers, and it can be used to delimit the scope of a statement such as `if/else`, `while`, and `for`. Blocks may be nested and optionally may contain declarations and/or statements. A block is also referred to as a compound statement. The empty block ({}) is equivalent to the null statement `;` except that the body of a function cannot be a null statement.

`bool`^C99 A macro, defined in stdbool.h, that expands to the keyword `_Bool`. For normal usage of the boolean type, it is strongly recommended you include stdbool.h and use this macro rather than using the `_Bool` keyword directly. In C++, `bool` is a keyword.

`_Bool`^C99 A keyword that provides support for a boolean type. Since it was invented by C99, by which time many programs already contained type synonyms or macros named using some form of the word bool, this keyword was spelled using one of the forms reserved for implementers. Unless you must mix both existing homegrown boolean machinery and this new keyword in the same source file, it is strongly recommended that you include stdbool.h and use its macro `bool` instead.

`__bool_true_false_are_defined`^C99 A macro, defined in stdbool.h, that expands to the integer constant 1. It is intended for supporting backwards compatibility by allowing code to determine whether the standard boolean machinery is supported. *See also* `bool`; `_Bool`; `false`; `true`.

braces The characters { and } that delimit a compound statement (block), initializer list, structure or union layout, enumeration definition, or a compound literal. Braces are always used in matching pairs, except perhaps in comments, string literals, and character constants.

`break` A keyword that causes termination of the innermost current `while`, `for`, or `do` loop, or `switch` statement. It may not be used in any other context. Control is transferred to the statement immediately following that being terminated. It is subtly different from `continue`. `break` only permits breaking out one level. To break out of more levels, use `goto`. It is used as follows:

```
break;
```

broken-down time The components of a calendar time contained in an object of type `struct tm` defined in time.h.

`bsearch` A function that searches an array of **`nmemb`** objects, the initial member of which is pointed to by **`base`**, for a member that matches the object pointed to by **`key`**.

```
#include <stdlib.h>
void *bsearch(const void *key, const void *base,
    size_t nmemb, size_t size,
    int (*compar)(const void *, const void *));
```

`size` specifies the size of each member in the array. The members of the array are assumed to be sorted in an ascending order corresponding to that expected by the comparison function pointed to by **`compar`**. **`compar`** is passed two arguments, the first pointing to the key object, and the second pointing to the array member. Based on the comparison, a negative, zero, or positive value is returned from **`compar`**. If no match is found, `NULL` is returned by **`bsearch`**; otherwise, a pointer to the matching member in the array is returned. If two members compare as equal, it is unspecified as to which member is matched.

`btowc`[C95] A function that indicates whether its argument `c` is a valid single-byte character in the initial shift state, and if so, converts that character to a wide character.

```
#include <stdio.h>
#include <wchar.h>
wint_t btowc(int c);
```

If `c` has the value EOF, or its value cast to type **`unsigned char`** does not constitute a valid single-byte character in the initial shift state, **`WEOF`** is returned; otherwise, the wide character representation of that character is returned.

`BUFSIZ` A macro, defined in stdio.h, that expands to an integer constant expression that is the size of the buffer to be used by **`setbuf`**. Standard C requires it to be at least 256.

C

C standard The formal definition of the C language, preprocessor, and run time library. *See also* ANSI C; ISO C.

"C" locale[C89] The one locale that every conforming implementation must support. The requirements for this locale are documented under each member of the structure `lconv`.

From a practical viewpoint, the `"C"` locale means "run in U.S.–English mode" and reflects exactly the same behavior we have always seen from the library. That is, `printf` uses a period for a decimal point, date and time formats reflect the U.S. style, and `isalpha` returns true only for the uppercase and lowercase Roman letters. By default, a C program runs in the `"C"` locale unless the `setlocale` function has been called (or the implementation's normal operating default locale is other than `"C"`). *See also* locale-specific behavior.

C++ programming language A language that was originally called "C with classes" and was developed by Bjarne Stroustrup at AT&T's Bell Laboratories, the birthplace of C and the UNIX operating system. C++ uses an object-oriented design and programming philosophy. A standard, called ISO/IEC 14892:1998, was published in 1998. Except for a few small areas, Standard C++ is a proper superset of C95; however, C99 contains numerous language and many library features not found in Standard C++. *See also* `__cplusplus`; identifier conflicts with C++; J16; WG21.

C89 The first ANSI C standard, produced in 1989 by committee X3J11.

C90 The first ISO C standard, produced in 1990 by committee WG14 in conjunction with committee X3J11. C90 is technically equivalent to C89.

C95 An amendment to C90, produced in 1995 by committee WG14 in conjunction with committee X3J11. The additions included digraphs and the header iso646.h, and many multibyte and wide character functions via the headers wchar.h and wctype.h. *See also* `__STDC_VERSION__`.

C99 The second ISO C standard, produced in 1999 by committee WG14 in conjunction with committee J11. Many of the new features resulted from work pioneered by NCEG and X3J11.1. *See also* `__STDC_VERSION__`.

C9X The working title used throughout the production of C99.

cabs[f|l][C99] A function that computes the complex absolute value of its argument `z`.

```
#include <complex.h>
double cabs(double complex z);
float cabsf(float complex z);
long double cabsl(long double complex z);
```

`cacos[f|l]`C99 A function that computes the complex arc cosine of its argument `z`, with branch cuts outside the interval $[-1, +1]$ along the real axis.

```
#include <complex.h>
double complex cacos(double complex z);
float complex cacosf(float complex z);
long double complex cacosl(long double complex z);
```

`cacosh[f|l]`C99 A function that returns the complex arc hyperbolic cosine of its argument `z`, with a branch cut at values less than 1 along the real axis.

```
#include <complex.h>
double complex cacosh(double complex z);
float complex cacoshf(float complex z);
long double complex cacoshl(long double complex z);
```

`calloc` A function that dynamically allocates contiguous memory for `nmemb` objects, each of whose size is `size` bytes.

```
#include <stdlib.h>
void *calloc(size_t nmemb, size_t size);
```

The space allocated is initialized to "all-bits-zero." Note that this is not guaranteed to be the same representation as floating-point zero or `NULL`. The value returned is of type `void *` and, as such, is assignment compatible with any data pointer type. Therefore, no explicit cast is needed (unlike in C++). This value is the address of the beginning of the allocated memory and is guaranteed to be suitably aligned for use in storing any object.

If the memory cannot be allocated, `NULL` is returned.

If `size` is zero, it is implementation defined as to whether `NULL` or a unique pointer is returned.

See also `free`; `malloc`; `realloc`.

`carg[f|l]`C99 A function that computes the argument (or *phase angle*) of its argument `z`, with a branch cut along the negative real axis.

```
#include <complex.h>
double carg(double complex z);
float cargf(float complex z);
long double cargl(long double complex z);
```

The value returned corresponds to the interval $[-\pi, +\pi]$.

carriage-return escape sequence An escape sequence, `\r`, which is used to represent the carriage-return character. This character is not often needed. For example, on systems where records are terminated by a carriage-return/line-feed pair, new-lines are translated to and from this pair on output and input, respectively. As such, there is no need to deal with the carriage return explicitly unless a text file containing such pairs is opened in binary mode. *See also* `fopen`.

`case` A keyword that is used only in the context of a `switch` statement to designate a switch value label. *See also* label, `case`.

case conversion *See* `tolower`; `toupper`; `towctrans`; `towlower`; `towupper`; `wctrans`.

`case` **label** *See* label, `case`.

case sensitivity The characteristic of a language, which allows it to distinguish between upper- and lowercase letters. C is a case-sensitive language; that is, the identifiers `ABC`, `abc`, `Abc`, and `AbC` are distinct. Note, however, that prior to C99, an implementation was permitted to ignore case in handling external names (i.e., those of `extern` functions and variables) because many linkers, librarians, and assemblers are not case sensitive.

C language keywords must be written in the correct case to be recognized as such. (Note that C99 added several keywords spelled in mixed case; e.g., `_Bool`.)

`casin[f|l]`[C99] A function that computes the complex arc sine of its argument `z`, with branch cuts outside the interval $[-1, +1]$ along the real axis.

```
#include <complex.h>
double complex casin(double complex z);
float complex casinf(float complex z);
long double complex casinl(long double complex z);
```

`casinh[f|l]`[C99] A function that returns the complex arc hyperbolic sine of its argument `z`, with branch cuts outside the interval $[-i, +i]$ along the imaginary axis.

```
#include <complex.h>
double complex casinh(double complex z);
float complex casinhf(float complex z);
long double complex casinhl(long double complex z);
```

cast operator The unary cast operator `()` has the general form

(*type*) *exp*

where the value of the expression *exp* is converted to a value having type *type*. Both *type* and *exp* must have scalar type except that a `void` expression is permitted if it is being cast to type `void`. (Note that *exp* may designate an array because such an expression is first converted to a pointer, which is a scalar. Similarly, *exp* may designate a function since such an expression is first converted to a pointer.) Type qualifiers are permitted in *type* but are vacuous. The result of a cast is not an lvalue, although some implementations may make it so. This operator associates left to right.

In some sense, a compound literal looks like a cast expression.

casting The operation of explicitly converting the value of an expression to a given type. Casting a value to type `void` causes that value to be explicitly discarded. *See also* cast operator.

`catan`[`f`|`l`][C99] A function that computes the complex arc tangent of its argument `z`, with branch cuts outside the interval $[-i, +i]$ along the imaginary axis.

```
#include <complex.h>
double complex catan(double complex z);
float complex catanf(float complex z);
long double complex catanl(long double complex z);
```

`catanh`[`f`|`l`][C99] A function that returns the complex arc hyperbolic tangent of its argument `z`, with branch cuts outside the interval $[-1, +1]$ along the real axis.

```
#include <complex.h>
double complex catanh(double complex z);
float complex catanhf(float complex z);
long double complex catanhl(long double complex z);
```

`catch` A C++ keyword that is not part of Standard C. If you think you might wish to move C code to a C++ environment in the future, you should refrain from using `catch` as an identifier in new C code you write.

category[C89] One of a number of components that, when combined, describe a locale. *See also* `LC_*` macros; locale, mixed.

`cbrt`[`f`|`l`][C99] A function that returns the real cube root of its argument **`x`**.

```
#include <math.h>
double cbrt(double x);
float cbrtf(float x);
long double cbrtl(long double x);
```

`ccos`[`f`|`l`][C99] A function that computes the complex cosine of its argument **`z`**.

```
#include <complex.h>
double complex ccos(double complex z);
float complex ccosf(float complex z);
long double complex ccosl(long double complex z);
```

`ccosh`[`f`|`l`][C99] A function that computes the complex hyperbolic cosine of its argument **`z`**.

```
#include <complex.h>
double complex ccosh(double complex z);
float complex ccoshf(float complex z);
long double complex ccoshl(long double complex z);
```

`ceil`[`f`|`l`] A function that computes the smallest integer value not less than its argument **`x`**.

```
#include <math.h>
double ceil(double x);
float ceilf(float x);
long double ceill(long double x);
```

The integer value computed is returned as a floating-point value.

The `float` and `long double` versions were an invention of C89, where they were optional; however, in C99, they are required.

`cerf`[`f`|`l`][C99] An optional complex error function that, if provided, must be declared in complex.h.

`cerfc`[`f`|`l`][C99] An optional complex complement function that, if provided, must be declared in complex.h.

`cexp`[`f`|`l`][C99] A function that returns the complex base-e exponential of its argument **`z`**.

```
#include <complex.h>
double complex cexp(double complex z);
float complex cexpf(float complex z);
long double complex cexpl(long double complex z);
```

cexp2[f|l]^{C99} An optional complex base-2 exponential function that, if provided, must be declared in complex.h.

cexpm1[f|l]^{C99} An optional complex base-e exponential minus one function that, if provided, must be declared in complex.h.

char An integer type keyword. A char is big enough to hold any character in the basic execution character set. Standard C requires it to be at least eight bits. Traditionally, char expressions were widened to int when used in expressions and as arguments to functions. However, Standard C allows them to be used as arguments without widening, provided a corresponding function prototype is in scope. *See also* char, plain; conversion, function arguments.

char, plain The type char used without either of the modifiers signed or unsigned. It is implementation defined as to whether a plain char is signed or unsigned. Some compilers provide an option to set the signedness.

character An abstract idea that means different things to different people. To convey an exact meaning, choose the appropriate term from the following list: char, multibyte character, single-byte character, or wide character.

Each character in a wide character set occupies the same amount of storage. Strictly speaking, ASCII and EBCDIC are wide character sets; each character simply occupies a single 8-bit byte. In the Unicode wide character set, each character occupies two 8-bit bytes.

character constant *See* constant, character.

character handling header *See* ctype.h.

character I/O functions The stdio.h functions fgetc, fgets, fputc, fputs, getc, getchar, gets, putc, putchar, puts, and ungetc.

character, multibyte^{C89} *See* multibyte character.

character, pushback *See* ungetc; ungetwc.

character set, execution^{C89} The set of characters available for use during the execution of a program. The basic execution character set must include all of the characters in the basic source character set, the null character, and the control characters representing alert, backspace, carriage return, and new line. The members of the extended-execution character set are locale specific and may be single-byte or multibyte characters.

character set, execution, extendedC89 *See* character set, execution.

character set, sourceC89 The set of characters available for use in writing source code. The basic source character set must include the 52 upper- and lowercase letters from the English alphabet, the digits 0–9, the graphic characters `! " # % & ' ( ) * + , - . / : ; < = > ? [ \ ] ^ _ { | } ~`, the space character, and control characters representing horizontal tab, vertical tab, and form feed. If any other characters are seen except inside character constants, comments, header names, and string literals, the behavior is undefined. The extended source character set may include other single-byte or multibyte characters.

character, single-byte A bit representation that fits into a byte. All source characters required to write C source are characters that can be represented in a single `char`. *See also* character, wide; multibyte character.

character string literal *See* string literal.

character testing functions The `is*` family of functions in ctype.h and its wide character counterpart wctype.h.

character, wideC89 A wide character is a character encoded in some manner into an object of some integer type. Standard C defines this type as `wchar_t` in a number of headers. Do not confuse a wide character with a multibyte character. C89 introduced minimal support for very large character sets in string literals, character constants, header names, and comments, and defined several functions in stdlib.h for conversion to and from multibyte representation. C95 significantly increased this level of support via the addition of several new headers and many functions.

`CHAR_BIT`C89 A macro, defined in limits.h, that designates the number of bits in a `char`. (Standard C requires that it be at least eight.) This macro expands to an integer constant expression suitable for use with a `#if` directive.

`CHAR_MAX`C89 A macro, defined in limits.h, that designates the maximum value for an object of type `char`. (Must be either `SCHAR_MAX` or `UCHAR_MAX` depending on whether a plain `char` is signed.) This macro expands to an integer constant expression suitable for use with a `#if` directive.

`CHAR_MIN`C89 A macro, defined in limits.h, that designates the minimum value for an object of type `char`. (Must be either `SCHAR_MIN` or zero depending on whether a plain `char` is signed.) This macro expands to an integer constant expression suitable for use with a `#if` directive.

`cimag[f|l]`C99 A function that returns the imaginary part of its argument `z` as a real.

```
#include <complex.h>
double cimag(double complex z);
float cimagf(float complex z);
long double cimagl(long double complex z);
```

class A term used in object-oriented programming that is also a keyword in C++. It is not part of Standard C. If you think you might wish to move C code to a C++ environment in the future, you should refrain from using `class` as an identifier in the new C code you write. This use of `class` is not to be confused with the storage class keywords in C.

`clearerr` A function that clears both the end-of-file and error indicators for the file pointed to by `stream`.

```
#include <stdio.h>
void clearerr(FILE *stream);
```

`clgamma[f|l]`[C99] An optional complex natural log of gamma function that, if provided, must be declared in complex.h.

`clock` A function that determines the amount of processor time used from the beginning of an implementation-defined era.

```
#include <time.h>
clock_t clock(void);
```

The era is related to the time at which the program started running and may be an approximation. The intent here is that `clock` gives the CPU time from the start of the program to the time `clock` is called.

The value returned has type `clock_t`, whose units are implementation defined. However, by definition, when this value is divided by `CLOCKS_PER_SEC`, the result is in seconds. If the processor time cannot be determined, or if the time cannot be represented in the return type, the value returned is `(clock_t)(-1)`.

`CLOCKS_PER_SEC`[C89] A macro, defined in time.h, that expands to the number of `clock_t` intervals in a second. For example, if `clock_t` is measured in milliseconds, the value of `CLOCKS_PER_SEC` will be 1,000.

`clock_t`[C89] A type, defined in time.h, that is an implementation-defined arithmetic type (not necessarily integer) capable of representing times. When two values of this type are obtained from calls during the same program execution, subtracting the first value from the second gives the time elapsed between those calls. *See also* `clock`; `CLOCKS_PER_SEC`.

`clog[f|l]`[C99] A function that returns the complex natural logarithm of its argument `z`, with a branch cut along the negative real axis.

```
#include <complex.h>
double complex clog(double complex z);
float complex clogf(float complex z);
long double complex clogl(long double complex z);
```

`clog10[f|l]`[C99] An optional complex base-10 log function that, if provided, must be declared in complex.h.

`clog1p[f|l]`[C99] An optional complex natural log function that, if provided, must be declared in complex.h.

`clog2[f|l]`[C99] An optional complex base-2 log function that, if provided, must be declared in complex.h.

colon A terminator for `case` and `default` labels in a `switch`, as well as for labels that are the object of a `goto` statement. It also precedes the width in a bit-field declaration, and is used as the second character of the conditional operator.

comma operator A binary operator, `,`, that causes its operands to be evaluated left to right. In the following example:

exp1 `,` *exp2*

exp1 is evaluated, and its value is discarded, so to be useful, this expression must contain a side effect. Then *exp2* is evaluated, and its value and type become the value and type of the whole expression. There is a sequence point at the comma. This operator associates left to right. (Except when used in the first and third expressions in a `for` statement, the comma operator is best restricted to macro definitions and not otherwise used overtly.) If a comma operator is used in the same context as a comma punctuator, it may be necessary to distinguish between the two. In the following example:

```
g(a, b, c);
h((a, b), c);
```

results in a call to `g` with three arguments and a call to `h` with only two. In the second case, the first comma is acting as an operator (as indicated by the grouping parentheses). The second comma is a punctuator separating the two arguments.

comma punctuator A token used as a punctuator, most often to separate macro and function arguments, declarators in a declaration, and initializer list expressions.

command line The set of arguments specified when a program is invoked at the operating system level or via a call to `system`. The count and contents of these arguments are made available to `main` via `argc` and `argv`. The existence of a command-line processor can be determined via the library routine `system`. Certain command-line processor-related issues regarding to arguments are outside the scope of the C standard; for example: Can an argument contain white space or double quotes? Will its letters' casing be preserved?

comment Text placed within code, that does not affect that code's operation, and that is intended to explain that code. The character sequences `/*` and `*/` delimit comments that are permitted to span multiple source lines but need not actually do so. C99 added C++'s `//`-style comments, which end at the next new-line. During source translation, an implementation recognizes each comment and replaces it with a single space. As such, `/*...*/`-style comments can be used anywhere white space is permitted; that is, between any two adjacent tokens. For example, the lines

```
/* */ a /* */ = /* */ b /* */ ; /* */
a = b;
```

contain identical token sequences. `/*...*/`-style comments do not nest in Standard C, although nesting is permitted in some nonstandard implementations. To disable a block of code containing `/*...*/`-style comments, use the following approach:

```
#if 0
        a = b + c; /* ... */
#endif
```

Consider the following code fragment:

```
int i = 20, j, *pi = &i;

j = 100/*pi;
```

At first glance it appears that 100 is being divided by the value of the `int` to which `pi` points. However, during tokenizing, the characters `/*` are recognized as the (presumably unintended) start of a comment. To resolve this, a space should follow the slash, or (better style suggests) the expression should be written as `100/(*pi)` instead.

common extensions Extensions that are widely implemented but are not universal. Extensions may include keywords (such as `fortran`), preprocessor directives (such as `#module`), or library functions (such as `open` and `close`). Support for `envp` and the allowance of `$` characters in identifiers are other examples.

common initial sequence A set of one or more initial members in two different structures, that have compatible types (and, for members that are bit-fields, the same widths).

common warning A warning issued by a translator to help the programmer locate nonsyntactic problems. However, these are not required by Standard C. Examples are "a statement can never be reached," "a function is called without a prototype in scope," and "an unrecognized pragma was found." As to whether an implementation issues such warnings is a marketplace issue and is referred to as "Quality of Implementation."

comparison functions The string.h functions `memcmp`, `strcmp`, `strcoll`, `strncmp`, and `strxfrm`, and their wide character counterparts in wchar.h, `wmemcmp`, `wcscmp`, `wcscoll`, `wcsncmp`, and `wcsxfrm`. Functions `bsearch` and `qsort` also take an argument that is a pointer to one of these functions or to a user-defined comparison function.

compatible type *See* type, compatible.

compiler A term used generically to mean a C language translator; it includes such tools as interpreters and incremental compilers.

`compl`[C95] A macro, defined in iso646.h, that expands to the token `~`. It allows programmers using source character sets (such as ISO 646) that are missing certain characters necessary for writing C programs to enter those characters using identifiers instead. Note that in C++, this name is a keyword.

complement operator A unary operator, `~`, that produces the bit-wise one's-complement of its operand. The operand must have integer type. The usual arithmetic conversions are performed on the operand, and the result has the promoted type. This operator associates right to left.

`complex`[C99] A macro, defined in complex.h, that expands to the keyword `_Complex`. For normal usage of the complex types, it is strongly recommended that you include complex.h and use this macro rather than using the `_Complex` keyword directly. There are three complex types: `float _Complex`, `double _Complex`, and `long double _Complex`, which can be written instead as `float complex`, `double complex`, and `long double complex`, respectively. *See also* `__STDC_IEC_559_COMPLEX__`.

`_Complex`[C99] A keyword that provides support for a family of complex types. Since it was invented by C99, by which time quite a few programs already contained type synonyms using some form of the word complex, this keyword was spelled using one of the forms reserved for implementers.

Unless you must mix both existing homegrown complex machinery and this new keyword in the same source file, it is strongly recommended that you include complex.h and use its macro `complex` instead.

Note that freestanding implementations are not required to provide complex types.

complex arithmetic[C99] Arithmetic based on objects having a real and an imaginary part. (In pre-C99 implementations, math.h is often extended to include functions and macros to assist with complex number processing.) *See also* `complex`; `_Complex`; complex.h.

complex.h[C99] A header that declares or defines the following names, all pertaining to complex arithmetic support:

Name	*Purpose*
`cabs`[`f`|`l`]	Complex absolute value
`cacos`[`f`|`l`]	Complex arc cosine
`cacosh`[`f`|`l`]	Complex hyperbolic arc cosine
`carg`[`f`|`l`]	Complex argument (*phase angle*)
`casin`[`f`|`l`]	Complex arc sine
`casinh`[`f`|`l`]	Complex hyperbolic arc sine
`catan`[`f`|`l`]	Complex arc tangent
`catanh`[`f`|`l`]	Complex hyperbolic arc tangent
`ccos`[`f`|`l`]	Complex cosine
`ccosh`[`f`|`l`]	Complex hyperbolic cosine
`cexp`[`f`|`l`]	Complex base-e exponential
`cimag`[`f`|`l`]	Obtain imaginary part
`clog`[`f`|`l`]	Complex natural logarithm
`complex`	Synonym for the type `_Complex`
`_Complex_I`	The constant i
`conj`[`f`|`l`]	Complex conjugate
`cpow`[`f`|`l`]	Complex power
`cproj`[`f`|`l`]	Complex Riemann sphere projection
`creal`[`f`|`l`]	Obtain real part
`csin`[`f`|`l`]	Complex sine
`csinh`[`f`|`l`]	Complex hyperbolic sine
`csqrt`[`f`|`l`]	Complex square root
`ctan`[`f`|`l`]	Complex tangent
`ctanh`[`f`|`l`]	Complex hyperbolic tangent
`I`	The constant i
`imaginary`	Synonym for the type `_Imaginary`
`_Imaginary_I`	The constant i

See future library directions.

`_Complex_I`^{C99} A macro, defined in complex.h, that expands to a constant expression of type `const float _Complex`, having a value of the imaginary unit *i*.

compliance The degree to which an implementation conforms to the requirements of a definition such as Standard C. While compliance can easily be claimed, it is usually subject to verification by using a formally accepted validation suite. *See also* implementation, conforming; program, conforming; program, strictly conforming.

composite type^{C89} *See* type, composite.

compound assignment operator *See* assignment operator, compound.

compound literal^{C99} An expression consisting of a parenthesized type name followed by a brace-enclosed list of initializers. This results in an unnamed object whose value is given by the initializer list.

If the type name specifies an array of unknown size, the size is determined by the initializer list, and the type of the compound literal is that of the completed array type. If the type name specifies an object type, the type of the compound literal is that specified by the type name. In either case, the result is an lvalue and can be modified.

If a compound literal occurs outside the body of a function, the resulting object has static storage duration, and its initializer must be made up of constant expressions; otherwise, it has automatic storage duration associated with the enclosing block, and its initializer need not be made up of constant expressions.

For example, the file scope definition

```
int *values = (int [4]){10, 20, 30};
```

initializes `values` to point to the first element of an array of four `int`, the first having the value 10, the second, 20, and the third, 30. The initializers expressions are required to be constant, since the unnamed object has static storage duration. Therefore, the fourth element takes on the value zero. The array elements can be modified.

The block scope definitions

```
int i = 10;
const int *counts = (int []){i, i * 2, i * 3};
```

initialize `counts` to point to the first element of an array of three `int`, the first having the value 10, the second, 20, and the third, 30. The initializer expressions are not required to be constant, since the unnamed object has automatic storage duration. The array elements cannot be modified.

A compound literal can be made `const` explicitly, as follows:

```
f((const int []){i, i * 2, i * 3});
```

Consider the case in which `Point` is a structure that contains the members `x` and `y`, in that order, and we wish to create a pair of unnamed Points and pass them by address to a function that draws a line between those points as in the following example:

```
drawLine(&(const struct point){-4, 3},
         &(const struct point){9, 2});
```

A compound literal can contain designated initializers. The following lines illustrate the previous example written without knowing the order of `Point`'s members:

```
drawLine(&(const struct point){.x = -4, .y = 3},
         &(const struct point){.x = 9, .y = 2});
```

compound statement *See* block.

concatenation functions The string.h functions `strcat` and `strncat` and their wide character counterparts in wchar.h, `wcscat`, and `wcsncat`.

conditional compilation The selection or rejection of source file lines based on the value of a translation-time integer constant expression, on the existence or nonexistence of a particular macro definition, or on a combination of both. It is effected using the preprocessor directives `#if`, `#ifdef`, `#ifndef`, `#else`, `#elif`, and `#endif`, and the preprocessor operator `defined`. The true and false selection paths may contain any language token or preprocessor directive. As such, conditional directives may be nested—to at least 8 levels in C89 and to 15 levels in C99.

All directives in a related set must reside in the same source file. That is, in the following example:

```
#ifdef DEBUG
#include "debug.h"
#endif
```

the header debug.h is not permitted to contain `#elif` or `#else` directives that belong to the outer set.

conditional operator A ternary operator, `?:`, that has the following form:

exp1 ? *exp2* : *exp3*

which evaluates to *exp2* if *exp1* tests true; otherwise it evaluates to *exp3*. (Only one of *exp2* and *exp3* is evaluated.) The type of the expression is the composite type of *exp2* and *exp3*. The first operand must have scalar type. The second and third operands must have either arithmetic types, compatible structure or union types, or `void` type; or they must be pointers to compatible types, or one a pointer and the other the null pointer constant, or one a pointer to an object or incomplete type and the other a pointer to `void`. This operator associates right to left. There is a sequence point at the `?`.

conforming implementation *See* implementation, conforming.

conforming program *See* program, conforming.

`conj[f|l]`[C99] A function that returns the complex conjugate of its argument `z`.

```
#include <complex.h>
double complex conj(double complex z);
float complex conjf(float complex z);
long double complex conjl(long double complex z);
```

`const`[C89] A keyword that is used as a type qualifier. It indicates that the object to which it applies cannot be modified in the scope of this declaration. Specifically, it causes it to be treated as a nonmodifiable lvalue. `const` was adapted from C++. While `const` is useful for partitioning data into read-only and read-write sections, `const` does not guarantee that an object will be physically write protected at run time. The `const` qualifier may also be applied to the underlying object in a pointer declaration. Consider the following cases:

```
char *ncpncc;
char * const cpncc;
const char *ncpcc;
const char * const cpcc;
```

`ncpncc` is a non-`const` pointer to a non-`const char`. Both the pointer and the `char` to which it points can be modified via this identifier.

`cpncc` is a `const` pointer to a non-`const char`. Only the `char` to which it points can be modified via this identifier; `cpncc` itself cannot be modified.

`ncpcc` is a non-`const` pointer to a `const char`. Only the pointer can be modified via this identifier; the `char` to which it points cannot be modified.

`cpcc` is a `const` pointer to a `const char`. Neither the pointer nor the `char` to which it points can be modified via this identifier.

Declarations containing the const qualifier also may contain the qualifiers restrict and volatile; the three are not related, nor are they mutually exclusive.

In C99, const may also be used inside any dimension of an array parameter (possibly along with restrict or static); for example

```
void copy(int s[const]);
```

The previous declaration is simply an alternate way of saying the following:

```
void copy(int * const s);
```

constant One of the token types in C. A constant represents a value that does not change. The kinds of constants are: character, enumeration, floating, and integer. String literals are in a token category of their own and are not considered constants.

constant, character A token of the form '*x*' where *x* is a sequence of printable graphic multibyte characters or escape sequences. Its type is int not char (unlike in C++). If the sequence contains more than one character, as in 'ab' and 'abcd', the value of the resulting character constant is implementation defined. Note that 'x' is quite different from "x", the latter being an array of two char. *See also* constant, character, wide.

constant, character, wide^{C89} A token of the form L'*x*' where *x* is a sequence of multibyte characters. The sequence may include escape sequences. A wide character constant has type wchar_t. *See also* constant, character; string literal, wide.

constant, enumeration Any one of the identifiers defined as part of an enumeration type. For example, red, green, and blue are enumeration constants in the following enumerated type definition:

```
enum color {red, green = 4, blue};
```

They have type int and take on the values 0, 4, and 5, respectively. Enumeration constants can be explicitly initialized as shown with green. As a result, there may be gaps in the set of initial values used, and there can also be duplicates. Enumeration constants share the same name space as variables and functions and are not limited to being used in the context of their parent enumerated type. To some extent, enumeration constants can be used in place of simple object-like macros.

constant expression An expression whose subexpressions are all constants. A constant expression can be evaluated at translation-time rather than at run time. There are three kinds of constant expression: address, arithmetic, and integer. Integer constant expressions are actually required in certain contexts; for example, in case labels, bit-field widths, and enumeration-constant initializers.

constant, floating A constant containing a significand part that may be followed by an exponent part and a suffix indicating its type. The exponent may be signed and it may be introduced with either `e` or `E`. The suffix `F` (or `f`) indicates the `float` type and the suffix `L` (or `l`) indicates the `long double` type. (These suffixes were an invention of C89.) The type of an unsuffixed floating constant is `double`.

Prior to C99, floating-point constants were written entirely in decimal. C99 allows the significand to be written in hexadecimal, provided a `0x` or `0X` prefix is present and the exponent is introduced by `p` (or `P`) instead of `e` (or `E`). While the exponent in a hexadecimal floating-point constant must be written in decimal, that exponent indicates the power of 2 (rather than 10) by which the significand part is to be scaled.

constant, integer A constant that begins with a digit but has no decimal point or exponent. It may have a prefix that specifies its base and a suffix that specifies its type. A prefix of `0` indicates octal base while `0x` or `0X` indicates hexadecimal. If no prefix is present, the base is taken as decimal. The suffix `L` (or `l`) indicates the `long int` type and the suffix `U` (or `u`) indicates `unsigned`. All possible combinations of `L` (or `l`) and `U` (or `u`) are permissible and equivalent. The `U` and `u` suffixes were an invention of C89.

C99 added the type `long long` along with the suffixes `ll` and `LL` (which are equivalent) that can be combined in either order with `u` or `U` to indicate the type `unsigned long long int`.

The type of an integer constant depends on its base and value as follows. It is the first of the corresponding list in which its value can be represented:

- In C89—Unsuffixed decimal: `int`, `long int`, `unsigned long int`; unsuffixed octal or hexadecimal: `int`, `unsigned int`, `long int`, `unsigned long int`; suffixed by the letter `u` or `U`: `unsigned int`, `unsigned long int`; suffixed by the letter `l` or `L`: `long int`, `unsigned long int`; suffixed by both the letters `u` or `U` and `l` or `L`: `unsigned long int`.
- In C99—Unsuffixed decimal: `int`, `long int`, `long long int`; unsuffixed octal or hexadecimal: `int`, `unsigned int`, `long int`, `unsigned long int`, `long long int`, `unsigned long long int`; suffixed by the letter `u` or `U`: `unsigned int`, `unsigned long int`,

unsigned long long int; decimal suffixed by the letter l or L: long int, long long int; octal or hexadecimal suffixed by the letter l or L: long int, unsigned long int, long long int, unsigned long long int; suffixed by both the letters u or U and l or L: unsigned long int, unsigned long long int; decimal suffixed by the letters ll or LL: long long int; octal or hexadecimal suffixed by the letters ll or LL: long long int, unsigned long long int; suffixed by both u or U and ll or LL: unsigned long long int.

constant, null pointer A pointer expression whose value is not, and never can be, the address of an object or function. It can be constructed from any integer constant expression having the value 0 or from such a constant cast to the type void *. The most common ways of representing a null pointer constant are 0, 0L, and NULL.

constant, type of *See* constant, floating; constant, integer.

const_cast A C++ keyword that is not part of Standard C. If you think you might wish to move C code to a C++ environment in the future, you should refrain from using const_cast as an identifier in new C code you write.

const-**qualified type**[C89] A type containing the const qualifier.

constraint A syntactic and semantic restriction by which the exposition of language elements is to be interpreted. An implementation must diagnose a constraint violation. The following are examples of constraints: "The operators [ ], ( ), and ? : shall occur in pairs, separated by expressions," "Each of the operands of the division, multiplication, and remainder operators shall have arithmetic type," and "Each # preprocessing token in the replacement list of a function-like macro shall be followed by a parameter as the next preprocessing token in the replacement line."

continue A statement that causes the current innermost iteration of a for, while, or do loop to be terminated and a new iteration (if any) to be started. It cannot be used in any other context. It is subtly different from break and has the following form:

```
continue;
```

contracted expression[C99] A floating-point expression (usually consisting of a multiply and add operation) may be *contracted*; that is, evaluated as though it were an atomic operation, thereby omitting intermediate rounding errors implied by the source code and the expression evaluation method. *See also* #pragma STDC FP_CONTRACT.

control character A member of an implementation-defined set of characters that are not printing characters. *See also* control wide character; `iscntrl`; `iswcntrl`.

control wide character^{C89} A member of a locale-specific set of wide characters that are not printing wide characters. *See also* control character; `iscntrl`; `iswcntrl`.

conversion The changing of operand values from one type to another. For example, in

```
double d;
int i = 5, j = 4;

d = i + (double)j;
```

the value of `i` is implicitly converted to `double` while that of `j` is explicitly converted using a cast.

conversion, array In almost all cases, an expression designating an array is converted to an expression of type "pointer to the first element of that array." The exceptions are when the expression is the operand of `sizeof` or the unary `&` operator, or it is a string literal used as the initializer of an array of characters or wide characters.

conversion, explicit The use of a cast operator to convert the value of an expression from one type to another.

conversion, function In almost all cases, a process in which an expression designating a function is converted to an expression of type "pointer to function." The exceptions are when the expression is the operand of `sizeof` or the unary `&` operator. (If `f` is a function, the expression `f` is not converted in `sizeof(f)`, thus producing the constraint violation that `sizeof` cannot be applied to function types.)

conversion, function arguments By default, a conversion in which expressions of type `signed` or `unsigned char` and `short` are widened to the corresponding flavor of `int` (as determined by the value preserving rule) when passed as arguments to a function. Similarly, `float` arguments get widened to `double`.

Standard C permits (but does not require) arguments of these "narrow" types to be passed without widening provided a prototype containing the corresponding narrow types is used for both the function definition and all its declarations. In such a case, an implementation may widen all, some, or none. For example, it may widen `char` and `short` but not `float`. Note that all arguments passed that correspond to an ellipses in a prototype are always widened.

Functions defined and declared without prototype notation always expect and get widened types. (That is why the `printf` family has no conversion specifiers for the types `char`, `short`, and `float`.)

conversion, implicit The automatic conversion of operand values from one type to another that occurs with some operators. For example, in the expression `i + d`, if `i` has type `int` and `d` has type `double`, the value of `i` is converted to `double`, the addition is performed, and the resulting type is also `double`. *See also* conversion; conversion, explicit.

conversion, integer type A conversion in which signed and unsigned `char`s, `short`s, and `int` bit-fields may be used wherever an `int` or `unsigned int` are expected. If their value can be represented in an `int`, that is the type to which they are converted, otherwise they are converted to `unsigned int`. *See also* unsigned preserving rule; value preserving rule.

conversion, pointer A `void` pointer is assignment compatible with all object and incomplete type pointers. As such, it may be converted to and from those types. A null pointer constant can be converted to any function pointer type. All other pointer types are incompatible with each other, however, they may be able to be cast one from the other producing useful results on some systems.

conversion specifier A character sequence of the general form $\%x$, where x may be one or more characters, used by the `printf` and `scanf` function family in interpreting formatted output and input argument lists, respectively. Sometimes called an edit mask.

conversion state[C80] The state in which a conversion between a given multibyte character sequence and a wide character sequence depends on the rules established by the `LC_CTYPE` category of the current locale. The current conversion state is stored in an object of type `mbstate_t`.

conversion, usual arithmetic The set of rules that dictates how operands of arithmetic type are converted when they meet across the operators `/`, `*`, `%`, `+`, `-`, `<<`, `>>`, `<`, `<=`, `>`, `>=`, `==`, `!=`, `&`, `^`, `|`, and the `:` in `?:`. The rules are as follows:

- If either operand has type `long double`, the other operand is converted to `long double`.
- If either operand has type `double`, the other operand is converted to `double`.
- If either operand has type `float`, the other operand is converted to `float`.
- Otherwise, the integer promotions are performed on both operands. Then, the following rules are applied:

- If both operands have the same type, no further conversion is needed.
- If both operands have signed integer types or both have unsigned integer types, the one with the type of lesser rank is converted to the type of the operand with greater rank.
- If the unsigned operand has greater or equal rank when compared to the other operand, the signed operand is converted to unsigned operand's type.
- If the signed operand's type can represent all of the values of the unsigned operand's type, the unsigned operand is converted to the type of the signed operand.
- Otherwise, both operands are converted to the unsigned type that corresponds to the type of the signed operand.

The addition of complex types in C99 required the following additional rules:

- If one operand has a real type and the other has a complex type, the value of the real type is converted to a complex type as follows: the real value becomes the real part of the complex result while the imaginary part of the complex result is set to positive or unsigned zero.
- If the operands are of different complex types, the conversion rules for the corresponding real types are followed.

conversion, `void` type A conversion in which the (nonexistent) value of a void expression is used as the operand in an explicit cast to type `void`.

copying functions The string.h functions `memcpy`, `memmove`, `strcpy`, and `strncpy`, and their wide character counterparts in string.h, `wmemcpy`, `wmemmove`, `wcscpy`, and `wcsncpy`.

`copysign[f|l]`[C99] A function that produces a value with the magnitude of `x` and the sign of `y`.

```
#include <math.h>
double copysign(double x, double y);
float copysignf(float x, float y);
long double copysignl(long double x, long double y);
```

If `x` is a NaN, the result is a NaN with the sign of `y`.

correctly rounded result[C99] The representation of a result that is nearest in value to what the result would be given unlimited range and precision; that is, the result with unlimited range and precision rounded to the representation used.

`cos`[`f`|`l`] A function that computes the cosine of its argument `x` (measured in radians).

```
#include <math.h>
double cos(double x);
float cosf(float x);
long double cosl(long double x);
```

If the magnitude of the argument is large, `cos` may produce a result with little or no significance.

The `float` and `long double` versions were an invention of C89, where they were optional; however, in C99, they are required.

`cosh`[`f`|`l`] A function that computes the hyperbolic cosine of its argument `x`.

```
#include <math.h>
double cosh(double x);
float coshf(float x);
long double coshl(long double x);
```

If the magnitude of the argument is too large, a range error occurs.

The `float` and `long double` versions were an invention of C89, where they were optional; however, in C99, they are required.

`__cplusplus` A macro that is predefined in C++ implementations only. It is intended to allow translation units (especially headers) containing C++-specific constructs to be shared between C and C++ programs. Its existence is tested for using `#ifdef`.

`cpow`[`f`|`l`]^{C99} A function that computes the complex power function x^y, with a branch cut for the first parameter along the negative real axis.

```
#include <complex.h>
double complex cpow(double complex x, double complex y);
float complex cpowf(float complex x, float complex y);
long double complex cpowl(long double complex x,
    long double complex y);
```

`cproj`[`f`|`l`]^{C99} A function that returns a projection of its argument `z` onto the Riemann sphere.

```
#include <complex.h>
double complex cproj(double complex z);
float complex cprojf(float complex z);
long double complex cprojl(long double complex z);
```

creal[f|l]^{C99} A function that returns the real part of its argument z.

```
#include <complex.h>
double creal(double complex z);
float crealf(float complex z);
long double creall(long double complex z);
```

cross-compilation A development environment in which source programs are compiled on one system (the host) but are intended to run on another (the target). The resulting program generally takes complete control of the target system; that is, it does not run under the control of an operating system. Such target systems are called "freestanding systems." *See also* environment, freestanding; environment, hosted.

csin[f|l]^{C99} A function that computes the complex sine of its argument z.

```
#include <complex.h>
double complex csin(double complex z);
float complex csinf(float complex z);
long double complex csinl(long double complex z);
```

csinh[f|l]^{C99} A function that computes the complex hyperbolic sine of its argument z.

```
#include <complex.h>
double complex csinh(double complex z);
float complex csinhf(float complex z);
long double complex csinhl(long double complex z);
```

csqrt[f|l]^{C99} A function that computes the complex square root of its argument z, with a branch cut along the negative real axis.

```
#include <complex.h>
double complex csqrt(double complex z);
float complex csqrtf(float complex z);
long double complex csqrtl(long double complex z);
```

ctan[f|l]^{C99} A function that computes the complex tangent of its argument z.

```
#include <complex.h>
double complex ctan(double complex z);
float complex ctanf(float complex z);
long double complex ctanl(long double complex z);
```

ctanh[f|l]^{C99} A function that computes the complex hyperbolic tangent of its argument z.

```
#include <complex.h>
double complex ctanh(double complex z);
float complex ctanhf(float complex z);
long double complex ctanhl(long double complex z);
```

`ctgamma[f|l]`[C99] An optional complex true gamma function that, if provided, must be declared in complex.h.

`ctime` A function that converts the calendar time pointed to by `timer` to a local time in the form of a string.

```
#include <time.h>
char *ctime(const time_t *timer);
```

A call to `ctime` is equivalent to

```
asctime(localtime(timer))
```

so the return value points to a string of the form identical to that returned by `asctime`.

ctype.h A header that contains various character testing and conversion functions. The `is*` family members return a zero or nonzero value based on the truth of their operation while the `to*` family members return a possibly case-converted value of their character argument.

The ctype.h header contains definitions or declarations for the following identifiers:

Name	*Purpose*
`isalnum`	Test if character is alphanumeric
`isalpha`	Test if character is alphabetic
`isblank`[C99]	Test if character is blank
`iscntrl`	Test if character is control
`isdigit`	Test if character is digit (0–9)
`isgraph`	Test if character is graphic
`islower`	Test if character is lowercase
`isprint`	Test if character is printable
`ispunct`	Test if character is punctuation
`isspace`	Test if character is space
`isupper`	Test if character is uppercase
`isxdigit`	Test if character is hex digit
`tolower`	Produce lowercase version
`toupper`	Produce uppercase version

The behavior of some functions is locale specific.

All functions take one `int` argument. However, the `int` argument must be either representable in an `unsigned char` or it must be the macro `EOF`. If the argument has any other value, the behavior is undefined.

See also future library directions; wctype.h.

currency displayC89 Monetary formatting information defined in a structure of type `lconv`. The macro `LC_MONETARY` can be used as the category argument to `setlocale` to select the currency display information to be used.

`currency_symbol`C89 An `lconv` structure member that is a pointer to a string containing the local currency symbol applicable to the current locale. If the string consists of `""`, this indicates that the value is not available in the current locale or is of zero length. In the `"C"` locale this member must have the value `""`.

`CX_LIMITED_RANGE` **pragma**C99 *See* `#pragma STDC CX_LIMITED_RANGE`.

D

`__DATE__` A predefined macro that expands to a string containing the date of compilation in the form `"Mmm dd yyyy"`. If the day is less than 10, its first position is a space. Examples are `Mar  2 1991` and `Mar 22 1991`. If the date is not available, an implementation-defined valid date is supplied. This macro can be used in any context where a string literal is permitted or required, for example,

```
char date[] = __DATE__;
printf("%s", __DATE__);
```

And because adjacent string literals are concatenated, the following is permitted:

```
printf(">%s<\n", "xxx" __DATE__ "xxx");
```

Note that there is no wide string version of this macro, so it was difficult to get the date string concatenated with wide strings; however, C99 allows wide and single-byte strings to be concatenated directly, so that operation becomes trivial.

This macro cannot be the subject of `#undef`.

date and time header *See* time.h.

`DBL_DIG`[C89] A macro, defined in float.h, that designates the number of decimal digits, such that a `double` value of that significance can be rounded into a floating-point number and back again without a change in those decimal digits.

`DBL_EPSILON`[C89] A macro, defined in float.h, that designates the difference between 1.0 and the least value greater than 1.0 that is representable in the `double` type.

`DBL_MANT_DIG`[C89] A macro, defined in float.h, that designates the number of base-`FLT_RADIX` digits in the floating-point significand of a `double` value.

`DBL_MAX`[C89] A macro, defined in float.h, that designates the maximum representable finite `double` number.

`DBL_MAX_10_EXP`[C89] A macro, defined in float.h, that designates the maximum integer such that 10 raised to that power is in a given range of representable finite floating-point numbers.

`DBL_MAX_EXP`[C89] A macro, defined in float.h, that designates the maximum integer such that `FLT_RADIX` raised to that power minus 1 is a representable finite floating-point number.

DBL_MIN[C89] A macro, defined in float.h, that designates the minimum normalized positive `double` number.

DBL_MIN_10_EXP[C89] A macro, defined in float.h, that designates the minimum negative integer such that 10 raised to that power is in a given range of normalized floating-point numbers.

DBL_MIN_EXP[C89] A macro, defined in float.h, that designates the minimum negative integer such that `FLT_RADIX` raised to that power minus 1 is a normalized floating-point number.

DECIMAL_DIG[C99] A macro, defined in float.h, that specifies the number of decimal digits such that any floating-point number in the widest supported floating type can be rounded to a floating-point number having that many decimal digits and back again without change to the value.

decimal constant *See* constant, integer.

decimal_point[C89] An `lconv` structure member that is a pointer to a string containing the decimal-point character used to format nonmonetary quantities. In the `"C"` locale this member must have the value `"."`. *See also* `mon_decimal_point`.

decimal point *See* radix point.

declaration A construct that declares the attributes of one or more identifiers. A definition (such as `static int i;`) is also a declaration, but a declaration (such as `extern int j;`) is not necessarily a definition. Prior to C99, declarations could optionally occur at the start of any block, prior to any statements. C99 permits them to occur after statements, so long as they occur prior to their first use. They also may occur outside of function definitions. A declaration must be terminated with a semicolon.

declaration specifiers Those parts of a declaration excluding any initializer; that is, the storage class specifier, type specifier, and type qualifier.

declarator The portion of a declaration that declares one identifier. For example, the declaration `int i, j[5], k(void);` contains three declarators: for `i`, `j`, and `k`. *See also* declaration.

declarator, full[C99] A declarator that is not part of another declarator. A sequence point exists at the end of a full declarator.

declarator, punctuation in Those punctuation characters permitted in declarators:

`()` is used in two different ways: to indicate the derived type "function returning" and to indicate precedence. For example, `int (*fp)(void)`, declares `fp` to be a pointer to a function having no arguments. Without the grouping parentheses, we would have `int *fp(void)`, in which case `fp` would be a function having no arguments and returning a pointer to an `int`.

`*` is used to indicate the derived type "pointer to" as in `int *pi` and `long (*pf)(int)`, for example.

`[ ]` is used to indicate the derived type "array of."

declarator type derivation *See* derived type.

decrement operator A unary operator, `--`, that may be used as either a prefix or postfix operator. The operand must have a scalar type and must be a modifiable lvalue. The value of x`--` is the value of x before it is decremented by 1, whereas the value of `--`x is the value of x after it is decremented by 1. The postfix version of this operator associates left to right while the prefix version associates right to left. (Prior to C89, the prefix and postfix versions had the same precedence. However, C89 elevated the precedence of the postfix version. This broke no correct existing code. It did, however, permit previously invalid constructs to be valid. For example, `p--->m` is now valid.) There is a corresponding increment operator `++`.

`default` A keyword used as a special label, but only in the context of a `switch` statement. A `switch` passes control to the `default` label if the controlling expression does not match any of the associated case label values. You cannot `goto` a `default` label because `goto` can be used only to transfer control to user-defined labels. *See also* labeled statement.

default argument promotions *See* conversion, function arguments.

`#define` A preprocessor directive used to define an object-like or function-like macro. *See also* `defined`; `#ifdef`; `#ifndef`; `#undef`. It is used as follows:

```
#define identifier  [replacement-list]
#define identifier( [identifier-list] ) \
                     [replacement-list]
```

`defined` A preprocessor operator that makes complex conditional compilation selection criteria much simpler to read and write. It is used to test if the macro specified as its operand is defined, and evaluates to 1 on true and 0 on false, for example,

```
#if defined M1 && !defined M2
        /* ... */
#endif
```

is equivalent to:

```
#ifdef M1
        #ifndef M2
                /* ... */
        #endif
#endif
```

Optional parentheses are permitted around the macro name operand of the `defined` operator.

Note that `defined` is not a keyword. It only has a special meaning when used in the context of a `#if` or `#elif` directive. In all other contexts this name may be safely used as an identifier.

`defined` cannot be the subject of a `#undef` or `#define` directive.

definition A declaration that causes storage to be reserved for an object or function named by an identifier. A definition (such as `static int i;`) is also a declaration, but a declaration (such as `extern int j;`) is not necessarily a definition.

definition, tentative^{C89} A definition that might be augmented by another definition for the same identifier, later in the same translation unit. A declaration of an identifier (that names an object) having file scope and no initializer, and without a storage class specifier or the specifier `static`, is a tentative definition.

`delete` A C++ keyword that is not part of Standard C. If you think you might wish to move C code to a C++ environment in the future, you should refrain from using `delete` as an identifier in new C code you write.

deprecated Synonym for obsolescent.

dereference *See* indirection.

derived type A type derived from another type. For example, `char *[10]` is derived from the type `char *`, which is in turn derived from the base type `char`. There are only three ways to derive a type from another type: *T2* is an array of *T1*; *T2* is a pointer to *T1*; and *T2* is a function returning *T1*. Not all possible derivations are permitted. For example, a function cannot return an array or a function, and you cannot have an array of functions, as indicated by the following table.

Valid Derived Type Combinations

Derived type	Pointer	Array	Function
Pointer to	yes	yes	yes
Array of	yes	yes	no
Function returning	yes	no	no

designated initializer[C99] An initializer for an array that can be written such that the numbers of the elements to be initialized explicitly are specified, as in the following:

```
enum Color {RED, GREEN, BLUE};
int counts[] = {[BLUE] = 10, [GREEN] = 15, [RED] = 20};
```

In the previous example, the element number is specified as an integer constant expression, as in `[BLUE] = 10`. The initializer list may be incomplete, as follows:

```
int values[10] = {1, 3, 5, [7] = 2, 4, 6};
```

In this case, elements 0, 1, 2, 7, 8, and 9 are given explicit values, while the elements 3, 4, 5, and 6 take on the value zero.

Members of a union or structure can also be designated explicitly, allowing a union to be initialized through any member (not just the first) and allowing a structure's member initializers to be specified in any order. An example is:

```
struct Point
{
        int x;
        int y;
};

struct Point p1 = {.y = 5, .x = 7};
```

Designated initializers can be used with compound literals.

diagnostic message An error message. A standard-conforming implementation must issue at least one diagnostic message for each translation unit containing one or more syntax rule or constraint violations. The format of any such message(s) is implementation defined. Note, though, that formal validation and procurement agencies may impose further requirements here. For example, in the U.S., FIPS validation requires that such messages indicate the name of the translation unit and as near as possible, the offending source line number.

Strictly speaking, an implementation that never issues more than one message per compilation (where the text of that message is "Yes, there's at least 1 error there.") could be a conforming implementation; however, marketplace forces likely would encourage the vendor to provide more and better quality messages.

diagnostics header *See* assert.h.

`difftime`[C89] A function that computes the difference between two calendar times using `time1 - time0`.

```
#include <time.h>
double difftime(time_t time1, time_t time0);
```

The return value indicates the number of seconds separating the two times.

digraph[C95] An alternate spelling for a source token that cannot be written solely using characters in the ISO-646 character set. The following digraphs are defined:

Digraphs

Spelling	*Equivalent Token*
`<:`	`[`
`:>`	`]`
`<%`	`{`
`%>`	`}`
`%:`	`#`
`%:%:`	`##`

direct I/O functions The stdio.h functions `fread` and `fwrite`.

`div`[C89] A function that computes the quotient and remainder when `numer` is divided by `denom`.

```
#include <stdlib.h>
div_t div(int numer, int denom);
```

If the division is inexact, the sign of the resulting quotient is that of the algebraic quotient, and the magnitude of the resulting quotient is the largest integer less than the magnitude of the algebraic quotient. If the result cannot be represented, the behavior is undefined. The value returned has the structure type `div_t`, which contains the two `int` members, `quot` and `rem`, in either order. *See also* `ldiv`; `lldiv`.

division assignment operator A binary operator, `/=`, that permits division and assignment to be combined such that *exp1* `/=` *exp2* is equivalent to *exp1* `=` *exp1* `/` *exp2* except that in the former, *exp1* is only evaluated once. Both operands must have arithmetic type, and the left operand must be a modifiable lvalue. The order of evaluation of the operands is unspecified. The type of the result is the type of *exp1*. This operator associates right to left.

Prior to C99, if either operand is negative the behavior is implementation defined. That is, the result could be the largest integer less than or equal to the algebraic quotient or the smallest integer greater than or equal to the algebraic quotient. In such cases, C99 requires truncation toward zero.

See also assignment operator, compound.

division, integer, with negative values *See* `div`; division operator; `ldiv`; `lldiv`.

division operator A binary operator, `/`, that causes the value of its left operand to be divided by the value of its second. Both operands must have arithmetic type. The order of evaluation of the operands is unspecified. The usual arithmetic conversions are performed on the operands. This operator associates left to right.

Prior to C99, if either operand is negative the behavior is implementation defined. That is, the result could be the largest integer less than or equal to the algebraic quotient or the smallest integer greater than or equal to the algebraic quotient. In such cases, C99 requires truncation toward zero.

See also `div`; `ldiv`; `lldiv`.

`div_t`[C89] A type, defined in stdlib.h, that is a structure type used as the implementation-defined return type of the `div` function. One possible definition for `div_t` is:

```
typedef struct {
        int quot;
        int rem;
} div_t;
```

The ordering of the members does not need to be specified. *See also* `ldiv_t`; `lldiv_t`.

domain error An error that occurs if an argument input to a math function is outside the domain over which that function is defined. In this case, an implementation-defined value is returned, and, in C89, `errno` is set to the macro `EDOM`. C99 changed things slightly. Specifically, if `math_errhandling & MATH_ERRNO` is nonzero, `errno` is set to `EDOM`; if `math_errhandling & MATH_ERREXCEPT` is nonzero, the "invalid" floating-point exception is raised.

dot operator A binary operator, `.`, that is used to select the right operand from the structure or union designated by the left operand. The order of evaluation of the operands is unspecified. The type of the left operand must be structure or union, and the right operand must be the name of a member in that structure or union. This operator produces an lvalue if the left operand is an lvalue. (One example where the expression is not an lvalue is `f().m`.) A dot expression can almost always be rewritten using the arrow operator. For example, `s.m` is equivalent to `(&s)->m`. Similarly, if `s` is a structure or union having storage class `register`, `s.m` is permitted while `(&s)->m` is not because you cannot take the address of a register variable. The type of the result of the dot operator is the type of the named member. This operator associates left to right.

`double` A keyword used for one of the three floating-point types. (The other two are `float` and `long double`.) Traditionally, `double` meant "double precision" while `float` implied "single precision." However, `double` is permitted to have the same precision as `float`. Some compilers accept `long float` as a synonym for `double`; however, this is not permitted by Standard C. *See also* floating type.

`double _Complex`[C99] *See* `complex`.

`double _Imaginary`[C99] *See* `imaginary`.

double quote escape sequence An escape sequence, `\"`, which represents the double quote character. A double quote character `"` can be included in a string literal only in its escape sequence form. However, in a character constant, it can occur either as `'\"'` or `'"'`.

`double_t`[C99] A type, defined in math.h, that is a floating type and is at least as wide as `double` and `float_t`. If the macro `FLT_EVAL_METHOD` evaluates to 0 or 1, `double_t` is `double`. If `FLT_EVAL_METHOD` evaluates to 2, `double_t` is `long double`. For other values of `FLT_EVAL_METHOD`, its exact type is implementation defined.

`double` **type conversion** *See* conversion, usual arithmetic.

`do/while` Two keywords used to implement a loop that executes at least once. The general form is

```
do
        statement
while ( expression );
```

The loop body *statement* is executed, then *expression* is evaluated. If it evaluates to true, this process is repeated. *expression* is a full expression.

`dynamic_cast` A C++ keyword that is not part of Standard C. If you think you might wish to move C code to a C++ environment in the future, you should refrain from using `dynamic_cast` as an identifier in new C code you write.

E

E∗ value macros *See* errno value macros.

EBCDIC An acronym for Extended Binary Coded Decimal Interchange Code. This 8-bit code can represent 256 different characters and is in common use on IBM mainframes. Standard C is not character set-specific. *See also* ASCII; Unicode.

edit mask *See* conversion specifier.

`EDOM` A macro, defined in errno.h, that is used to indicate a domain error. It expands to an implementation-defined positive integer value. *See also* `errno`.

`EILSEQ`[C95] A macro, defined in errno.h, that is used to indicate an illegal sequence error. It expands to an implementation-defined positive integer value. *See also* `errno`; error, encoding.

element type The type of an array element. Each member of an array is an element.

`#elif` A preprocessor directive used as a short form for a nested `#else` with `#if`. It is used as follows:

`#elif` *constant-expression*

If *constant-expression* contains any identifiers that are not currently defined as macros, they are assumed (for this directive only) to be macros defined with value 0. In C89, *constant-expression* is evaluated as though each term had type `long int`. In C99, all signed integer types and all unsigned integer types act like the types `intmax_t` and `uintmax_t`, respectively.

ellipsis[C89] A punctuator that is used in function declarations and definitions to indicate a variable argument list. The only standard library functions that use this notation are the `printf` and `scanf` families. The standard header stdarg.h declares machinery for accessing arguments in a variable argument list. The behavior is undefined if you call a function that expects a variable argument list, but you do not have a prototype containing an ellipsis in scope. The rule then, is to always `#include <stdio.h>` before you call `printf` and `scanf` even though these functions have an `int` return type. *See also* conversion, function arguments.

C99 added the capability to have macros with a variable number of arguments. *See also* `__VA_ARGS__`.

#else A preprocessor directive used to indicate the false path of a conditional compilation directive set. Used with **#if**, **#ifdef**, **#ifndef**, **#elif**, and **#endif**. It has the following form:

```
#else
```

else statement *See* if/else.

empty statement *See* null statement.

encoding scheme A set of rules for parsing a stream of bytes into a group of coded characters. The meaning of a multibyte character can vary if the encoding scheme provides state-dependent encoding via shift sequences. Standard C requires that no encoding scheme have a byte with value zero as the second or subsequent byte of a multibyte character. This restriction allows many of the traditional string manipulation functions to be used transparently with strings containing multibyte characters.

Encoding schemes for wide characters are quite simple—all characters have the same internal width and each character has a unique value. (Note, however, that in Unicode, some characters, such as accented letters not given their own alternate encoding, are encoded as two wide characters: the letter, followed by the accent.)

Examples of encoding schemes are: ASCII, EBCDIC, EUC, JIS, Shift-JIS, ISO/IEC 10646.UCS-2 (also known as Unicode), and ISO/IEC 10646.UCS-4. *See also* __STDC_ISO_10646__.

#endif A preprocessor directive used to indicate the end of a conditional compilation directive set containing one or more of the following: **#if**, **#ifdef**, **#ifndef**, **#elif**, and **#else**. It has the following form:

```
#endif
```

end-of-file indicator One of the members stored in a FILE object. It is used by the standard I/O library functions in conjunction with the file system to indicate whether or not the end of file has been reached for the corresponding file. This member is accessed by feof and clearerr. The end-of-file indicator is cleared by fopen, freopen, ungetc, and ungetwc.

end-of-file macro *See* EOF; WEOF.

end-of-line indicator The character sequence used in a particular environment to indicate the end of a line of source or data input. For example, it might be a carriage-return/line-feed pair, or just a line-feed. In any case, C treats this indicator as a single new-line character.

entry An identifier reserved for future use as a keyword in the original definition of C. It is not part of Standard C.

`enum` The keyword used to specify an enumerated type and to declare identifiers for objects of that type; for example,

```
enum color {red, green = 4, blue};
enum color car_color;
```

The identifier `color` is the enumerated type tag, which is optional. The identifiers `red`, `green`, and `blue` are enumeration constants. (For convenience, a comma is permitted after the final enumeration constant.) Unless it contains an initializer, the first such constant in an enumeration has the value 0. Subsequent constants take on the value of one more than the previous constant except when overridden by an initializer. Constants within the same enumeration may have the same value, and the range of values represented need not be continuous.

enumerated type A set of related integer values, each of which is referred to as an enumeration constant. The type optionally may have a tag (and is declared somewhat like a structure or union). An object of an enumerated type maps to an implementation-defined integer type. The type checking for operations on enumerated objects is very weak. *See also* `enum`.

enumeration constant An identifier used inside the definition of an enumerated type. It is a translation-time constant expression of type `int` and may have an explicit initializer. Enumeration constants share the same name space as variables, functions, and typedef names. Unlike members defined within structures and unions, enumeration constants are never qualified with `.` and `->` operators. Instead, they can be used in any context where a translation-time constant expression is permitted (except in `#if` and `#elif` directives). *See also* `enum`.

enumeration tag *See* tag.

environment *See* environment list.

environment, freestanding[C89] A system in which a program does not run under the control of an operating system. Often, freestanding programs do not have access to a command-line processor or a file system. (An operating system is a special case of such an environment.) A C89 translator for a freestanding environment must provide the headers float.h, limits.h, and stddef.h. A C99 translator for a freestanding environment must also provide iso646.h, stdarg.h, stdbool.h, and stdint.h. Any library facilities available to the freestanding program are implementation defined. *See also* environment, hosted; `__STDC_HOSTED__`.

environment functions The stdlib.h functions `abort`, `atexit`, `_Exit`, `exit`, `getenv`, and `system`.

environment, hosted[C89] A system in which a program runs under the control of an operating system. Typically, hosted programs have access to a command-line processor and a file system. A conforming hosted C translator must implement all of the standard runtime library. *See also* environment, freestanding; `__STDC_HOSTED__`.

environment list A list of environment strings. What (if any) strings exist and how they are created or changed is implementation defined. This mechanism is often used on systems as a way to pass information (such as directory and file names) from an operating system shell or command level to an application program. Standard C provides `getenv` to access this list. *See also* `envp`.

environment variables The entries in an environment list.

environmental considerations Issues pertaining to translation and execution character sets, device character display semantics, signals and interrupts, and environmental limits.

environmental limits[C89,C99] Minimum "capacity" requirements placed on a conforming translator. A conforming implementation must be able to handle translation units of a minimum complexity. The values shown below are in pairs with the first representing C99 and the second (in parentheses) representing C89.

According to Standard C, "The implementation shall be able to translate and execute at least one program that contains at least one instance of every one of the following limits:

- 127 (15) nesting levels of compound statements, iteration control structures, and selection control structures
- 63 (8) nesting levels of conditional inclusion
- 12 (12) pointer, array, and function declarators (in any combinations) modifying an arithmetic, a structure, a union, or an incomplete type in a declaration
- 63 (31) nesting levels of parenthesized declarators within a full declarator
- 63 (32) nesting levels of parenthesized expressions within a full expression
- 63 (31) significant initial characters in an internal identifier or a macro name
- 31 (6) significant initial characters in an external identifier
- 4095 (511) external identifiers in one translation unit
- 511 (127) identifiers with block scope declared in one block

- 4,085 (1,024) macro identifiers simultaneously defined in one translation unit
- 127 (31) parameters in one function definition
- 127 (31) arguments in one function call
- 127 (31) parameters in one macro definition
- 127 (31) arguments in one macro invocation
- 4,095 (509) characters in a logical source line
- 4,095 (509) characters in a character-string literal or wide-string literal (after concatenation)
- 65,535 (32,767) bytes in an object (in a hosted environment only)
- 15 (8) nesting levels for headers
- 1,023 (257) `case` labels for a `switch` statement (excluding those for any nested `switch` statements)
- 1,023 (127) members in a single structure or union
- 1,023 (127) enumeration constants in a single enumeration
- 63 (15) levels of nested structure or union definitions in a single structure declaration list"

Standard C also requires an implementer to document the integer and floating type properties in limits.h and float.h.

`envp` An array of pointers to the strings specified as environment variables. It is commonly used as the third argument passed to `main`. `envp` is not defined by Standard C but is a permitted extension.

`EOF` A macro, defined in stdio.h, that is the negative integer constant expression returned by numerous functions to indicate an end-of-file condition. *See also* end-of-file indicator.

equality The testing of two expressions to see if their values are equal. This requires the `==` operator, which should not be confused with the assignment operator `=`.

equality operator A binary operator, `==`, that compares the values of its two operands for equality. Both operands must have scalar types and must be either both arithmetic, both pointers to qualified or unqualified versions of compatible types, one a pointer to `void` and the other a pointer to an object or incomplete type, or one a pointer and the other the null pointer constant. The order of evaluation of the operands is unspecified. The result has type `int` and value 0 (if false) or 1 (if true). This operator associates left to right. Note that the equality operator must not be confused with the assignment operator `=`. The two are easily confused and can be interchanged syntactically. However, their semantics are quite different. For example, in

```
if (a = b) /* ... */
```

the value of b is assigned to a and the value of a is tested for truth. In the following:

```
if (a == b) /* ... */
```

the values of a and b are compared for equality.

equals punctuator A punctuator used in initializers in object definitions and enumeration constants.

`ERANGE` A macro, defined in errno.h, that is used to indicate a range error. It expands to an implementation-defined positive integer value. *See also* `errno`.

`erf[f|l]`[C99] A function that computes the error function of `x`.

```
#include <math.h>
double erf(double x);
float erff(float x);
long double erfl(long double x);
```

where the error function is defined by $\frac{2}{\sqrt{\pi}} \int_0^x e^{-t^2} dt$.

`erfc[f|l]`[C99] A function that computes the complementary error function of `x`.

```
#include <math.h>
double erfc(double x);
float erfcf(float x);
long double erfcl(long double x);
```

where the complementary error function is defined by $1 - erf(x)$; that is, $1 - \frac{2}{\sqrt{\pi}} \int_x^\infty e^{-t^2} dt$. A range error occurs if `x` is too large.

`errno` A modifiable lvalue that is declared in errno.h and designates the memory location via which the standard library can communicate error values. Historically, `errno` has been declared using `extern int errno`; however, Standard C permits it to be a macro. There are only three standard values defined for `errno`: `EDOM`, `EILSEQ`, and `ERANGE`.

errno is cleared (set to 0) during program startup; however, no library routine is required to clear errno. Therefore, it is the programmer's responsibility to clear errno each time immediately before calling a library routine that is documented as having the ability to set it.

See also errno value macros; perror; strerror.

errno **value macros** Macros that define valid values for errno. They are required to be named E∗ where ∗ starts with an uppercase letter or digit. C89 defined only two such macros: EDOM and ERANGE; C95 added EILSEQ. Other implementation-defined macros of this form may exist. *See also* future library directions.

errno.h A header that contains definitions or declarations for the following identifiers:

Name	*Purpose*
EDOM	Argument out of domain
EILSEQ[C95]	Illegal sequence indicator
ERANGE	Result out of range
errno	Error number storage location

It also may contain other implementation-defined macros (named E∗) against which the value of errno can be compared. *See also* future library directions.

#error[C89] A preprocessor directive used to display a message on stderr and to terminate translation. It is used as follows:

```
#error [preprocessor-tokens]
```

error, domain *See* domain error.

error, encoding[C95] An error that occurs if the character sequence presented to mbrtowc (when it is called directly, or indirectly from some other library function) does not form a valid multibyte character, or if the value passed to the underlying wcrtomb does not correspond to a valid multibyte character. When an encoding error occurs within the wide-character and byte I/O functions, they store the value of the macro EILSEQ in errno.

error handling functions The stdio.h functions clearerr, feof, ferror, and perror.

error indicator One of the members stored in a FILE object. It is used by the standard I/O library functions in conjunction with the file system to indicate whether or not a read/write error has occurred on the corresponding file. *See also* clearerr; ferror.

error, range *See* range error.

escape sequence A sequence of source characters used to represent the code for one logical character. While displayable characters (such as A, b, ?, and +) may be represented as themselves directly, nondisplayable characters (such as backspace and new-line) must be represented using an escape sequence (such as `\b` and `\n`, respectively). Displayable characters can also be represented using either their octal or hexadecimal internal representation. The following table lists the escape sequences and their meanings:

Sequence	*Meaning*
`\"`	Double quote
`\'`	Single quote
`\0`	Null character
`\?`[C89]	Question mark
`\\`	Backslash
`\a`[C89]	Terminal alert
`\b`	Backspace
`\`*ddd*	Octal value *ddd*
`\f`	Form-feed
`\n`	New-line
`\r`	Carriage return
`\t`	Horizontal tab
`\v`	Vertical tab
`\x`*h..h*	Hexadecimal value *h..h*

See also future language directions.

EUC A scheme commonly used to encode Japanese text in multibyte characters. It is an abbreviation for Extended UNIX Code. *See also* JIS; Shift-JIS.

evaluation The act of performing an operation on one or more operands to produce a value (e.g., `a + b`), a designator (e.g., `*pc`), a side effect (e.g., `++i`), or a combination thereof (e.g., `*pc = g(a + b++)`). *See* order of evaluation.

exception *See* signal.

exclusive OR assignment operator *See* OR assignment operator, bitwise exclusive.

exclusive OR operator *See* OR operator, bitwise exclusive.

`exit` A function that causes normal program termination to occur.

```
#include <stdlib.h>
void exit(int status);
```

First, the functions registered by `atexit` are called in the reverse order of their registration. Then, all open output files are flushed, open files are closed, and temporary files created by `tmpfile` are removed. Control is then returned to the host environment, to which it is given the exit code `status`. *See also* `abort`.

`_Exit`[C99] A function that causes normal program termination to occur.

```
#include <stdlib.h>
void _Exit(int status);
```

Unlike with `exit`, no functions registered by `atexit` or signal handlers registered by `signal` are called. The `status` argument has the same meaning as in `exit`. It is implementation defined as to whether open streams are flushed or closed, or temporary files are removed.

exit code The `int` value returned by a user program to its calling environment when it returns from `main`, or from a call to `exit` or `abort`. The code's meaning is implementation defined except that zero and the object-like macro `EXIT_SUCCESS` signify success while `EXIT_FAILURE` indicates failure. Prior to C89, a value of 0 did not mean "success" on some systems.

Prior to C99, the exit code was undefined if you dropped through the outermost closing brace of `main`. However, C99 requires this to be equivalent to `return 0;` Explicitly returning from `main` without specifying a value results in an undefined exit code.

`EXIT_FAILURE`[C89] A macro, defined in stdlib.h, that is used as the implementation-defined failure exit code value that can be used with `exit` or `abort`. It expands to an integer expression (that is not necessarily constant). *See also* `EXIT_SUCCESS`.

`EXIT_SUCCESS`[C89] A macro, defined in stdlib.h, that is used as the implementation-defined success exit code value that can be used with `exit`. It expands to an integer expression (that is not necessarily constant). *See also* `EXIT_FAILURE`.

`exp[f|l]` A function that computes the exponential function of its argument `x`.

```
#include <math.h>
double exp(double x);
float expf(float x);
long double expl(long double x);
```

If the magnitude of the argument is too large, a range error occurs.

The `float` and `long double` versions were an invention of C89, where they were optional; however, in C99, they are required.

`exp2[f|l]`C99 A function that computes the base-2 exponential function of its argument `x`.

```
#include <math.h>
double exp2(double x);
float exp2f(float x);
long double exp2l(long double x);
```

If the magnitude of the argument is too large, a range error occurs.

`explicit` A C++ keyword that is not part of Standard C. If you think you might wish to move C code to a C++ environment in the future, you should refrain from using `explicit` as an identifier in new C code you write.

explicit conversion A conversion achieved by using a cast operator.

`expm1[f|l]`C99 A function that computes the base-e minus 1 exponential function of its argument `x`; that is, $e^x - 1$.

```
#include <math.h>
double expm1(double x);
float expm1f(float x);
long double expm1l(long double x);
```

If the value of the argument is positive and too large, a range error occurs.

exponential and logarithmic functions The math.h functions `exp`, `exp2`, `expm1`, `frexp`, `ldexp`, `log`, `log10`, `log1p`, `log2`, and `modf`, and their `float` and `long double` counterparts for both floating and complex types.

`export` A C++ keyword that is not part of Standard C. If you think you might wish to move C code to a C++ environment in the future, you should refrain from using `export` as an identifier in new C code you write.

expression A valid sequence of operators and operands that specifies how to compute a value (e.g., `a + b`), how to generate side effects (e.g., `f()`, `++i`, or `j--`), or both (e.g., `a + g() + ++k`).

expression, full An expression that is not part of another expression. There is a sequence point at the end of a full expression. Each of the following is a full expression: an initializer; the expression in an expression statement; the controlling expression of an `if`, `switch`, `while`, or `do` statement; each of the three (optional) expressions of a `for` statement; and the (optional) expression in a `return` statement.

expression, parenthesized Any expression contained within parentheses. The type and value of the parenthesized expression is the same as the type and value of the same expression without parentheses. A parenthesized expression is a primary expression. If expression *exp* is an lvalue, function designator, or void expression, then `(` *exp* `)` is, respectively, an lvalue, function designator, or void expression. This gives rise to the following correct, but odd-looking, expressions:

```
(((i))) = 6
((printf))("Hello")
```

expression statement An expression statement has the form

expression ;

Such an expression is a full expression. Most C statements are expression statements, as in the following examples:

```
i++;
f(i, j, k);
a = b + c - g();
x += y;
```

The following are also acceptable (but vacuous) expression statements; it is a quality-of-implementation issue whether an implementation identifies such vacuous statements or generates code for them:

```
i;
10 + j * k;
*pc + 3;
```

extended integer types[C99] Signed and unsigned integer types beyond those required by the standard. An implementation may support these, in which case they are subject to the rules of the standard with respect to signed and unsigned type behavior.

`extern` A keyword used to indicate a storage class that signifies an identifier is defined, either later in the same translation unit or in a separate translation unit. If a function declaration does not include a class keyword, `extern` is assumed.

external definition A non-`static` function definition or a non-`static` variable definition outside of a function definition. *See also* scope, file.

external name An identifier exported to the development environment. It may be visible to tools such as assemblers, linkers, object libraries, and debuggers; and its length of significance and case distinction may be limited. (C89 permits external name significance to be as few as 6 characters and to be monocase only, while C99 requires at least 31 characters of significance.) Also, underscores might be mapped to some other character. *See also* internal name; future language directions.

external object definition The defining instance of an external object. *See also* definition, tentative.

F

F suffix *See* constant, floating.

f suffix For the use of this construct in a floating-point constant, *see* constant, floating. For use with math library function names in C89, *see* future library directions.

fabs[f|l] A function that computes the absolute value of its floating-point argument x.

```
#include <math.h>
double fabs(double x);
float fabsf(float x);
long double fabsl(long double x);
```

The float and long double versions were an invention of C89, where they were optional; however, in C99, they are required.

false One of the two possible truth values, true and false. In C, an expression tests true if its value is nonzero; otherwise it tests false. Logical tests, such as if (x), are equivalent to, and treated as, if (x != 0). As such, logical tests may be performed on pointer expressions as well as arithmetic expressions because a zero-valued pointer expression represents the null pointer constant. *See also* false.

By definition, logical, relational, and equality expressions have type int and value 0 (false) or 1 (true).

false[C99] A macro, defined in stdbool.h, that expands to the integer constant 0. It is intended for use in contexts involving the bool macro (or its underlying type, _Bool.) *See also* true.

fclose A function that causes the stream pointed to by stream to be flushed and the corresponding file to be closed.

```
#include <stdio.h>
int fclose(FILE *stream);
```

If fclose successfully closes the stream, it returns a zero. If the stream was already closed or an error occurs, EOF is returned. If a program terminates abnormally, there is no guarantee that streams open for output will have their buffers flushed. It is permissible to close the files pointed to by stdin, stdout, and stderr.

fdim[f|l][C99] A function that determines the positive difference between its arguments.

```
#include <math.h>
double fdim(double x, double y);
float fdimf(float x, float y);
long double fdiml(long double x, long double y);
```

A range error may occur.

`FE_ALL_EXCEPT`^{C99} A macro, defined in fenv.h, that is the bitwise-OR of all floating-point exception macros defined by the implementation.

`feclearexcept`^{C99} A function that clears the supported floating-point exceptions represented by its argument.

```
#include <fenv.h>
void feclearexcept(int excepts);
```

`FE_DFL_ENV`^{C99} A macro, defined in fenv.h, that represents the default floating-point environment, as installed at program startup. It expands to an expression of type `const fenv_t *`.

`FE_DIVBYZERO`^{C99} *See* floating-point exception macro.

`FE_DOWNWARD`^{C99} *See* rounding direction.

`fegetenv`^{C99} A function that stores the current floating-point environment in the object pointed to by `envp`.

```
#include <fenv.h>
void fegetenv(fenv_t *envp);
```

`fegetexceptflag`^{C99} A function that stores an implementation-defined representation of the states of the floating-point status flags indicated by the argument `excepts` in the object pointed to by `flagp`.

```
#include <fenv.h>
void fegetexceptflag(fexcept_t *flagp, int excepts);
```

`fegetround`^{C99} A function that returns the current rounding direction.

```
#include <fenv.h>
int fegetround(void);
```

The value returned should correspond to one of the rounding direction macros. It will be a negative value if there is no such rounding direction macro or the current rounding direction cannot be determined.

`feholdexcept`C99 A function that saves the current floating-point environment in the object pointed to by **envp**, clears the floating-point status flags, and then installs a non-stop mode, if available, for all floating-point exceptions.

```
#include <fenv.h>
int feholdexcept(fenv_t *envp);
```

`FE_INEXACT`C99 *See* floating-point exception macro.

`FE_INVALID`C99 *See* floating-point exception macro.

`FENV_ACCESS` **pragma**C99 *See* `#pragma STDC FP_ACCESS`.

fenv.hC99 A header that provides a number of types, macros, and functions which give access to the current floating-point environment. The following table lists their names and purpose.

Name	*Purpose*
`FE_ALL_EXCEPT`	All FP exceptions ORed together
`FE_DFL_ENV`	Default FP environment
`FE_DIVBYZERO`	FP exception macro
`FE_DOWNWARD`	Rounding direction
`FE_INEXACT`	FP exception macro
`FE_INVALID`	FP exception macro
`FE_OVERFLOW`	FP exception macro
`FE_TONEAREST`	Rounding direction
`FE_TOWARDZERO`	Rounding direction
`FE_UNDERFLOW`	FP exception macro
`FE_UPWARD`	Rounding direction
`feclearexcept`	Clear given FP exceptions
`fegetenv`	Store current FP environment
`fegetexceptflag`	Store FP status
`fegetround`	Get rounding mode
`feholdexcept`	Save current FP environment
`fenv_t`	Type that represents an FP environment
`feraiseexcept`	Raise given FP exceptions
`fesetenv`	Set current FP environment
`fesetexceptflag`	Set given FP exception flags
`fesetround`	Set rounding mode
`fetestexcept`	Test FP status flags
`feupdateenv`	Save currently raised FP exceptions
`fexcept_t`	Type that represents FP status flags

`fenv_t`C99 A type, defined in fenv.h, that is capable of representing a floating-point environment.

`feof` A function that tests the end-of-file indicator for the file pointed to by `stream`.

```
#include <stdio.h>
int feof(FILE *stream);
```

Zero is returned if the end-of-file indicator is clear; nonzero if it is set.

`FE_OVERFLOW`[C99] *See* floating-point exception macro.

`feraiseexcept`[C99] A function that raises the supported floating-point exceptions represented by its argument.

```
#include <fenv.h>
void feraiseexcept(int excepts);
```

`ferror` A function that tests the error indicator for the file pointed to by `stream`.

```
#include <stdio.h>
int ferror(FILE *stream);
```

Zero is returned if the error indicator is clear; nonzero if it is set.

`fesetenv`[C99] A function that establishes the floating-point environment represented by the object pointed to by `envp`.

```
#include <fenv.h>
void fesetenv(const fenv_t *envp);
```

`fesetexceptflag`[C99] A function that sets the floating-point status flags indicated by the argument `excepts` to the states stored in the object pointed to by `flagp`. No exceptions are raised.

```
#include <fenv.h>
void fesetexceptflag(const fexcept_t *flagp, int excepts);
```

`fesetround`[C99] A function that establishes the rounding direction represented by its argument `round`, provided that argument equals the value of a supported rounding direction macro.

```
#include <fenv.h>
int fesetround(int round);
```

`fetestexcept`[C99] A function that determines which of a specified subset of the floating-point exception flags are currently set.

```
#include <fenv.h>
int fetestexcept(int excepts);
```

`FE_TONEAREST`[C99] *See* rounding direction.

`FE_TOWARDZERO`[C99] *See* rounding direction.

`FE_UNDERFLOW`[C99] *See* floating-point exception macro.

`feupdateenv`[C99] A function that saves the currently raised floating-point exceptions in its automatic storage, installs the floating-point environment represented by the object pointed to by `envp`, and then raises the saved floating-point exceptions.

```
#include <fenv.h>
void feupdateenv(const fenv_t *envp);
```

`FE_UPWARD`[C99] *See* rounding direction.

`fexcept_t`[C99] A type, defined in fenv.h, that represents the floating-point status flags.

`fflush` A function that flushes an open stream's I/O buffer. If the stream were being written, any unwritten data in the output buffer is written.

```
#include <stdio.h>
int fflush(FILE *stream);
```

`fflush` should be used only with streams open for output or open for update and currently in output mode. If the stream is not open for output, or if it is open for update and the immediately previous operation is other than output, the behavior is undefined. However, some implementations permit input streams to be `fflush`ed reliably. A zero value is returned on success; an `EOF` is returned if a write error occurs. If a program terminates abnormally, there is no guarantee that streams open for output will have their buffers flushed. If `stream` is the null pointer, all files currently open for output are flushed.

`fgetc` A function that gets the next character (if any) from the file pointed to by `stream`.

```
#include <stdio.h>
int fgetc(FILE *stream);
```

The character is read as an `unsigned char` and returned as an `int`. If end-of-file is detected, `fgetc` returns `EOF`, and the end-of-file indicator is set for that stream. (`feof` can be used to test this indicator.) If a read error occurs, `EOF` is returned and the error indicator is set for that stream. (`ferror` can be used to test this indicator.) *See also* `fgetwc`; `getwc`.

`fgetpos`[C89] A function that stores the current value of the stream's file position indicator in the object pointed to by `pos`.

```
#include <stdio.h>
int fgetpos(FILE * restrict stream,
    fpos_t * restrict pos);
```

`fgetpos` was invented to handle very large files whose file position indicator cannot be represented in a `long int` (as required by `ftell`).

The object stored in `pos` is suitable for use by `fsetpos` to restore the file to that previous position. `fgetpos` returns zero on success. On failure, a nonzero value is returned, and `errno` is set to an implementation-defined positive value.

`fgets` A function that reads at most $n-1$ characters from the file pointed to by `stream` into the array pointed to by `s`. A `'\0'` is appended to `array` after the last read character.

```
#include <stdio.h>
char *fgets(char * restrict s, int n,
    FILE * restrict stream);
```

If a new-line is encountered, or end-of-file occurs, no more characters are read. If seen, a new-line is included in the array (unlike `gets`). If `fgets` succeeds, it returns `s`. If an end-of-file condition is encountered and no characters have been read yet, `NULL` is returned and the contents of the array pointed to by `s` are unchanged. `NULL` is also returned on a read error; however, the contents of the array are then indeterminate. *See also* `fgetws`.

`fgetwc`[C95] A function that gets the next wide character (if any) from the file pointed to by `stream`.

```
#include <stdio.h>
#include <wchar.h>
wint_t fgetwc(FILE *stream);
```

The wide character is read as a `wchar_t` and returned as a `wint_t`. If end-of-file is detected, `fgetwc` returns `WEOF`, and the end-of-file indicator is set for that stream. If a read error occurs, `WEOF` is returned, and the error indicator is set for that stream. *See also* `fgetc`; `getc`.

`fgetws`[C95] A function that reads at most $n-1$ wide characters from the file pointed to by `stream` into the array pointed to by `s`. A wide `'\0'` is appended to `array` after the last read character.

```
#include <stdio.h>
#include <wchar.h>
wchar_t *fgetws(wchar_t * restrict s, int n,
    FILE * restrict stream);
```

See also `fgets`.

field An item input by the `scanf` function family or output by the `printf` function family. Each field has a corresponding conversion specifier.

`__FILE__` A predefined object-like macro that expands to the name of the source file as a string. This macro can be used in any context where a string literal is permitted or required; for example,

```
char fname[] = __FILE__;
printf("%s", __FILE__);
```

Because adjacent string literals are concatenated, the following is also permitted:

```
printf(">%s<\n", "xxx" __FILE__ "xxx");
```

Some implementations include the file's full path name (such as device and directory as well as name), others do not. This macro cannot be the subject of `#undef`.

Note that there is no wide string version of this macro, so it was difficult to get the filename string concatenated with wide strings; however, C99 allows wide and single-byte strings to be concatenated directly, so that operation becomes trivial. *See also* `#line`.

file A term that has the usual data processing meaning. When a file is opened by a standard library function, a stream is associated with it. The file is specified in all subsequent operations on, and accesses to, that file via a stream, which is represented as a `FILE` pointer.

`FILE` An object type capable of containing the "current context" of an open file. This information includes buffering details, error and end-of-file flags, file position indicator, and other unspecified members. A program never needs to create `FILE` objects directly. Instead, they are created and managed by library functions.

file access functions The stdio.h functions `fclose`, `fflush`, `fopen`, `freopen`, `setbuf`, and `setvbuf`.

file closing *See* `abort`; `exit`; `_Exit`; `fclose`; `freopen`.

file creation *See* `fopen`; `tmpfile`.

file name The names of files for which the attributes and format of those on external media (such as disks or tapes) is specific to each operating system. As such, Standard C places no requirements on file names nor does it rely on them. Functions such as `fopen` simply expect a file name to be represented as a null-terminated array of `char`. *See also* `FILENAME_MAX`.

While most implementations actually represent headers as text files (with the same name) on disk, it is not required.

The file names used by `tmpfile` and `tmpnam` are unspecified.

file opening *See* `fopen`; `freopen`; `tmpfile`.

file operation functions The stdio.h functions `remove`, `rename`, `tmpfile`, and `tmpnam`.

file pointer A pointer to an object of type `FILE`.

file position indicator A member that is part of each `FILE` object and has type `fpos_t`. When files on devices supporting positioning requests are opened for read or write, the file position indicator is set to the start of the file. If the file is opened for append, the indicator is set either to the start or to the end of the file, as defined by the implementation. This indicator is maintained by the file positioning and I/O functions and is not accessed directly by application programmers. *See also* file positioning functions.

file positioning functions The stdio.h functions `fgetpos`, `fseek`, `fsetpos`, `ftell`, and `rewind`.

file, source The file containing the text of the program to be translated. *See also* translation unit.

`FILENAME_MAX`^{C89} A macro, defined in stdio.h, that expands to an integer constant expression that represents the maximum length of a file name string that can be used with the implementation.

flexible array member^{C99} The last member whose type is an incomplete array, which is present in a structure that has more than one named member; for example,

```
struct message {
        int count;
        char text[];    // flexible array member
};
```

Such structures are typically used as follows:

```
message *pm;

pm = malloc(sizeof(struct message) + (N * sizeof(char)));
```

where N is the the number of elements represented by count.

float A keyword used for one of the three floating-point types. (The other two are double and long double.) Traditionally, double meant "double precision" while float implied "single precision." float expressions traditionally were widened to double when used in expressions and as arguments to functions. However, Standard C allows them to be used without widening if no prototype is in scope or, if a prototype is in scope yet it contains an ellipses in the appropriate place. *See also* conversion, function arguments; floating type.

float _Complex[C99] *See* complex.

float.h[C89,C99] A header that contains a family of macros that describe the floating-point properties of the target system. While Standard C requires certain minima (or maxima), it is intended that an implementation will document its actual values. The macros have FLT, DBL, and LDBL prefixes which designate the types float, double, and long double, respectively. (Note that several generic floating-point attributes have the prefix FLT, even though they are not float-specific.) The following is the complete set of macros:

DBL_DIG	FLT_DIG	LDBL_DIG
DBL_EPSILON	FLT_EPSILON	LDBL_EPSILON
DBL_MANT_DIG	FLT_MANT_DIG	LDBL_MANT_DIG
DBL_MAX	FLT_MAX	LDBL_MAX
DBL_MAX_10_EXP	FLT_MAX_10_EXP	LDBL_MAX_10_EXP
DBL_MAX_EXP	FLT_MAX_EXP	LDBL_MAX_EXP
DBL_MIN	FLT_MIN	LDBL_MIN
DBL_MIN_10_EXP	FLT_MIN_10_EXP	LDBL_MIN_10_EXP
DBL_MIN_EXP	FLT_MIN_EXP	LDBL_MIN_EXP
DECIMAL_DIG[C99]		
FLT_EVAL_METHOD[C99]	FLT_RADIX	FLT_ROUNDS

All integer value macros except FLT_ROUNDS are guaranteed to expand to a translation-time constant expression suitable for use with #if. *See also* environmental limits.

float _Imaginary[C99] *See* imaginary.

floating-point exception macro[C99] A macro, defined in fenv.h, that indicates that implementation supports the corresponding floating-point exception. The defined set contains FE_DIVBYZERO, FE_INEXACT,

FE_INVALID, FE_OVERFLOW, and FE_UNDERFLOW. Other implementation-defined macros whose names begin with FE_ and an uppercase letter, may also be defined. These macros must expand to integer constant expressions such that bitwise-ORing of all combinations of the macros results in distinct values.

floating suffix, `f` or `F`[C89] *See* constant, floating.

floating suffix, `l` or `L`[C89] *See* constant, floating.

floating type A type that is represented using an exponent and fractional part. There are three such types: `float`, `double`, and `long double` (which was an invention of C89). An object of type `long double` must have as least as much range and precision as that of type `double`, which, in turn, must have at least as much as `float`. As such, two or more of the three types could map to the same representation. The header float.h can be used to determine the attributes of an implementation's floating-point types. All floating types are arithmetic types.

`float_t`[C99] A type, defined in math.h, that is a floating type at least as wide as `float`. If the macro `FLT_EVAL_METHOD` evaluates to 0, `float_t` is `float`. If `FLT_EVAL_METHOD` evaluates to 1, `float_t` is `double`. If `FLT_EVAL_METHOD` evaluates to 2, `float_t` is `long double`. The exact type is implementation defined for other values of `FLT_EVAL_METHOD`. *See* `double_t`

`floor[f|l]` A function that computes the largest integer value not greater than its argument `x`.

```
#include <math.h>
double floor(double x);
float floorf(float x);
long double floorl(long double x);
```

The integer value computed is returned as a `double`.

The `float` and `long double` versions were an invention of C89, where they were optional; however, in C99, they are required.

`FLT_DIG`[C89] A macro, defined in float.h, that designates the number of decimal digits, such that a `float` value of that significance can be rounded into a floating-point number and back again without change in those decimal digits.

`FLT_EPSILON`[C89] A macro, defined in float.h, that designates the difference between 1.0 and the least value greater than 1.0 that is representable in the `float` type.

`FLT_EVAL_METHOD`^C99 A macro, defined in float.h, that indicates how floating-point operations are evaluated with respect to range and precision. Its value can be one of the following:

-1 Indeterminable.

0 Evaluate all operations and constants to the range and precision of the type.

1 Evaluate operations and constants of type `float` and `double` to the range and precision of `double`, and `long double` to `long double`.

2 Evaluate all operations and constants to the range and precision of `long double`.

Other All other negative values indicate implementation-defined behavior.

`FLT_MANT_DIG`^C89 A macro, defined in float.h, that designates the number of base-`FLT_RADIX` digits in the floating-point significand of a `float` value.

`FLT_MAX`^C89 A macro, defined in float.h, that designates the maximum representable finite `float` number.

`FLT_MAX_10_EXP`^C89 A macro, defined in float.h, that designates the maximum integer such that 10 raised to that power is in a given range of representable finite floating-point numbers.

`FLT_MAX_EXP`^C89 A macro, defined in float.h, that designates the maximum integer such that `FLT_RADIX` raised to that power minus 1 is a representable finite floating-point number.

`FLT_MIN`^C89 A macro, defined in float.h, that designates the minimum normalized positive `float` number.

`FLT_MIN_10_EXP`^C89 A macro, defined in float.h, that designates the minimum negative integer such that 10 raised to that power is in a given range of normalized floating-point numbers.

`FLT_MIN_EXP`^C89 A macro, defined in float.h, that designates the minimum negative integer such that `FLT_RADIX` raised to that power minus 1 is a normalized floating-point number.

`FLT_RADIX`^C89 A macro, defined in float.h, that designates the radix of exponent representation. This macro expands to a translation-time constant expression suitable for use with `#if`.

`FLT_ROUNDS`^C89 A macro, defined in float.h, that designates the current mode of rounding behavior. Standard C defines the following modes:

-1 Indeterminable

0 Toward zero

1 To nearest

2 Toward positive infinity

3 Toward negative infinity

All other values specify implementation-defined rounding behavior.

`fma[f|l]`[C99] A function that computes a fused multiply-and-add, $(x \times y) + z$, as a single operation.

```
#include <math.h>
double fma(double x, double y, double z);
float fmaf(float x, float y, float z);
long double fmal(long double x, long double y,
    long double z);
```

`fma` may provide a more accurate result than performing a multiply followed by a separate add since only the final result is rounded, as opposed to rounding the result of the multiply, followed by rounding the result of the add.

`fmax[f|l]`[C99] A function that determines the maximum numeric value of its arguments.

```
#include <math.h>
double fmax(double x, double y);
float fmaxf(float x, float y);
long double fmaxl(long double x, long double y);
```

If one argument is a NaN and the other numeric, the numeric value is returned.

`fmin[f|l]`[C99] A function that determines the minimum numeric value of its arguments.

```
#include <math.h>
double fmin(double x, double y);
float fminf(float x, float y);
long double fminl(long double x, long double y);
```

If one argument is a NaN and the other numeric, the numeric value is returned.

`fmod[f|l]` A function that computes the floating-point remainder of `x/y`.

```
#include <math.h>
double fmod(double x, double y);
float fmodf(float x, float y);
long double fmodl(long double x, long double y);
```

The value returned is $x - i \times y$, where i is an integer such that, if y is nonzero, the result has the same sign as x and a magnitude less than that of y. If y is 0, it is implementation defined whether or not a domain error occurs, or if `fmod` returns 0.

The `float` and `long double` versions were an invention of C89, where they were optional; however, in C99, they are required.

`fopen` A function that opens the file whose name is pointed to by `filename`, in the mode specified by `mode`.

```
#include <stdio.h>
FILE *fopen(const char * restrict filename,
    const char * restrict mode);
```

`mode` points to a string whose initial character contents must be one of the following sequences: `"r"`, `"w"`, `"a"`, `"rb"`, `"wb"`, `"ab"`, `"r+"`, `"w+"`, `"a+"`, `"rb+"`, `"wb+"`, `"ab+"`, `"r+b"`, `"w+b"`, or `"a+b"`. Mode `r` signifies read, `w` signifies write (or create if the file does not already exist), and `a` signifies append mode. In the absence of mode `b`, the file is deemed to be a text stream, while `b` signifies a binary stream. The `+` mode indicates that the file is to be open for update. The set of modes `"r?+"` is equivalent to the set `"r+?"`.

If `fopen` succeeds, it returns a `FILE` pointer to the opened stream. On failure, it returns `NULL`. Note that an implementation may limit the number of currently open files—`FOPEN_MAX` specifies the number permitted—in which case `fopen` will fail if you attempt to exceed this number. The error and end-of-file indicators are cleared.

The standard streams `stderr`, `stdin`, and `stdout` are opened automatically at program startup. *See also* `FOPEN_MAX`; `freopen`.

`FOPEN_MAX`[C89] A macro, defined in stdio.h, that expands to an integer constant expression representing the minimum number of files that the implementation guarantees you can have open simultaneously. Standard C requires `FOPEN_MAX` to be at least eight, including `stdin`, `stdout`, and `stderr`. Earlier versions of it were called `SYS_MAX` and `OPEN_MAX`. Files created by `tmpfile` count against this limit.

`for` A looping construct that evaluates its criteria before each iteration of the loop like `while` and unlike `do/while` which always executes at least once. It has the following form:

```
for ( [ exp1 ]; [ exp2 ]; [ exp3 ] )
        statement
```

First, *exp1* is evaluated for the side effects it contains. Then, *exp2* is evaluated. If it tests false, the body of the `for` statement is bypassed. If it tests true, *statement* is executed and *exp3* is evaluated for its side effects. The process is then repeated starting with *exp2*.

All three expressions are optional. If the first is missing, there is no initialization. If the second is missing, it is as if a true expression were present. If the third is missing, there is nothing to do at the end of each iteration. A `for` construct can always be rewritten as a `while` construct and vice versa. Each of *exp1*, *exp2*, and *exp3* is a full expression.

C99 permits *exp1* to be a declaration, whose identifiers' scope ends at the end of the loop body.

form-feed One of the white space characters allowed in source text and as input to certain library functions.

form-feed escape sequence An escape sequence, `\f`, which represents the form-feed character.

formatted I/O An input/output capability provided by the `scanf` and `printf` functions families, respectively. The `printf` family provides formatted output capabilities to the standard output stream (usually directed to the screen or terminal printer), to files, and to memory. The `scanf` family handles formatted input from these same places.

`FP_*` **value macros** *See* number classification macro.

`fpclassify`^C99 A macro, defined in math.h, that classifies its argument value as having one of the following categories: infinite, NaN, normal, subnormal, zero, or implementation defined.

```
#include <math.h>
int fpclassify(real-floating-type x);
```

The value returned is one of the number classification macros.

`FP_CONTRACT` **pragma**^C99 *See* `#pragma STDC FP_CONTRACT`.

`FP_FAST_FMA`^C99 An optional macro, defined in math.h, which indicates that, in general, the `fma` function executes about as fast as, or faster than, a multiply and an add of `double` operands. *See also* the macros `FP_FAST_FMAF` and `FP_FAST_FMAL`.

`FP_FAST_FMAF`^C99 An optional macro, defined in math.h, which indicates that, in general, the `fma` function executes about as fast as, or faster than, a multiply and an add of `float` operands. *See also* `FP_FAST_FMA` and `FP_FAST_FMAL`.

`FP_FAST_FMAL`C99 An optional macro, defined in math.h, which indicates that, in general, the `fma` function executes about as fast as, or faster than, a multiply and an add of `long double` operands. *See also* `FP_FAST_FMA` and `FP_FAST_FMAF`.

`FP_ILOGB0`C99 A macro, defined in math.h, that expands to one of the integer constant expressions `INT_MIN` or `-INT_MAX`. This macro's value is returned by the function `ilogb` if its argument is zero.

`FP_ILOGBNAN`C99 A macro, defined in math.h, that expands to one of the integer constant expressions `INT_MIN` or `INT_MAX`. This macro's value is returned by the function `ilogb` if its argument is a NaN.

`FP_INFINITE`C99 *See* number classification macro.

`FP_NAN`C99 *See* number classification macro.

`FP_NORMAL`C99 *See* number classification macro.

`fpos_t`C89 A type, defined in stdio.h, that is large enough to hold the largest possible file position indicator for the implementation. *See* `fgetpos`; `fsetpos`.

`fprintf` A function that writes formatted output to the file specified by `stream` in a format specified by `format`. It is a more general version of `printf`.

```
#include <stdio.h>
int fprintf(FILE * restrict stream,
    const char * restrict format, ...);
```

A call to `printf` is equivalent to a call to `fprintf` using the stream `stdout`. For a discussion of `format` and the value returned, *see* `printf`. *See also* `fwprintf`.

`FP_SUBNORMAL`C99 *See* number classification macro.

`fputc` A function that writes the character specified by `c` (converted to `unsigned char`) to the file pointed to by `stream`.

```
#include <stdio.h>
int fputc(int c, FILE *stream);
```

On success, the character written is returned. If a write error occurs, `EOF` is returned, and the error indicator is set for that stream. (`ferror` can be used to test this indicator.) *See also* `fputc`; `putc`; `putwc`.

`fputs` A function that writes the string pointed to by `s` to the file pointed to by `stream`.

```
#include <stdio.h>
int fputs(const char * restrict s,
    FILE * restrict stream);
```

The `'\0'` terminating the string is not written. Unlike `puts`, `fputs` does not append a new-line to the output. `fputs` returns `EOF` if an error occurs; otherwise, it returns a nonnegative value. *See also* `fputws`.

`fputwc`[C95] A function that writes the wide character specified by `c` to the file pointed to by `stream`.

```
#include <stdio.h>
#include <wchar.h>
wint_t fputwc(wchar_t c, FILE *stream);
```

On success, the wide character written is returned. If a write error occurs, `WEOF` is returned, and the error indicator is set for that stream. *See also* `fputc`.

`fputws`[C95] A function that writes the wide string pointed to by `s` to the file pointed to by `stream`.

```
#include <stdio.h>
#include <wchar.h>
int fputws(const wchar_t * restrict s,
    FILE * restrict stream);
```

The wide null terminating the string is not written. `EOF` is returned if an error occurs; otherwise, a nonnegative value is returned. *See also* `fputs`.

`FP_ZERO`[C99] *See* number classification macro.

`frac_digits`[C89] An `lconv` structure member that is a nonnegative number representing the number of fractional digits (those after the decimal point) to be displayed in a formatted monetary quantity. A value of `CHAR_MAX` indicates that the value is not available in the current locale. In the `"C"` locale this member must have the value `CHAR_MAX`.

`fread` A function that reads up to `nmemb` elements each of size `size` into the array pointed to by `ptr` from the file pointed to by `stream`.

```
#include <stdio.h>
size_t fread(void * restrict ptr, size_t size,
    size_t nmemb, FILE * restrict stream);
```

If an error occurs, the file position indicator's value is indeterminate. If a partial element is read, its value is indeterminate. The value returned is the number of elements successfully read. This number may be less than nmemb if end-of-file is detected or if an error occurs. If either size or nmemb is 0, a zero is returned and the contents of the array pointed to by ptr remains intact. *See also* fwrite.

free A function that causes the space (previously allocated by calloc, malloc, or realloc) pointed to by ptr to be freed.

```
#include <stdlib.h>
void free(void *ptr);
```

If ptr is NULL, free does nothing. Otherwise, if ptr is not a value previously returned by one of these three allocation functions, the behavior is undefined. The value of a pointer that refers to space that has been freed is indeterminate, and such pointers should not be dereferenced. Note that free has no way to communicate an error if one is detected.

freestanding environment[C89] *See* environment, freestanding; cross-compilation.

freopen A function that is almost identical to fopen except that freopen recycles an existing FILE pointer that points to a currently open file.

```
#include <stdio.h>
FILE *freopen(const char * restrict filename,
    const char * restrict mode, FILE * restrict stream);
```

The arguments filename and mode are the same as for fopen. If freopen succeeds, it returns the value of stream; otherwise it returns NULL. freopen first tries to close the file associated with stream. Any failure encountered in this attempt is ignored. The error and end-of-file indicators are cleared.

frexp[f|l] A function that breaks a floating-point number value into a normalized fraction and an integer power of 2.

```
#include <math.h>
double frexp(double value, int *exp);
float frexpf(float value, int *exp);
long double frexpl(long double value, int *exp);
```

The integer power is stored at the location pointed to by exp and the fractional part is the return value. The value returned has magnitude of

0 or is in the interval $[1/2, 1)$, and `value` equals $x \times 2^{*exp}$. If `value` is 0, both the return value and `*exp` are 0.

The `float` and `long double` versions were an invention of C89, where they were optional; however, in C99, they are required.

`friend` A C++ keyword that is not part of Standard C. If you think you might wish to move C code to a C++ environment in the future, you should refrain from using `friend` as an identifier in new C code you write.

`fscanf` A function that reads formatted input from the file specified by `stream` in a format specified by `format`. It is a more general version of `scanf`.

```
#include <stdio.h>
int fscanf(FILE * restrict stream,
    const char * restrict format, ...);
```

Note, that all arguments must be passed by address. A call to `scanf` is equivalent to a call to `fscanf` using the stream `stdin`. For a discussion of `format` and the value returned, *see* `scanf`. *See also* `fwscanf`.

`fseek` A function that sets the current value of the stream's file position indicator to an `offset` based on the value of `whence`.

```
#include <stdio.h>
int fseek(FILE *stream, long int offset,
    int whence);
```

`whence` may be any one of the three macros `SEEK_SET`, `SEEK_CUR`, or `SEEK_END`, which represent, respectively, the start of the file, the current file position, and the end of the file. On success, `fseek` clears the end-of-file indicator, discards any pushed back characters for that stream and returns zero. On failure, it returns a nonzero value.

For very large files whose file position indicator cannot be represented in a `long int` (as required by `fseek`), use `fsetpos`. *See also* `ftell`.

`fsetpos`[C89] A function that sets the file position indicator for the file pointed to by `stream` to the value of the object pointed to by `pos`.

```
#include <stdio.h>
int fsetpos(FILE *stream, const fpos_t *pos);
```

On success, `fsetpos` returns zero, clears the end-of-file indicator, and discards characters pushed back via `ungetc`. On failure, a nonzero value is returned and errno is set to an implementation-defined positive value. *See also* fgetpos; fseek.

ftell A function that returns the current value of the stream's file position indicator.

```
#include <stdio.h>
long int ftell(FILE *stream);
```

On failure, -1L is returned and errno is set to an implementation-defined positive value. For very large files whose file position indicator cannot be represented in a long int (as required by ftell), use fgetpos. *See also* fseek.

full declarator *See* declarator, full.

full expression *See* expression, full.

fully buffered stream A stream in which characters are intended to be sent to or received from the host environment as a block when some buffer is filled. *See also* _IOFBF; setvbuf.

__func__[C99] A predefined identifier that is implicitly declared in each function as if the following declaration

```
static const char __func__[] = "function-name";
```

occurred immediately following the opening brace of that function's definition; *function-name* is the name of the parent function.

function The basic executable module in a C program. It is synonymous with a subroutine or procedure in other languages. All C functions have the same general format, including main. A function may expect arguments, produce a return value, both, or neither. In C, function definitions do not nest.

function argument *See* argument.

function body That part of a function's definition delimited by { and } that immediately follows the declarator part that introduces the definition; for example,

```
void f(int i, double d)
{                   /* body begins here */
        ...
}                   /* body ends here */
```

```
void f(i, d)
int i;
double d;
{                    /* body begins here */
          ...
}                    /* body ends here */
```

function call The act of invoking a function using the function call operator `()`.

function call operator A primary operator, `()`, that has the following general form:

exp1 `(` [*exp2* [`,` *exp3*] ...] `)`

where *exp1* designates the function to be called and *exp2, exp3,* ... are the arguments passed to that function. The order of evaluation of all the expressions is unspecified, but there is a sequence point after all expressions have been evaluated, just before the function is actually called. The type of the result is that returned by the function—it can be any scalar, structure, or union type, or the incomplete type `void`. This operator associates left to right.

function declarator The part of a declaration having the following form:

D `(` *parameter-type-list* `)`

as in `void f(int i, double d)`, or:

D `(` *identifier-list*$_{opt}$ `)`

as in `void f(i, d)`.

See also future language directions.

function definition A mechanism for defining a function. It has the following general form:

declaration-specifiers$_{opt}$ *declarator*
declaration-list$_{opt}$ *compound-statement*

where *compound-statement* is the function's body. *See also* future language directions.

function designator An expression that has a function type. In most cases, such an expression is converted to a pointer to that function. The most common way to designate a function is simply to use its name. However, a function also can be designated by dereferencing a pointer to it. For example, given the following declarations:

```
void f(int);
void (*pf)(int) = f;
void (**pf)(int) = &pf;
```

the function `f` can be designated by the expressions `f`, `*pf`, and `**ppf`.

See also conversion, function.

function library A collection of functions that may be defined by Standard C, extra functions provided by an implementer, third-party or user-written functions, or a combination of all three.

function name An identifier used to name a function. Function names share the same name space as enumeration constants, variables, and `typedef` names.

function parameter *See* parameter.

function prototype A function declaration that includes a parameter type list. Each parameter optionally may include an identifier, which has no effect. Prototypes were adapted by C89 from the C++ language, for example,

```
void f(int [i], double [d]);
```

is a prototype that declares `f` to be a function that takes one `int` argument and one `double` argument and returns no value. If present, the parameter names must be unique within that prototype. The "old-style" declaration for this function would be as follows:

```
void f();
```

Essentially, a prototype is an old-style function declaration that has argument list information. A new style of defining a function was also defined by C89. It also uses the prototype notation.

function return The explicit or implicit return from a called function to its caller. *See also* `return`.

function type A type that describes a function. This type information includes both the argument list and the return type. *See also* function designator.

function type conversion *See* conversion, function.

future directions Guidance contained in Standard C to implementers and users with regard to areas in which future revision might take place. Language standards are revised periodically, either to correct shortcomings or, more likely, to add support for new devices, application classes, and environments. (With ANSI and ISO standards, this typically takes place every 10 years.) For specific details *see* future language directions; future library directions. A future standard revision might even drop support for features declared obsolescent in previous versions.

future language directions Guidance contained in Standard C to implementers and users with regard to areas in which language revision might occur, due to a revision of the standard, or language may be added as an extension to a conforming implementation. The following items are taken directly from the C89 and C99 standards:

Array parameters C89 and C99: The use of two parameters declared with an array type (prior to their adjustment to pointer type) in separate lvalues to designate the same object is an obsolescent feature.

Character escape sequences C89 and C99: Lowercase letters as escape sequences are reserved for future standardization. Other characters may be used in extensions.

External names C89: Restriction of the significance of an external name to fewer than 31 characters or to only one case is an obsolescent feature that is a concession to existing implementations. C99: Restriction of the significance of an external name to fewer than 255 characters (considering each universal character name or extended source character as a single character) is an obsolescent feature that is a concession to existing implementations.

Floating types C99: Future standardization may include additional floating-point types, including those with range, precision, or both greater than `long double`.

Function declarators C89 and C99: The use of function declarators with empty parentheses (not prototype-format parameter type declarators) is an obsolescent feature.

Function definitions C89 and C99: The use of function definitions with separate parameter identifier and declaration lists (not prototype-format parameter type and identifier declarators) is an obsolescent feature.

Pragma directives C99: Pragmas whose first preprocessing token is `STDC` are reserved for future standardization.

Predefined macro names C99: Macro names beginning with `__STDC__` are reserved for future standardization.

Storage-class specifiers C89: The placement of a storage-class specifier other than at the beginning of the declaration specifiers in a declaration is an obsolescent feature. C99: Declaring an identifier with internal linkage at file scope without the static storage-class specifier is an obsolescent feature.

future library directions Guidance contained in Standard C to implementers and users with regard to areas in which library revision might occur due to a revision of the standard or by the addition of extensions to a conforming implementation. The following list is taken directly from the C89 and C99 standards:

The following names are grouped under individual headers for convenience. **All external names described below are reserved no matter what headers are included by the program.**

Complex arithmetic `<complex.h>` C99: The function names `cerf`, `cerfc`, `cexp2`, `cexpm1`, `clog10`, `clog1p`, `clog2`, `clgamma`, and `ctgamma`, and the same names suffixed with `f` or `l` may be added to the declarations in the complex.h header.

Character handling `<ctype.h>` C89 and C99: Function names that begin with `is` or `to` and a lowercase letter (followed by any combination of digits, letters, and underscores) may be added to the declarations in the ctype.h header.

Errors `<errno.h>` C89 and C99: Macros that begin with `E` and a digit or `E` and an uppercase letter (followed by any combination of digits, letters, and underscores) may be added to the declarations in the errno.h header.

Format conversion of integer types `<inttypes.h>` C99: Macro names beginning with `PRI` or `SCN` followed by any lowercase letter or `X` may be added to the macros defined in the inttypes.h header.

Localization `<locale.h>` C89 and C99: Macros that begin with `LC_` and an uppercase letter (followed by any combination of digits, letters, and underscores) may be added to the definitions in the locale.h header.

Mathematics `<math.h>` C89: The names of all existing functions declared in the math.h header, suffixed with `f` or `l`, are reserved respectively for corresponding functions with `float` and `long double` arguments and return values. (C99 requires these functions.)

Signal handling `<signal.h>` C89 and C99: Macros that begin with either `SIG` and an uppercase letter or `SIG_` and an uppercase letter (followed by any combination of digits, letters, and underscores) may be added to the definitions in the signal.h header.

Boolean type and values `<stdbool.h>` C99: The ability to undefine and perhaps then redefine the macros `bool`, `true`, and `false` is an obsolescent feature.

Integer types `<stdint.h>` C99: Typedef names beginning with `int` or `uint` and ending with `_t` may be added to the types defined in the stdint.h header. Macro names beginning with `INT` or `UINT` and ending with `_MAX`, `_MIN`,or `_C` may be added to the macros defined in the stdint.h header.

Input/output `<stdio.h>` C89 and C99: Lowercase letters may be added to the conversion specifiers in `fprintf` and `fscanf`. Other characters may be used in extensions. C99: The use of `ungetc` on a binary stream where the file position indicator is zero prior to the call is an obsolescent feature.

General utilities `<stdlib.h>` C89 and C99: Function names that begin with `str` and a lowercase letter (followed by any combination of digits, letters, and underscores) may be added to the declarations in the stdlib.h header.

String handling `<string.h>` C89 and C99: Function names that begin with `str`, `mem`, or `wcs` and a lowercase letter (followed by any combination of digits, letters, and underscores) may be added to the declarations in the string.h header.

Extended multibyte and wide character utilities `<wchar.h>` C99: Function names that begin with `wcs` and a lowercase letter may be added to the declarations in the wchar.h header. Lowercase letters may be added to the conversion specifiers and length modifiers in `fwprintf` and `fwscanf`. Other characters may be used in extensions.

Wide character classification and mapping utilities `<wctype.h>` C99: Function names that begin with `is` or `to` and a lowercase letter may be added to the declarations in the wctype.h header.

`fwide`^{C95} A function that determines the orientation of the stream pointed to by `stream`.

```
#include <stdio.h>
#include <wchar.h>
int fwide(FILE *stream, int mode);
```

If `mode` has a positive value, the function attempts to make the stream wide oriented. If `mode` has a negative value, the function attempts to make the stream byte oriented. Otherwise, `mode` is zero and the stream's orientation is not altered.

A positive return value indicates the stream has wide orientation; a negative return value indicates the stream has byte orientation; a zero return value indicates the stream has no orientation.

`fwprintf`[C95] A function that is the wide character analog of `fprintf`.

```
#include <stdio.h>
#include <wchar.h>
int fwprintf(FILE * restrict stream,
    const wchar_t * restrict format, ...);
```

`fwrite` A function that writes up to `nmemb` elements each of size `size` from the array pointed to by `ptr` to the file pointed to by `stream`.

```
#include <stdio.h>
size_t fwrite(const void * restrict ptr, size_t size,
    size_t nmemb, FILE * restrict stream);
```

If an error occurs, the file position indicator's value is indeterminate. The value returned is the number of elements successfully written. This number may be less than `nmemb` if an error occurs. *See also* `fread`.

`fwscanf`[C95] A function that is the wide character analog of `fscanf`.

```
#include <stdio.h>
#include <wchar.h>
int fwscanf(FILE * restrict stream,
    const wchar_t * restrict format, ...);
```

◇ ◇ ◇

G

gamma functions[C99] *See* `lgamma`; `tgamma`.

general utility library[C89] *See* stdlib.h.

`getc` A function that gets the next character (if any) from the file pointed to by `stream`.

```
#include <stdio.h>
int getc(FILE *stream);
```

`getc` is equivalent to `fgetc` except that `getc` is permitted to be an unsafe macro. *See also* `getwc`.

`getchar` A function that gets the next character (if any) from `stdin`.

```
#include <stdio.h>
int getchar(void);
```

`getchar()` is equivalent to `getc(stdin)`. Therefore, `getchar` may be implemented as an unsafe macro. *See also* `getwchar`.

`getenv` A function that searches an environment list for a string that matches that pointed to by `name`.

```
#include <stdlib.h>
char *getenv(const char *name);
```

The environment list is maintained by the host environment, and the set of names available is implementation defined. It is possible that an implementation does not even support environment strings, in which case `getenv` could always fail.

The value returned is a pointer to a string that "matches" the string pointed to by `name`. If no match is found, `NULL` is returned. The behavior is undefined if you attempt to modify the contents of the string pointed to by the return value. *See also* `envp`.

`gets` A function that reads characters from `stdin` into the array pointed to by `s` until a new-line or end-of-file is encountered.

```
#include <stdio.h>
char *gets(char *s);
```

A `'\0'` is appended after the last-read character in the array. If a new-line is encountered, it is discarded (unlike `fgets`, which retains it). If

gets succeeds, it returns `s`. If an end-of-file condition is encountered and no characters have been read yet, `NULL` is returned and the contents of the array pointed to by `s` are unchanged. `NULL` is also returned on a read error; however, the contents of the array are then indeterminate.

`getwc`[C95] A function that returns the next wide character from the input stream pointed to by **stream**, or `WEOF` if there are no more wide characters.

```
#include <stdio.h>
#include <wchar.h>
wint_t getwc(FILE *stream);
```

This function is equivalent to **fgetwc**, except that if it is implemented as a macro, it might evaluate **stream** more than once.

`getwchar`[C95] A function that returns the next wide character from the standard input stream, or `WEOF` if there are none.

```
#include <wchar.h>
wint_t getwchar(void);
```

GMT Abbreviation for Greenwich Mean Time. *See* Universal Time Coordinated.

`gmtime` A function that converts the calendar time pointed to by **timer** into a broken-down time, expressed as Greenwich Mean Time (GMT).

```
#include <time.h>
struct tm *gmtime(const time_t *timer);
```

The value returned is a pointer to the converted object or `NULL` if GMT is not available. GMT is now called Universal Time Coordinated (UTC).

`goto` A keyword used to implement an unconditional branch statement to a user-defined label elsewhere within the same function. The general form is as follows:

`goto` *identifier*;

identifier:
    statement

For information about nonlocal branches *see* `longjmp`.

greater-than operator A binary operator, `>`, that compares the values of its operands. Both operands either must have arithmetic type or be pointers to compatible object or incomplete types. The order of evaluation of the operands is unspecified. The result has type `int` and value 0 (if false) or 1 (if true). This operator associates left to right.

greater-than-or-equal-to operator A binary operator, `>=`, that compares the values of its operands. Both operands either must have arithmetic type or be pointers to compatible object or incomplete types. The result has type `int` and value 0 (if false) or 1 (if true). This operator associates left to right.

grouping The manner in which subexpressions are delineated when an expression contains more than one operator. The operators have an order of precedence that is used to determine the grouping of terms. The default operator precedence can be documented or overridden via the use of grouping parentheses. Grouping is not related to order of evaluation of the individual terms. *See also* parentheses punctuator.

`grouping`[C89] An `lconv` structure member that is a pointer to a string whose elements indicate the size of each group of digits in formatted nonmonetary quantities. If the string consists of `""`, the value is not available in the current locale or is of zero length. In the `"C"` locale this member must have the value `""`. The elements are interpreted according to the following:

`CHAR_MAX` No further grouping is to be performed.

`0` The previous element is to be repeatedly used for the remainder of the digits.

other The integer value is the number of digits that constitute the current group. The next element is examined to determine the size of the next group of digits before the current group.

H

header An entity whose contents are made available via the `#include` preprocessor directive. A header does not need to exist as a text file—it can be stored as a binary file or defined internally within the translator. Typically, a header contains function declarations and macro definitions. It also may contain `typedef` and structure, union, and enumeration declarations. Headers can be nested up to some implementation-defined depth (at least 8 in C89, 15 in C99). Standard headers are accessed using the following notation:

`#include` <*header-name*>

while programmer-defined headers are accessed using

`#include` "*header-name*"

header, name of A header name preprocessing token which has one of the following forms:

<*h-char-sequence*>
"*q-char-sequence*"

where *h-char-sequence* may contain any member of the source character set except the new-line character and `>`; and where *q-char-sequence* may contain any member of the source character set except the new-line character and `"`.

Header names are only recognized as such in the context of a `#include` directive.

If the characters `'`, `\`, `"`, or `/*` occur in the sequence between the `<` and `>` delimiters, the behavior is undefined. Similarly, if the characters `'`, `\`, or `/*` occur in the sequence between the `"` delimiters, the behavior is undefined. As such, sequences of characters that resemble escape sequences cause undefined behavior. (MS-DOS/Windows directory names use a backslash to separate subdirectories. Therefore, a directive such as `#include "\abc.h"` has undefined behavior.)

header, standard A header that is required by Standard C. Each library routine defined by Standard C is declared in a corresponding standard header, the names and purposes of which are as follows:

Header	*Purpose*
assert.h	Program diagnostic purposes
complex.h^{C99}	Complex arithmetic
ctype.h	Character testing and conversion
errno.h	Various error-checking facilities
fenv.h^{C99}	Floating-point environment
float.h	Floating type characteristics
inttypes.h^{C99}	Integer format conversion
iso646.h^{C95}	Alternate Token Spellings
limits.h	Integer type sizes
locale.h	Internationalization support
math.h	Math functions
setjmp.h	Nonlocal jump facility
signal.h	Signal handling
stdarg.h	Variable argument support
stdbool.h^{C99}	Boolean type and values
stddef.h	Miscellaneous
stdint.h^{C99}	Integer types
stdio.h	Input/output functions
stdlib.h	General utilities
string.h	String functions
tgmath.h^{C99}	Type-generic math
time.h	Date and time functions
wchar.h^{C95}	Multibyte and wide-character processing
wctype.h^{C95}	Wide-character classification and mapping

All external identifiers declared in the standard headers are reserved, whether or not their associated header is referenced.

Standard headers may be included in any order and multiple times in the same scope without producing ill effects. The exception is assert.h, which, if included multiple times, can behave differently depending on the existence of the macro `NDEBUG`.

You should include a standard header only at file scope in your program.

heap Memory that may be dynamically allocated and released by a user program using the library functions `calloc`, `free`, `malloc`, and `realloc`.

hexadecimal constant *See* constant, integer.

hexadecimal escape sequence A sequence of the form \x*h..h* that represents the character having a bit pattern with value *h..h* hexadecimal. As shown, the length of the sequence of hexadecimal digits is not limited by Standard C, while that for an octal sequence is.

horizontal-tab character One of the white space characters allowed in source text.

horizontal-tab escape sequence An escape sequence, `\t`, which represents the horizontal tab character.

hosted environment[C89] *See* environment, hosted.

`HUGE_VAL`[C89] A macro, defined in math.h, that expands to a positive `double` expression that is not necessarily representable as a `float`. It is returned from some math functions to indicate an unrepresentably large value. On some implementations, it may equal infinity. Prior to C99, it was not required to be a constant expression. The name `HUGE_VAL` replaced what many implementations previously called `HUGE`. *See also* `HUGE_VALF` and `HUGE_VALL`.

`HUGE_VALF`[C99] A macro, defined in math.h, that expands to a positive `float` constant expression and is returned from some math functions to indicate an unrepresentably large value. On some implementations, it may equal infinity. *See also* `HUGE_VAL` and `HUGE_VALL`.

`HUGE_VALL`[C99] A macro, defined in math.h, that expands to a positive `long double` constant expression and is returned from some math functions to indicate an unrepresentably large value. On some implementations, it may equal infinity. *See also* `HUGE_VAL` and `HUGE_VALF`.

hyperbolic functions The math.h functions `acosh`, `asinh`, `atanh`, `cosh`, `sinh`, and `tanh`, and their `float` and `long double` counterparts, for both floating and complex types.

`hypot[f|l]`[C99] A function that computes the hypotenuse of a right triangle given the two sides `x` and `y`, without undue underflow or overflow.

```
#include <math.h>
double hypot(double x, double y);
float hypotf(float x, float y);
long double hypotl(long double x, long double y);
```

A range error may occur.

I

`I`^{C99} A macro, defined in complex.h, that expands to `_Complex_I` if the macro `_Imaginary_I` is not defined; otherwise, it expands to `_Imaginary_I`.

I18N An abbreviation for internationalization, a word that has 18 letters between its first and last letter. *See also* L10N.

identifier A name consisting of a sequence of characters that can be used to name a variable, function, enumeration constant, type synonym, structure, union or enumerated type tag or member, label, or macro. An identifier must begin with a letter or an underscore and may contain alphanumeric and underscore characters.

While K&R stated that the first eight characters were significant, C89 requires that identifiers be significant in at least the first 31 (C99 requires 63) characters and be case distinct. (Note that due to linker and other restrictions, the length of significance of external names may be as few as 6 in C89 and 31 in C99. Prior to C99, they also may be converted to one case only.)

As a rule, to avoid conflicts between user-written and vendor-supplied identifiers, do not invent an identifier whose name begins with an underscore. (While the requirements are not quite this strict, this rule is much simpler to remember.)

Two identifiers may designate different entities within the same scope provided they are in different name spaces.

identifier conflicts with C++ Conflicts arising when C++-only keywords are used in a C program and that program is compiled in a C++ environment. To avoid such conflicts, you should refrain from using the following as identifiers in new C code you write: `asm`, `catch`, `class`, `const_cast`, `delete`, `dynamic_cast`, `explicit`, `export`, `friend`, `mutable`, `namespace`, `new`, `operator`, `private`, `protected`, `public`, `reinterpret_cast`, `static_cast`, `template`, `this`, `throw`, `try`, `typeid`, `typename`, `using`, and `virtual`.

C++ also has the keywords `bool`, `false`, and `true`, which while they are not keywords in Standard C, they exist in C99 as macro names defined in the header stdbool.h. C99 added the keyword `inline`, which C++ already had. C89 defined `wchar_t` as a type synonym while C++ makes this a keyword.

identifier linkage *See* linkage.

identifier list A comma-separated list of identifiers.

identifier name space *See* name space.

identifier, reserved Keywords that are special identifiers in that they are reserved words. As such, they cannot be used as user-defined identifiers. Also, all external names declared in the standard headers are reserved *whether or not* their parent header is actually included. *See also* future library directions.

identifier scope *See* scope.

identifier type *See* type.

IEC The International Electrotechnical Commission, a body that develops standards. *See also* ISO.

IEC 559 *See* IEEE Floating-Point Arithmetic Standards.

IEC 60559 *See* IEEE Floating-Point Arithmetic Standards.

IEEE The Institute of Electrical and Electronics Engineers, a U.S.–based organization that is involved, among other things, in producing various computer-related hardware and software standards and specifications.

IEEE 754 *See* IEEE Floating-Point Arithmetic Standards.

IEEE 854 *See* IEEE Floating-Point Arithmetic Standards.

IEEE Floating-Point Arithmetic Standards IEEE Standard for Binary Floating-Point Arithmetic (ANSI/IEEE Std 754-1985) known internationally first as IEC 559:1989 (and then as IEC 60559:1989) and IEEE Standard for Radix-Independent Floating-Point Arithmetic (ANSI/IEEE Std 854-1987). C99 added extensive support for floating-point environments adhering to these standards.

`#if` A preprocessor directive used to begin a conditional compilation "block" based on the truth of an integer constant expression. It must have a corresponding **`#endif`** directive and, optionally, **`#else`** or **`#elif`** directives. It is used as follows:

`#if` *constant-expression*

If *constant-expression* contains any identifiers that are not currently defined as macros, they are assumed (for this directive only) to be macros defined with value 0. *constant-expression* is evaluated as though each term had type `long int`. In C99, all signed integer types and all unsigned integer types act like the types `intmax_t` and `uintmax_t`, respectively. *See also* comment.

`#ifdef` A preprocessor directive used to begin a conditional compilation "block" based on the existence of a macro definition. It must have a corresponding `#endif` directive and, optionally, a `#else` or `#elif` directive. It is used as follows:

```
#ifdef identifier
```

`if/else` A construct involving these two keywords that allows control to be directed based on the truth value of a scalar expression. The true and false paths must consist of only one statement each. If more than one is needed, a block must be used. It is used as follows:

```
if ( expression )
        statement
[ else
        statement ]
```

Note that *expression* is a full expression. If it contains no relational or equality operator, inequality to zero is implied; for example, `if (p)` is equivalent to `if (p != 0)`.

`#ifndef` A preprocessor directive used to begin a conditional compilation "block" based on the nonexistence of a macro definition. It must have a corresponding `#endif` directive and, optionally, a `#else` or `#elif` directive. It is used as follows:

```
#ifndef identifier
```

`ilogb[f|l]`[C99] A function that returns the exponent of `x`.

```
#include <math.h>
int ilogb(double x);
int ilogbf(float x);
int ilogbl(long double x);
```

If `x` is zero, `FP_ILOGB0` is returned. If `x` is infinite, `INT_MAX` is returned. If `x` is a NaN, `FP_ILOGBNAN` is returned. If `x` is zero, a range error may result.

`imaginary`[C99] A macro, defined in complex.h, that is defined only if the implementation supports imaginary types according to the standard's Annex G. It expands to the keyword `_Imaginary`. For normal usage of the imaginary type, it is strongly recommended that you include complex.h and use this macro rather using the `_Imaginary` keyword directly. There are three imaginary types: `float _Imaginary`, `double _Imaginary`, and `long double _Imaginary`, which can be written instead as `float imaginary`, `double imaginary`, and `long double imaginary`, respectively.

_Imaginary[C99] A keyword that provides support for an imaginary type. Since it was invented by C99, by which time quite a few programs already contained type synonyms using some form of the word complex, this keyword was spelled using one of the forms reserved for implementers. Unless you must mix both existing homegrown complex machinery and this new keyword in the same source file, it is strongly recommended that you include complex.h and use its macro `imaginary` instead.

Note that implementations are not required to provide imaginary types.

_Imaginary_I[C99] A macro, defined in complex.h, that is defined only if the implementation supports imaginary types according to the standard's Annex G. It expands to a constant expression of type `const float _Imaginary`, having a value of the imaginary unit i.

imaxabs[C99] A function that computes the absolute value of its argument.

```
#include <inttypes.h>
intmax_t imaxabs(intmax_t j);
```

imaxdiv[C99] A function that computes `numer/denom` and `numer % denom` in a single operation.

```
#include <inttypes.h>
imaxdiv_t imaxdiv(intmax_t numer, intmax_t denom);
```

The quotient and the remainder are returned in a structure of type `imaxdiv_t`.

imaxdiv_t[C99] A type, defined in inttypes.h, that is a structure that contains (in either order) the members `quot` (representing a quotient) and `rem` (representing a remainder), each of which has type `intmax_t`. *See also* `imaxdiv`.

implementation A C translation environment. It collectively refers to the preprocessor, compiler, and run-time library for a given host system. It is used primarily to mean "compiler" or "interpreter."

implementation, conforming A C translation environment that conforms to the standard specification for C. Specifically, a hosted implementation that conforms to C89 must contain all of the library functions, whereas the set of library facilities provided by a conforming freestanding implementation is implementation defined, beyond having to provide float.h, limits.h, stdarg.h, and stddef.h. C99 requires three extra freestanding headers: iso646.h, stdbool.h, and stdint.h.

See also `__STDC__`; `__STDC_VERSION__`.

implementation limits *See* environmental limits.

implementation-defined behavior Given a correct program construct and correct data, if the runtime behavior depends on the characteristics of the implementation, then that behavior is deemed to be implementation defined. Such behavior shall be documented by that implementation. For example, whether or not a `char` is sign extended on conversion to `int` is implementation defined, as is whether a plain `int` bit-field is signed.

implicit conversion *See* conversion; conversion, explicit; conversion, implicit.

implicit function declaration The implicit process that occurs if the compiler comes across an identifier for which it has no visible declaration in scope, and that identifier is the expression that immediately precedes a function call operator. The identifier is implicitly declared as follows:

```
extern int identifier();
```

Note that no prototype information is assumed. Consider the following example:

```
void a(void)
{
        void f(void);

        f();
}

void b(void)
{
        int i;

        i = f(10); /* discrepancy not detected */
}
```

Because the declaration of function `f` only has block scope, the compiler forgets about it at the end of its parent block. As such, no prototype is in scope of the second call to `f`, and the compiler is not able to detect the argument list or return type mismatches. (This can be avoided by placing the function declaration at file scope.)

Note that C99 does not support implicit function declarations.

implicit `int` The assumption of type `int`, when no type keyword exists in a declaration. Prior to C99, if a type were omitted in numerous contexts, type `int` was assumed. Such occurrences of "implicit `int`" are not permitted by C99.

`#include` A preprocessor directive used to include a standard or programmer-defined header. It is used as follows:

```
#include <preprocessor-tokens>
#include "preprocessor-tokens"
#include identifier
```

where *preprocessor-tokens* is either the name of a header or a series of tokens that after preprocessor expansion, together form the name of a header.

The third case was an invention of C89 and is permitted, provided the identifier is a macro that expands to a character sequence of the form specified in either of the first two cases. *See also* header, name of.

inclusive OR assignment operator *See* OR assignment operator, bitwise inclusive.

inclusive OR operator *See* OR operator, bitwise inclusive.

incomplete type *See* type, incomplete.

increment operator A unary operator, `++`, that may be used as either a prefix or postfix operator. The operand must have a scalar type and be a modifiable lvalue. The value of x`++` is the value of x before it is incremented by 1, whereas the value of `++`x is the value of x after it is incremented by 1. The postfix version of this operator associates left to right, while the prefix version associates right to left. (Prior to C89, the prefix and postfix versions had the same precedence. However, C89 elevated the precedence of the postfix version. This broke no correct existing code. It did, however, permit previously invalid constructs to be valid. For example, `p++->m` is now valid.) There is a corresponding decrement operator `--`.

indirection The act of getting at an object or function via a pointer to that object or function. It is achieved using the unary `*` indirection operator.

indirection operator A unary operator, `*`, that is used to get at an object or function indirectly via a pointer to it. Indirection on a pointer is often called dereferencing. This operator associates right to left. When applied to data pointers, it always produces an lvalue. Given the following declarations:

```
double d;
double *pd = &d;
double **ppd = &pd;

double df(void);
double (*pf)(void) = df;
```

the expression `*pd` designates the `double` object to which `pd` points; the expression `**pd` designates the `double` object to which `*pd` points; and the expression `*pf` designates the function to which `pf` points.

inequality operator A binary operator, `!=`, that compares the values of its operands for inequality. Its operands must have scalar types and must be either both arithmetic, both pointers to qualified or unqualified versions of compatible types, one a pointer to `void` and the other a pointer to an object or incomplete type, or one a pointer and the other the null pointer constant. The order of evaluation of the operands is unspecified. The result has type `int` and value 0 (if false) or 1 (if true). This operator associates left to right.

`INFINITY`^{C99} A macro, defined in math.h, that expands to a constant expression of type `float` that represents the value positive or unsigned infinity, if an infinity value is available. Otherwise, it expands to a positive constant of type `float` that overflows at compile time, thus causing a diagnostic.

initialization The act of defining an object's initial value. Objects that have automatic storage duration and are not explicitly initialized have indeterminate values. Objects that have static storage duration and are not explicitly initialized have a value of zero cast to their type. (In the case of aggregate objects, the value zero is cast to all subordinate scalar members; for unions, it is cast to the first member.) C89 added the ability to explicitly initialize unions and automatic aggregates; however, such initializers must be translation-time constant expressions. C99 added the ability to initialize given elements of an array, and given members of structures and unions via designated initializers. *See also* initializer.

initializer A construct of the following format used in initialization:

{ *initializer-list* }

If the object being initialized has scalar type, the delimiting { and } may be omitted (and usually are). *initializer-list* is a comma-separated list of initializers. Nested initializers are used to initialize nested structures, arrays of structures, multidimensional arrays, and the like. *See also* compound literal.

initializer, string literal An initializer for an array of `char`. There are two ways of writing such an initializer, as follows:

```
char c1[] = {'o', 'n', 'e', '\0'};
char c2[] = "one";
```

In the case of `c2`, the initializer has the form of a string literal. The initializer expression has type "array of 4 `char`" as you would expect. However, this array type is not converted to the address of the first element. Instead, it is recognized as an abbreviation for the first case. Note, though, that in the following case, the array consists of only three characters—there is no trailing `'\0'` placed in `c3`. The following is an example:

```
char c3[3] = "one";
```

`inline`[C99] A type specifier used on a function which suggests to the translator that calls to that function should be as fast as possible; that is, the function should be "inlined." However, whether or not this suggestion is followed, is implementation defined. `inline` is also a C++ keyword.

`int` An integer type keyword. Standard C requires it to represent at least 16 bits. Typically, it maps onto the native data type for a given machine's architecture (its word or register size, for example). Except when used with a bit-field, a plain `int` is signed. *See also* integer type.

`int_curr_symbol`[C89] An `lconv` structure member that is a pointer to a string containing the international currency symbol applicable to the current locale. The first three characters contain the alphabetic international currency symbol in accordance with those specified in *ISO 4217 Codes for the Representation of Currency and Funds.* The fourth character (immediately preceding the null character) is the character used to separate the international currency symbol from the monetary quantity. If the string consists of `""`, this indicates that the value is not available in the current locale or is of zero length. In the `"C"` locale this member must have the value `""`. Examples are "`CHF␣`" (Switzerland, franc), "`ITL␣`" (Italy, lira), "`NOK␣`" (Norway, krona), and "`NLG␣`" (Netherlands, guilder), where ␣ represents a space.

integer arithmetic functions The stdlib.h functions `abs`, `div`, `labs`, `ldiv`, `llabs` and `lldiv`.

integer constant *See* constant, integer.

integer constant expression An expression involving only integer constants, enumeration constants, character constants, `sizeof` expressions (not having a VLA operand), and floating constants that are immediate operands of casts. When an integer constant expression is required by a preprocessor directive (such as `#if` and `#elif`), further restrictions are applied. Specifically, enumeration constants and casts are not permitted. `sizeof` expressions are permitted but are not required to be supported here.

integer promotions *See* conversion, integer type.

integer suffix *See* constant, integer.

integer type In C89, the following types: `char`, `short int`, `int`, and `long int`, and their unsigned counterparts. C99 added `long long int`. These types are listed in nondecreasing order of their precision. As such, one or more of the types could map to the same representation. Both signed and unsigned versions are available. The header limits.h can be used to determine the attributes of an implementation's integer types. All integer types are arithmetic types. *See also* `char`, plain.

integer type conversion *See* conversion, usual arithmetic.

integer type, exact-widthC99 *See* `int`*N*`_t`; `uint`*N*`_t`

integer types, extendedC99 Integer types that are supported by an implementation, beyond the requirements of the standard.

integer type, minimum-widthC99 *See* `int_least`*N*`_t`; `uint_least`*N*`_t`.

integer type, minimum-width, fastestC99 *See* `int_fast`*N*`_t`; `uint_fast`*N*`_t`.

integral Prior to C99, when used as an adjective, a term that was equivalent to integer. C99 used integer instead.

internal name A name not exported outside of a source module. That is, it is not seen, nor resolved, by the linker. Its length of significance is at least 31 characters in C89, 63 in C99. Internal names are case-distinct. *See also* external name.

internationalization The process of providing support for, and integrating better with, translation or execution environments other than the original "U.S. English" mode. Commonly abbreviated as I18N. *See also* localization; locale.

interrupt *See* signal.

`INT_FAST`*N*`_MAX`C99 A macro, defined in stdint.h, that indicates the maximum value of the corresponding fastest minimum-width signed integer type, `int_fast`*N*`_t`. It expands to an integer constant expression suitable for use with a `#if` directive.

`INT_FAST`*N*`_MIN`[C99] A macro, defined in stdint.h, that indicates the minimum value of the corresponding fastest minimum-width signed integer type, `int_fast`*N*`_t`. It expands to an integer constant expression suitable for use with a `#if` directive.

`int_fast8_t`[C99] *See* `int_fast`*N*`_t`.

`int_fast16_t`[C99] *See* `int_fast`*N*`_t`.

`int_fast32_t`[C99] *See* `int_fast`*N*`_t`.

`int_fast64_t`[C99] *See* `int_fast`*N*`_t`.

`int_fast`*N*`_t`[C99] A type, defined in stdint.h, that is the fastest signed integer type with a width of at least *N* bits, such that no signed integer type with lesser size has at least the specified width. For example, `int_fast16_t` denotes a signed integer type with a width of at least 16 bits. The following types must be defined: `int_fast8_t`, `int_fast16_t`, `int_fast32_t`, and `int_fast64_t`. Other types of this form are optional. *See also* `INT_FAST`*N*`_MAX`; `INT_FAST`*N*`_MIN`; `uint_fast`*N*`_t`.

`int_frac_digits`[C89] An `lconv` structure member that is a nonnegative number representing the number of fractional digits (those after the decimal point) to be displayed in an internationally formatted monetary quantity. A value of `CHAR_MAX` indicates that the value is not available in the current locale. In the `"C"` locale this member must have the value `CHAR_MAX`.

`INT_LEAST`*N*`_MAX`[C99] A macro, defined in stdint.h, that indicates the maximum value of the corresponding minimum-width signed integer type, `int_least`*N*`_t`. It expands to an integer constant expression suitable for use with a `#if` directive.

`INT_LEAST`*N*`_MIN`[C99] A macro, defined in stdint.h, that indicates the minimum value of the corresponding minimum-width signed integer type, `int_least`*N*`_t`. It expands to an integer constant expression suitable for use with a `#if` directive.

`int_least8_t`[C99] *See* `int_least`*N*`_t`.

`int_least16_t`[C99] *See* `int_least`*N*`_t`.

`int_least32_t`[C99] *See* `int_least`*N*`_t`.

`int_least64_t`[C99] *See* `int_least`*N*`_t`.

`int_least`*N*`_t`[C99] A type, defined in stdint.h, that is a signed integer type with a width of at least *N* bits, such that no signed integer type with lesser size has at least the specified width. For example, `int_least16_t` denotes a signed integer type with a width of at least 16 bits. The following types must be defined: `int_least8_t`, `int_least16_t`, `int_least32_t`, and `int_least64_t`. Other types of this form are optional. *See also* INT_LEAST*N*_MAX; INT_LEAST*N*_MIN; `uint_least`*N*`_t`.

INT_MAX^{C89} A macro, defined in limits.h, that designates the maximum value for an object of type `int`. It must be at least 32,767 (16 bits). This macro expands to an integer constant expression suitable for use with a `#if` directive.

INTMAX_C^{C99} A function-like macro, defined in stdint.h, that has the form `INTMAX_C(`*value*`)` and expands to an integer constant with the specified value and type `intmax_t`. *value* is a decimal, octal, or hexadecimal constant whose value does not exceed the limits for the corresponding type.

INTMAX_MAX^{C99} A macro, defined in stdint.h, that indicates the maximum value of the corresponding greatest-width signed integer type, `intmax_t`. It expands to an integer constant expression suitable for use with a `#if` directive.

INTMAX_MIN^{C99} A macro, defined in stdint.h, that indicates the minimum value of the corresponding greatest-width signed integer type, `intmax_t`. It expands to an integer constant expression suitable for use with a `#if` directive.

intmax_t^{C99} A type, defined in stdint.h, that is a signed integer type capable of representing any value of any signed integer type, including extended types. Preprocessor arithmetic is done using this type. *See also* INTMAX_MAX; INTMAX_MIN; `uintmax_t`.

INT_MIN^{C89} A macro, defined in limits.h, that designates the minimum value for an object of type `int`. It must be at least −32,767 (16 bits). This macro expands to an integer constant expression suitable for use with a `#if` directive.

int_n_cs_precedes^{C99} An `lconv` structure member that is a nonnegative number that is set to 1 or 0 if the `int_curr_symbol` respectively precedes or succeeds the value for a negative internationally formatted monetary quantity. A value of CHAR_MAX indicates that the value is not available in the current locale. In the `"C"` locale this member must have the value CHAR_MAX.

int_n_sep_by_space^{C99} An `lconv` structure member that is a nonnegative number that is set to 1 or 0 if the `int_curr_symbol` respectively is or is not separated by a space from the value for a negative internationally formatted monetary quantity. A value of CHAR_MAX indicates that the value is not available in the current locale. In the `"C"` locale this member must have the value CHAR_MAX.

int_n_sign_posn[C99] An `lconv` structure member that is a nonnegative number that is set to a value indicating the positioning of the `negative_sign` for a negative internationally formatted monetary quantity. The value is interpreted according to the following:

0 Parentheses surround the quantity and `int_curr_symbol`.

1 The sign string precedes the quantity and `int_curr_symbol`.

2 The sign string succeeds the quantity and `int_curr_symbol`.

3 The sign string immediately precedes the `int_curr_symbol`.

4 The sign string immediately succeeds the `int_curr_symbol`.

`CHAR_MAX` indicates that the value is not available in the current locale.

In the `"C"` locale this member must have the value `CHAR_MAX`.

INT*N*_C[C99] A function-like macro, defined in stdint.h, that has the form

```
INTN_C(value)
```

and expands to a signed integer constant with the specified value and type `int_leastN_t`. *value* is a decimal, octal, or hexadecimal constant whose value does not exceed the limits for the corresponding type..

INT*N*_MAX[C99] A macro, defined in stdint.h, that indicates the maximum value of the corresponding exact-width signed integer type, `intN_t`. It expands to an integer constant expression suitable for use with a `#if` directive.

INT*N*_MIN[C99] A macro, defined in stdint.h, that indicates the minimum value of the corresponding exact-width signed integer type, `intN_t`. It expands to an integer constant expression suitable for use with a `#if` directive.

int*N*_t[C99] A type, defined in stdint.h, that designates a signed integer type having width *N*, no padding bits, and a two's complement representation. For example, `int16_t` denotes a signed integer type with a width of exactly 16 bits.

Such types are optional, but if an implementation provides integer types with widths of 8, 16, 32, or 64 bits, it must define the corresponding typedef names. *See also* `INTN_MAX`; `INTN_MIN`; `uintN_t`.

int_p_cs_precedes[C99] An `lconv` structure member that is a nonnegative number that is set to 1 or 0 if the `int_curr_symbol` respectively precedes or succeeds the value for a nonnegative internationally formatted monetary quantity. A value of `CHAR_MAX` indicates that the value is not available in the current locale. In the `"C"` locale this member must have the value `CHAR_MAX`.

int_p_sep_by_space[C99] An lconv structure member that is a nonnegative number that is set to 1 or 0 if the int_curr_symbol respectively is or is not separated by a space from the value for a nonnegative internationally formatted monetary quantity. A value of CHAR_MAX indicates that the value is not available in the current locale. In the "C" locale this member must have the value CHAR_MAX.

int_p_sign_posn[C99] An lconv structure member that is a nonnegative number that is set to a value indicating the positioning of the positive_sign for a nonnegative internationally formatted monetary quantity. The value is interpreted according to the following:

0 Parentheses surround the quantity and int_curr_symbol.

1 The sign string precedes the quantity and int_curr_symbol.

2 The sign string succeeds the quantity and int_curr_symbol.

3 The sign string immediately precedes the int_curr_symbol.

4 The sign string immediately succeeds the int_curr_symbol.

CHAR_MAX indicates that the value is not available in the current locale.

In the "C" locale this member must have the value CHAR_MAX.

INTPTR_MAX[C99] A macro, defined in stdint.h, that indicates the maximum value of the corresponding pointer-holding signed integer type, intptr_t. It expands to an integer constant expression suitable for use with a #if directive.

INTPTR_MIN[C99] A macro, defined in stdint.h, that indicates the minimum value of the corresponding pointer-holding signed integer type, intptr_t. It expands to an integer constant expression suitable for use with a #if directive.

intptr_t[C99] An optional type, defined in stdint.h, that designates a signed integer type such that any valid pointer to void can be converted to this type and back again, with the result comparing equal to the original pointer. *See also* INTPTR_MAX; INTPTR_MIN; uintptr_t.

inttypes.h[C99] A header that includes stdint.h and, for hosted implementations, extends it with functions relating to greatest-width integers.

This header contains definitions or declarations for the following identifiers:

Name	*Purpose*
`imaxabs`	Absolute value
`imaxdiv`	Quotient and remainder
`imaxdiv_t`	Structure type used by `imaxdiv`
`PRIdFAST`*N*	Output conversion specifier for `int_fast`*N*`_t`
`PRIdLEAST`*N*	Output conversion specifier for `int_least`*N*`_t`
`PRIdMAX`	Output conversion specifier for `intmax_t`
`PRId`*N*	Output conversion specifier for `int`*N*`_t`
`PRIdPTR`	Output conversion specifier for `intptr_t`
`PRIiFAST`*N*	Output conversion specifier for `int_fast`*N*`_t`
`PRIiLEAST`*N*	Output conversion specifier for `int_least`*N*`_t`
`PRIiMAX`	Output conversion specifier for `intmax_t`
`PRIiN`	Output conversion specifier for `int`*N*`_t`
`PRIiPTR`	Output conversion specifier for `intptr_t`
`PRIoFAST`*N*	Output conversion specifier for `uint_fast`*N*`_t`
`PRIoLEAST`*N*	Output conversion specifier for `uint_least`*N*`_t`
`PRIoMAX`	Output conversion specifier for `uintmax_t`
`PRIoN`	Output conversion specifier for `uint`*N*`_t`
`PRIoPTR`	Output conversion specifier for `uintptr_t`
`PRIuFAST`*N*	Output conversion specifier for `uint_fast`*N*`_t`
`PRIuLEAST`*N*	Output conversion specifier for `uint_least`*N*`_t`
`PRIuMAX`	Output conversion specifier for `uintmax_t`
`PRIuN`	Output conversion specifier for `uint`*N*`_t`
`PRIuPTR`	Output conversion specifier for `uintptr_t`
`PRIxFAST`*N*	Output conversion specifier for `uint_fast`*N*`_t`
`PRIXFAST`*N*	Output conversion specifier for `uint_fast`*N*`_t`
`PRIXLEAST`*N*	Output conversion specifier for `uint_least`*N*`_t`
`PRIxLEAST`*N*	Output conversion specifier for `uint_least`*N*`_t`
`PRIxMAX`	Output conversion specifier for `uintmax_t`
`PRIXMAX`	Output conversion specifier for `uintmax_t`
`PRIx`*N*	Output conversion specifier for `uint`*N*`_t`
`PRIX`*N*	Output conversion specifier for `uint`*N*`_t`
`PRIxPTR`	Output conversion specifier for `uintptr_t`
`PRIXPTR`	Output conversion specifier for `uintptr_t`
`SCNdFAST`*N*	Input conversion specifier for `int_fast`*N*`_t`
`SCNdLEAST`*N*	Input conversion specifier for `int_least`*N*`_t`
`SCNdMAX`	Input conversion specifier for `intmax_t`
`SCNd`*N*	Input conversion specifier for `int`*N*`_t`
`SCNdPTR`	Input conversion specifier for `intptr_t`
`SCNiFAST`*N*	Input conversion specifier for `int_fast`*N*`_t`
`SCNiLEAST`*N*	Input conversion specifier for `int_least`*N*`_t`
`SCNiMAX`	Input conversion specifier for `intmax_t`
`SCNi`*N*	Input conversion specifier for `int`*N*`_t`
`SCNiPTR`	Input conversion specifier for `intptr_t`

Name	*Purpose*
SCNoFAST*N*	Input conversion specifier for uint_fast*N*_t
SCNoLEAST*N*	Input conversion specifier for uint_least*N*_t
SCNoMAX	Input conversion specifier for uintmax_t
SCNo*N*	Input conversion specifier for uint*N*_t
SCNoPTR	Input conversion specifier for uintptr_t
SCNuFAST*N*	Input conversion specifier for uint_fast*N*_t
SCNuLEAST*N*	Input conversion specifier for uint_least*N*_t
SCNuMAX	Input conversion specifier for uintmax_t
SCNu*N*	Input conversion specifier for uint*N*_t
SCNuPTR	Input conversion specifier for uintptr_t
SCNxFAST*N*	Input conversion specifier for uint_fast*N*_t
SCNxLEAST*N*	Input conversion specifier for uint_least*N*_t
SCNxMAX	Input conversion specifier for uintmax_t
SCNx*N*	Input conversion specifier for uint*N*_t
SCNxPTR	Input conversion specifier for uintptr_t
strtoimax	Convert string to signed integer
strtoumax	Convert string to unsigned integer
wcstoimax	Convert wide string to signed integer
wcstoumax	Convert wide string to unsigned integer

In these names, *N* represents the width of the type in bits.

See future library directions.

_IOFBF A macro, defined in stdio.h, that can be used as the third argument to setvbuf to indicate that a stream is fully buffered. *See also* _IOLBF; _IONBF.

_IOLBF A macro, defined in stdio.h, that can be used as the third argument to setvbuf to indicate that a stream is line buffered. *See also* _IOFBF; _IONBF.

_IONBF A macro, defined in stdio.h, that can be used as the third argument to setvbuf to indicate that a stream is not buffered. *See also* _IOFBF; _IOLBF.

is prefix *See* future library directions.

isalnum A locale-specific function that tests if its argument c is alphabetic (isalpha) or decimal numeric (isdigit).

```
#include <ctype.h>
int isalnum(int c);
```

A zero value is returned for false, a nonzero for true. *See also* iswalnum.

`isalpha` A locale-specific function that tests if its argument `c` is an alphabetic character.

```
#include <ctype.h>
int isalpha(int c);
```

In the `"C"` locale, this means that either `isupper` or `islower` is true. In other locales, other implementation-defined characters may be included in the `isalpha` set, provided they are not in the `iscntrl`, `isdigit`, `ispunct`, or `isspace` sets as well. *See also* `iswalpha`.

A zero value is returned for false, a nonzero for true.

`isblank`C99 A function that tests for any character that is a standard blank character or is one of a locale-specific set of characters for which `isspace` is true and which is used to separate words within a line of text.

```
#include <ctype.h>
int isblank(int c);
```

The standard blank characters are the following: space (`' '`) and horizontal tab (`'\t'`). In the `"C"` locale, `isblank` returns true for the standard blank characters only. *See also* `isspace`; `iswblank`; `iswspace`.

`iscntrl` A function that tests to see if its argument `c` is one of an implementation-defined set of control characters.

```
#include <ctype.h>
int iscntrl(int c);
```

In ASCII, the control characters have values 0 through 0x1f, and 0x7f. In EBCDIC, the control characters have values less than 0x40 (except that 0x29, 0x30, 0x31, and 0x3e are not control characters.)

A zero value is returned for false, a nonzero for true. *See also* `iswcntrl`.

`isdigit` A function that tests to see if its argument `c` is one of the decimal digits 0–9.

```
#include <ctype.h>
int isdigit(int c);
```

A zero value is returned for false, a nonzero for true. *See also* `iswdigit`.

`isfinite`C99 A macro, defined in math.h, that indicates whether its argument has a finite (that is, not infinite or NaN) value.

```
#include <math.h>
int isfinite(real-floating x);
```

A zero value is returned for false, a nonzero for true.

`isgraph` A locale-specific function that tests if its argument `c` is any printable character except a space.

```
#include <ctype.h>
int isgraph(int c);
```

A zero value is returned for false, a nonzero for true. *See also* `iswgraph`.

`isgreater`C99 A macro, defined in math.h, that indicates whether its first argument is greater than its second.

```
#include <math.h>
int isgreater(real-floating x, real-floating y);
```

A zero value is returned for false, a nonzero for true. Unlike the corresponding relational operator `>`, this function does not raise the "invalid" floating-point exception when `x` and `y` are unordered (i.e., either is a NaN).

`isgreaterequal`C99 A macro, defined in math.h, that indicates whether its first argument is greater than or equal to its second.

```
#include <math.h>
int isgreaterequal(real-floating x, real-floating y);
```

A zero value is returned for false, a nonzero for true. Unlike the corresponding relational operator `>=`, this function does not raise the "invalid" floating-point exception when `x` and `y` are unordered (i.e., either is a NaN).

`isinf`C99 A macro, defined in math.h, that indicates whether its argument is a positive or negative infinity.

```
#include <math.h>
int isinf(real-floating x);
```

A zero value is returned for false, a nonzero for true.

`isless`C99 A macro, defined in math.h, that indicates whether its first argument is less than its second.

```
#include <math.h>
int isless(real-floating x, real-floating y);
```

A zero value is returned for false, a nonzero for true. Unlike the corresponding relational operator `<`, this function does not raise the "invalid" floating-point exception when `x` and `y` are unordered (i.e., either is a NaN).

islessequal[C99] A macro, defined in math.h, that indicates whether its first argument is less than or equal to its second.

```
#include <math.h>
int islessequal(real-floating x, real-floating y);
```

A zero value is returned for false, a nonzero for true. Unlike the corresponding relational operator `<=`, this function does not raise the "invalid" floating-point exception when `x` and `y` are unordered (i.e., either is a NaN).

islessgreater[C99] A macro, defined in math.h, that indicates whether its first argument is either less than or greater than its second.

```
#include <math.h>
int islessgreater(real-floating x, real-floating y);
```

A zero value is returned for false, a nonzero for true. It behaves like `x < y || x > y`, but it does not raise the "invalid" floating-point exception when `x` and `y` are unordered (i.e., either is a NaN).

islower A locale-specific function that tests if its argument `c` is a lowercase alphabetic character.

```
#include <ctype.h>
int islower(int c);
```

In the `"C"` locale, lowercase letters are the Roman letters a–z inclusive. In other locales, other implementation-defined characters may be included in the `isalpha` set, provided they are not in the `iscntrl`, `isdigit`, `ispunct`, or `isspace` sets as well.

A zero value is returned for false, a nonzero for true. *See also* `iswlower`.

isnan[C99] A macro, defined in math.h, that indicates whether its argument is a NaN.

```
#include <math.h>
int isnan(real-floating x);
```

A zero value is returned for false, a nonzero for true.

`isnormal`[C99] A macro, defined in math.h, that indicates whether its argument is normal (that is, not zero, subnormal, infinite, or NaN).

```
#include <math.h>
int isnormal(real-floating x);
```

A zero value is returned for false, a nonzero for true.

ISO Acronym for the International Organization for Standardization, the international counterpart of national standards bodies. A Joint Technical Committee, JTC 1, has been set up between ISO and IEC (International Electrotechnical Commission) to produce standards for programming languages, among other things. JTC 1 standards are most often referred to as ISO Standards. *See also* ISO C.

ISO C The formal definition of the C language, preprocessor, and run-time library as accepted by ISO in 1989 and then again in 1999. This standard was produced by committee WG14. *See also* Standard C.

ISO 4217 Codes for the representation for currencies and funds A standard referred to when the currency part of the locale structure type `lconv` was defined. *See also* `int_curr_symbol`.

ISO 646 Invariant Code Set A coding scheme used primarily in Europe that is missing nine critical source characters needed in C programming. *See also* digraph; trigraph.

iso646.h[C95] A header that provides a family of macros that allow programmers using source character sets (such as ISO 646) missing certain characters necessary for writing C programs, to enter those characters using identifiers instead. The macros defined here are `and`, `and_eq`, `bitand`, `bitor`, `compl`, `not`, `not_eq`, `or`, `or_eq`, `xor`, and `xor_eq`. Note that in C++, these are implemented as keywords instead.

ISO/IEC 10646 A character set family. Most people use it to mean ISO/IEC 10646.UCS-2.

ISO/IEC 10646.UCS-2 A two-byte per character character set based on Unicode.

ISO/IEC 10646.UCS-4 A four-byte per character character set.

ISO/IEC 646 *See* digraph; ISO 646 Invariant Code Set; trigraph.

`isprint` A locale-specific function that tests if its argument `c` is any printable character, including a space.

```
#include <ctype.h>
int isprint(int c);
```

A zero value is returned for false, a nonzero for true. *See also* `iswprint`.

`isprint` subsumes `isgraph`'s functionality.

`ispunct` A locale-specific function that tests if its argument `c` is any printable character, except a space, or any character for which `isalnum` tests true.

```
#include <ctype.h>
int ispunct(int c);
```

A zero value is returned for false, a nonzero for true. *See also* `iswpunct`.

`isspace` A locale-specific function that tests if its argument `c` is any of the white space characters.

```
#include <ctype.h>
int isspace(int c);
```

In the `"C"` locale, the set of characters is space, form feed, new-line, carriage return, horizontal tab, and vertical tab. In other locales, other implementation-defined characters may be added to the above set, provided they do not test true for `isalnum`.

A zero value is returned for false, a nonzero for true. *See also* `isblank`; `iswblank`; `iswspace`.

`isunordered`[C99] A macro, defined in math.h, that indicates whether its arguments are unordered (i.e., either is a NaN).

```
#include <math.h>
int isunordered(real-floating x, real-floating y);
```

A zero value is returned for false, a nonzero for true.

`isupper` A locale-specific function that tests if its argument `c` is an uppercase alphabetic character.

```
#include <ctype.h>
int isupper(int c);
```

In the `"C"` locale, uppercase letters are the Roman letters A–Z inclusive. In other locales, other implementation-defined characters may be included in the `isalpha` set, provided they are not in the `iscntrl`, `isdigit`, `ispunct`, or `isspace` sets as well.

A zero value is returned for false, a nonzero for true. *See also* `iswupper`.

`isxdigit` A function that tests if its argument `c` is a hexadecimal digit. The set of valid characters are the digits 0–9 and the letters A–F and a–f.

```
#include <ctype.h>
int isxdigit(int c);
```

A zero value is returned for false, a nonzero for true. *See also* `iswxdigit`.

`iswalnum`^{C95} A locale-specific function that tests if its wide character argument `wc` is alphabetic (`iswalpha`) or decimal numeric (`iswdigit`).

```
#include <wctype.h>
int iswalnum(wint_t wc);
```

A zero value is returned for false, a nonzero for true. *See also* `isalnum`.

`iswalpha`^{C95} A locale-specific function that tests if its wide character argument `wc` is an alphabetic character.

```
#include <wctype.h>
int iswalpha(wint_t wc);
```

In the `"C"` locale, this means that either `iswupper` or `iswlower` is true. In other locales, other implementation-defined characters may be included in the `isalpha` set, provided they are not in the `iswcntrl`, `iswdigit`, `iswpunct`, or `iswspace` sets as well. *See also* `isalpha`.

A zero value is returned for false, a nonzero for true.

`iswblank`^{C99} A function that tests if its wide character argument `wc` is a blank wide character or is one of a locale-specific set of wide characters for which `iswspace` is true and that is used to separate words within a line of text.

```
#include <wctype.h>
int iswblank(wint_t wc);
```

The standard blank wide characters are: space (`L' '`) and horizontal tab (`L'\t'`). In the `"C"` locale, `iswblank` returns true only for the standard blank characters. *See also* `iswspace`.

`iswcntrl`^{C95} A function that tests to see if its wide character argument `wc` is one of an implementation-defined set of control characters.

```
#include <wctype.h>
int iswcntrl(wint_t wc);
```

A zero value is returned for false, a nonzero for true. *See also* `iscntrl`.

`iswctype`C95 A function that tests whether the wide character `wc` has the property described by `desc`.

```
#include <wctype.h>
int iswctype(wint_t wc, wctype_t desc);
```

The setting of the `LC_CTYPE` category when this function is called must be the same as that during the call to `wctype` that produced the value `desc`.

A zero value is returned for false, a nonzero for true.

`iswdigit`C95 A function that tests to see if its wide character argument `wc` is one of the decimal digits 0–9.

```
#include <wctype.h>
int iswdigit(wint_t wc);
```

A zero value is returned for false, a nonzero for true. *See also* `isdigit`.

`iswgraph`C95 A locale-specific function that tests if its wide character argument `wc` is any printable character except a space.

```
#include <wctype.h>
int iswgraph(wint_t wc);
```

A zero value is returned for false, a nonzero for true. *See also* `isgraph`.

`iswlower`C95 A locale-specific function that tests if its wide character argument `wc` is a lowercase alphabetic character.

```
#include <wctype.h>
int iswlower(wint_t wc);
```

In the `"C"` locale, lowercase letters are the Roman letters a–z inclusive. In other locales, other implementation-defined characters may be included in the `iswalpha` set, provided they are not in the `iswcntrl`, `iswdigit`, `iswpunct`, or `iswspace` sets as well.

A zero value is returned for false, a nonzero for true. *See also* `islower`.

iswprint^{C95} A locale-specific function that tests if its wide character argument wc is any printable character, including a space.

```
#include <wctype.h>
int iswprint(wint_t wc);
```

A zero value is returned for false, a nonzero for true. *See also* isprint. isprint subsumes isgraph's functionality.

iswpunct^{C95} A locale-specific function that tests if its wide character argument wc is any printable character except a space, or any character for which neither iswspace nor iswalnum tests true.

```
#include <wctype.h>
int iswpunct(wint_t wc);
```

A zero value is returned for false, a nonzero for true. *See also* ispunct.

iswspace^{C95} A locale-specific function that tests if its wide character argument wc is any of the white space characters.

```
#include <ctype.h>
int isspace(int c);
```

In the "C" locale, the set of characters is space, form feed, new-line, carriage return, horizontal tab, and vertical tab. In other locales, other implementation-defined characters may be added to the above set, provided they do not test true for iswalnum, iswgraph, or iswpunct.

A zero value is returned for false, a nonzero for true. *See also* isblank, isspace, iswblank.

iswupper^{C95} A locale-specific function that tests if its wide character argument wc is an uppercase alphabetic character.

```
#include <wctype.h>
int iswupper(wint_t wc);
```

In the "C" locale, uppercase letters are the Roman letters A–Z inclusive. In other locales, other implementation-defined characters may be included in the iswalpha set, provided they are not in the iswcntrl, iswdigit, iswpunct, or iswspace sets as well.

A zero value is returned for false, a nonzero for true. *See also* isupper.

`iswxdigit`^{C95} A function that tests if its wide character argument `wc` is a hexadecimal digit. The set of valid characters are the digits 0–9 and the letters A–F and a–f.

```
#include <wctype.h>
int iswxdigit(wint_t wc);
```

A zero value is returned for false, a nonzero for true. *See also* `isxdigit`.

iteration statements The `while`, `do`, and `for` statements.

J

J11 Known formally as NCITS/J11, a U.S. standards' committee that is responsible for the production and maintenance of what is generally known as the ANSI C standard. It was formerly called X3J11. Its ISO counterpart is WG14. *See also* NCEG; Standard C; X3J11.1.

J16 Known formally as NCITS/J16, a U.S. standards' committee that is responsible for the production and maintenance of what is generally known as the ANSI C++ standard. It was formerly called X3J16. Its ISO counterpart is WG21.

JIS A scheme commonly used to encode Japanese text in multibyte characters. *See also* EUC; Shift-JIS.

`jmp_buf` An array type of suitable size to store the "current program context." Used by `setjmp` and `longjmp` to save and restore a program context, respectively. This type is defined in setjmp.h.

jump statements The `break`, `continue`, `goto`, and `return` statements.

jump table A commonly used programming data structure that is implemented in C as an array of function pointers. Given the following declarations:

```
int transact0(void *);
int transact1(void *);
int transact2(void *);
int transact3(void *);

int (*jtable[])(void *) = {
        transact0,
        transact1,
        transact2,
        transact3
};
```

the transaction-processing function that corresponded to transaction type t would be called using

```
value = (*jtable[t])(record);
```

Standard C also permits that function to be called using the following:

```
value = jtable[t](record);
```

That is, the left operand of a function call operator may be either an expression that designates a function or an expression that is a pointer to a function.

K

K&R The book *The C Programming Language* by Brian W. Kernighan and Dennis M. Ritchie. When the first edition was written in 1978, it was the definitive reference book for C. Although the second edition was published in 1988, the name K&R is normally used to mean the first edition. The second edition was further revised in 1990 to include the final ANSI C Standard. (The 1988 version was based on a near-final draft.) Appendix A of the first edition was one of the base documents used by X3J11 in producing C89.

Kernighan, B.W. A Distinguished Member of the Bell Labs Computer Science Research Center. He is the "K" in K&R.

keyword One of a set of identifier-like tokens that has a predefined meaning and is reserved by the language. As such, it cannot be used as a user-defined identifier.

Name	*Purpose*
`auto`	Storage class
`_Bool`^{C99}	Type specifier
`break`	Jump statement
`case`	Label (in `switch` only)
`char`	Type specifier
`_Complex`^{C99}	Type specifier
`const`^{C89}	Type qualifier
`continue`	Jump statement
`default`	Label (in `switch` only)
`do`	Iteration statement
`double`	Type specifier
`else`	Optional path in `if`
`enum`	Type specifier
`extern`	Storage class
`float`	Type specifier
`for`	Iteration statement
`goto`	Jump statement
`if`	Selection statement
`_Imaginary`^{C99}	Type specifier
`inline`^{C99}	Function specifier
`int`	Type specifier
`long`	Type specifier
`register`	Storage class
`restrict`^{C99}	Type qualifier

Name	*Purpose*
`return`	Jump statement
`short`	Type specifier
`signed`[C89]	Type specifier
`sizeof`	Translation-time operator
`static`	Storage class
`struct`	Type specifier
`switch`	Selection statement
`typedef`	Declare type synonym
`union`	Type specifier
`unsigned`	Type specifier
`void`	Type specifier
`volatile`[C89]	Type qualifier
`while`	Iteration statement

The `entry` keyword reserved in the original definition of C is not reserved by Standard C.

L

`L` **prefix**[C89] A prefix used to introduce a wide character constant or wide string literal.

`L` **suffix** For use in a floating-point constant, *see* constant, floating. For use in an integer constant, *see* constant, integer.

`l` **suffix** For use in a floating-point constant, *see* constant, floating. For use in an integer constant, *see* constant, integer. For use with math library function names in C89, *see* future library directions.

L10N An abbreviation for localization, a word that has 10 letters between its first and last letter. *See also* I18N.

label A user-defined identifier, followed by a colon, that can appear before a statement. Such a label can be used only in conjunction with a matching `goto` statement. The two other label formats, `case` and `default`, are used only with the `switch` construct and cannot be the object of a `goto`. *See also* labeled statement.

label, `case` A label involving the `case` keyword that is used only in the context of a `switch` statement. It consists of a translation-time integer constant expression followed by a colon, and it must precede a statement. Duplicate case labels are not permitted within a given switch. A `switch` passes control to a particular `case` label if the controlling expression matches that label's value. *See also* labeled statement.

label, `default` A label involving the `default` keyword that is used only in the context of a `switch` statement. A switch passes control to the `default` label if the value of the controlling expression does not match any of that switch's `case` labels. *See also* labeled statement.

labeled statement A statement preceded by a label; for example,

identifier : *statement*
`case` *constant-expression* : *statement*
`default` : *statement*

`labs` A function that computes the absolute value of its `long int` argument `j`.

```
#include <stdlib.h>
long int labs(long int j);
```

The behavior is undefined if the result cannot be represented. For example, the absolute value of the most negative number cannot be represented in two's complement. On such a system, the absolute value very likely will be the same as the original value; that is, the absolute value of this most negative value might be negative! *See also* `abs`; `llabs`.

layout The data mapping declared in a structure or union type definition; not to be confused with an actual instance of a structure or union object; for example,

```
struct tag {
        int i;
        double d;
};
```

`LC_*` **macros**C89 A family of macros, defined in locale.h, that expand to distinct integer constant expressions and that are intended for use as the first argument (category) to the `setlocale` function. Standard C has reserved names beginning with `LC_` followed by an uppercase letter for use by implementations so they may add other locale categories. The standard macros are: `LC_ALL`, `LC_COLLATE`, `LC_CTYPE`, `LC_MONETARY`, `LC_NUMERIC`, and `LC_TIME`. *See also* future library directions.

`LC_ALL`C89 A macro, defined in locale.h, that is used as the first argument to `setlocale` to select a whole locale. (The other `LC_*` macros select only a partial locale.) Its use implies all the other `LC_*` categories for that locale.

`LC_COLLATE`C89 A macro, defined in locale.h, that is used as the first argument to `setlocale` to select that part of a locale having to do with collation in the functions `strcoll` and `strxfrm`.

`LC_CTYPE`C89 A macro, defined in locale.h, that is used as the first argument to `setlocale` to select that part of a locale having to do with character handling and multibyte functions (in ctype.h and stdlib.h, respectively), and wide characters (in wchar.h and wctype.h).

`LC_MONETARY`C89 A macro, defined in locale.h, that is used as the first argument to `setlocale` to select that part of a locale having to do with the monetary formatting information returned by `localeconv`.

`LC_NUMERIC`C89 A macro, defined in locale.h, that is used as the first argument to `setlocale` to select that part of a locale having to do with the selection of a decimal point character in formatted I/O and string conversion functions, and nonmonetary formatting information returned by `localeconv`.

`lconv`C89 A structure type, defined in locale.h, that is the key to defining a locale. It contains the following members in any order (other members also may exist):

currency_symbol	int_n_sign_posn[C99]	n_cs_precedes
decimal_point	int_p_cs_precedes[C99]	n_sep_by_space
frac_digits	int_p_sep_by_space[C99]	n_sign_posn
grouping	int_p_sign_posn[C99]	positive_sign
int_curr_symbol	mon_decimal_point	p_cs_precedes
int_frac_digits	mon_grouping	p_sep_by_space
int_n_cs_precedes[C99]	mon_thousands_sep	p_sign_posn
int_n_sep_by_space[C99]	negative_sign	thousands_sep

LC_TIME[C89] A macro, defined in locale.h, that is used as the first argument to `setlocale` to select that part of a locale to do with the behavior of the `strftime` function.

LDBL_DIG[C89] A macro, defined in float.h, that designates the number of decimal digits, such that a `long double` value of that significance can be rounded into a floating-point number and back again without change in those decimal digits.

LDBL_EPSILON[C89] A macro, defined in float.h, that designates the difference between 1.0 and the least value greater than 1.0 that is representable in the `long double` type.

LDBL_MANT_DIG[C89] A macro, defined in float.h, that designates the number of base-FLT_RADIX digits in the floating-point significand of a `long double` value.

LDBL_MAX[C89] A macro, defined in float.h, that designates the maximum representable finite `long double` number.

LDBL_MAX_10_EXP[C89] A macro, defined in float.h, that designates the maximum integer such that 10 raised to that power is in a given range of representable finite floating-point numbers.

LDBL_MAX_EXP[C89] A macro, defined in float.h, that designates the maximum integer such that `FLT_RADIX` raised to that power minus 1 is a representable finite floating-point number.

LDBL_MIN[C89] A macro, defined in float.h, that designates the minimum normalized positive `long double` number.

LDBL_MIN_10_EXP[C89] A macro, defined in float.h, that designates the minimum negative integer such that 10 raised to that power is in a given range of normalized floating-point numbers.

LDBL_MIN_EXP[C89] A macro, defined in float.h, that designates the minimum negative integer such that `FLT_RADIX` raised to that power minus 1 is a normalized floating-point number.

`ldexp[f|l]` A function that multiplies a floating-point number `x` by 2^{exp}.

```
#include <math.h>
double ldexp(double x, int exp);
float ldexpf(float x, int exp);
long double ldexpl(long double x, int exp);
```

A range error may result. The value returned is $x \times 2^{exp}$.

The `float` and `long double` versions were an invention of C89, where they were optional; however, in C99, they are required.

`ldiv`^{C89} A function that computes the quotient and remainder when `numer` is divided by `denom`.

```
#include <stdlib.h>
ldiv_t ldiv(long int numer, long int denom);
```

If the division is inexact, the sign of the resulting quotient is that of the algebraic quotient, and the magnitude of the resulting quotient is the largest integer less than the magnitude of the algebraic quotient. If the result cannot be represented, the behavior is undefined. The value returned has the structure type `ldiv_t`, which contains the two `long int` members, `quot` and `rem`, in either order. *See also* `div`; `lldiv`.

`ldiv_t`^{C89} A type, defined in stdlib.h, that is a structure type used as the implementation-defined return type of the `ldiv` function. A possible definition for `ldiv_t` is:

```
typedef struct {
        long int quot;
        long int rem;
} ldiv_t;
```

The ordering of the members does not need to be specified. *See also* `div_t`; `lldiv_t`.

left-shift assignment operator A binary operator, `<<=`, that permits left shift and assignment to be combined such that *exp1* `<<=` *exp2* is equivalent to *exp1* `=` *exp1* `<<` *exp2* except that in the former, *exp1* is only evaluated once. Both operands must have integer type, and the left operand must be a modifiable lvalue. The order of evaluation of the operands is unspecified. If the value of the right operand is negative, or equal to or greater than the number of bits in the promoted left operand, the behavior is undefined. The type of the result is the type of *exp1*. This operator associates right to left. *See also* assignment operator, compound.

left-shift operator A binary operator, <<, that causes the value of its left operand to be shifted left by the number of bits specified by its right operand. Both operands must have integer type. The order of evaluation of the operands is unspecified. This operator associates left to right. The usual arithmetic conversions are performed on the operands. The result has the type of the left operand after promotion. If the value of the right operand is negative, or equal to or greater than the number of bits in the promoted left operand, the behavior is undefined.

less-than operator A binary operator, <, that compares the values of its two operands. Both operands must either have arithmetic type or be pointers to compatible object or incomplete types. The order of evaluation of the operands is unspecified. The result has type `int` and value 0 (if false) or 1 (if true). This operator associates left to right.

less-than-or-equal-to operator A binary operator, <=, that compares the values of its operands. Both operands must either have arithmetic type or be pointers to compatible object types or incomplete types. The order of evaluation of the operands is unspecified. The result has type `int` and value 0 (if false) or 1 (if true). This operator associates left to right.

letter One of the 52 uppercase and lowercase alphabetic Latin characters required to be in the execution character set.

lexical element One of a set of fundamental units that, when combined in a proper sequence, make up a valid C program. *See also* token.

`lgamma[f|l]`[C99] A function that computes the natural logarithm of the absolute value of gamma of `x`.

```
#include <math.h>
double lgamma(double x);
float lgammaf(float x);
long double lgammal(long double x);
```

If the value of `x` is too large, a range error occurs. A range error may also occur if `x` is nonpositive. The value returned is $log_e|\Gamma(x)|$.

lifetime A lay term for "storage duration."

limits, environmental *See* environmental limits.

limits, numerical *See* environmental limits; float.h; limits.h.

limits, translation *See* environmental limits.

limits.h[C89,C99] A header that contains a family of macros which describe the integer properties of the target system. (There is also one macro used for multibyte processing purposes.) While Standard C requires certain minima (or maxima), it is intended that an implementation will document its exact values. The complete set of macros is as follows:

CHAR_BIT	LLONG_MAX[C99]	SCHAR_MAX	UINT_MAX
CHAR_MAX	LLONG_MIN[C99]	SCHAR_MIN	ULLONG_MAX[C99]
CHAR_MIN	LONG_MAX	SHRT_MAX	ULONG_MAX
INT_MAX	LONG_MIN	SHRT_MIN	USHRT_MAX
INT_MIN	MB_LEN_MAX	UCHAR_MAX	

All these macros are guaranteed to expand to a translation-time constant expression suitable for use with `#if`. C99 requires `UCHAR_MAX` to be $2^{CHAR\_BIT} - 1$.

`__LINE__` A predefined macro that expands to the current source line number as a decimal constant. (The type of the constant is unspecified but it must have at least the range of `int`.) The following is an example of its use:

```
printf("%lu", (unsigned long)__LINE__);
```

This macro cannot be the subject of `#undef`. *See also* `#line`.

`#line` A preprocessor directive used to override the current source filename or line number during translation. It is used as follows:

`#line` *line-number* ["*source-file-name*"]

This directive is not seen often except in code generated under program control by some kind of preprocessor. Standard C allows macro expansion in this directive. *See also* `__FILE__`; `__LINE__`.

line buffered stream A stream in which characters are intended to be sent to or received from the host environment as a block when a new-line is encountered. *See also* `_IOLBF`; `setvbuf`.

line, logical The concatenation of physical source lines that (except for the last) end in a backslash/new-line continuation character.

line, physical A source line terminated by a new-line character. Multiple physical source lines may be concatenated into a logical line.

linkage The form of coupling (if any) between occurrences of the same identifier when used as an object or function name. Standard C defines three forms of linkage: none, internal, and external. Examples of these three forms are an automatic variable, a static function, and external variable, respectively. *See also* scope; storage duration.

linkage, external A form of linkage in which two or more declarations of a given identifier designate the same object or function. Such identifiers are "exported" from the object module created by the translator and the objects or functions they designate may be accessed by name from any translation unit in which the identifiers are declared. Examples are non-`static` functions and external variables.

linkage, internal A form of linkage in which an identifier that has file scope and designates an object or function, and is `static`. Such identifiers are not "exported" from the object module created by the translator and the objects or functions they designate cannot be accessed by name from any translation unit other than that in which the identifiers are defined.

linkage, no A situation in which an identifier that designates an object and has neither external nor internal linkage. Examples are formal parameters, identifiers other than those designating objects and functions, and non-`extern` block scope identifiers. Such identifiers are private to the blocks in which they are defined.

`LL` **suffix**[C99] *See* constant, integer.

`ll` **suffix**[C99] *See* constant, integer.

`llabs`[C99] A function that computes the absolute value of its `long long int` argument `j`.

```
#include <stdlib.h>
long long int llabs(long long int j);
```

The behavior is undefined if the result cannot be represented. For example, the absolute value of the most negative number cannot be represented in two's complement. On such a system, the absolute value very likely will be the same as the original value; that is, the absolute value of this most negative value might be negative! *See also* `abs`; `labs`.

`lldiv`[C99] A function that computes the quotient and remainder when `numer` is divided by `denom`.

```
#include <stdlib.h>
lldiv_t lldiv(long long int numer, long long int denom);
```

If the division is inexact, the sign of the resulting quotient is that of the algebraic quotient, and the magnitude of the resulting quotient is the largest integer less than the magnitude of the algebraic quotient. If the result cannot be represented, the behavior is undefined. The value returned has the structure type `lldiv_t`, which contains the two `long long int` members, `quot` and `rem`, in either order. *See also* `div`; `ldiv`.

`lldiv_t`[C99] A type, defined in stdlib.h, that is a structure type used as the implementation-defined return type of the `lldiv` function. A possible definition for `lldiv_t` is

```
typedef struct {
        long long int quot;
        long long int rem;
} lldiv_t;
```

The ordering of the members does not need to be specified. *See also* `div_t`; `ldiv_t`.

`LLONG_MAX`[C99] A macro, defined in limits.h, that designates the maximum value for an object of type `long long int`. This value must be at least 9,223,372,036,854,775,807 (64 bits). This macro expands to an integer constant expression suitable for use with a `#if` directive.

`LLONG_MIN`[C99] A macro, defined in limits.h, that designates the minimum value for an object of type `long long int`. This value must be at least -9,223,372,036,854,775,807 (64 bits). This macro expands to an integer constant expression suitable for use with a `#if` directive.

`llrint[f|l]`[C99] A function that rounds its argument to the nearest integer value, according to the current rounding direction.

```
#include <math.h>
long int lrint(double x);
long int lrintf(float x);
long int lrintl(long double x);
```

A range error may occur.

`llround[f|l]`[C99] A function that returns the rounded integer value of its argument, rounding halfway cases away from zero, regardless of the current rounding direction.

```
#include <math.h>
long long int llround(double x);
long long int llroundf(float x);
long long int llroundl(long double x);
```

A range error may occur.

local A term pertaining to the scope of an identifier in that it is not visible outside its containing and subordinate blocks. *See also* linkage.

locale^{C89} A description of a cultural (or some other) environment. By default, a C program runs in the "C" locale unless the `setlocale` function has been called (or the implementation's normal operating default locale is other than "C"). In the "C" locale, the ctype.h routines have their traditional U.S.–English meaning. When a locale other than "C" is selected, the set of characters qualifying for a particular character type test may be extended to include other implementation-defined characters. For example, implementations running in Western Europe likely will include characters such as ä, ß, æ, Å, Ø, or Ł. Whether these test true with `isalpha` is implementation defined, based on the current locale. *See also* locale-specific behavior; `MB_LEN_MAX`.

locale, mixed^{C89} A composite locale comprised of a set of conventions representing two or more distinct nationalities, cultures, or languages. For example, a Swiss locale might include some German aspects as well as some French or Italian aspects. *See also* category; `LC_*` macros.

`localeconv`^{C89} A function that causes a structure of type `struct lconv` to be initialized with values corresponding to the current locale so that they can be interrogated by the programmer and used to format currency, floating-point data, etc., as needed. The address of this structure is returned.

```
#include <locale.h>
struct lconv *localeconv(void);
```

Undefined behavior results if the structure pointed to by the return value is modified by the caller.

locale.h^{C89} A header that was created as a place to declare routines and types useful in establishing library run-time environments that support cultural and language representations (called locales) in other than the "U.S.–English" mode provided by traditional C. (This traditional locale is known as the "C" locale.)

This header contains definitions or declarations for the following identifiers:

Name	*Purpose*
`LC_ALL`	`setlocale` category
`LC_COLLATE`	`setlocale` category
`LC_CTYPE`	`setlocale` category
`LC_MONETARY`	`setlocale` category
`LC_NUMERIC`	`setlocale` category
`LC_TIME`	`setlocale` category
`struct lconv`	Numeric format structure
`localeconv`	Setup locale information
`NULL`	Null pointer constant
`setlocale`	Establish a new locale

The key to defining a locale is the type `struct lconv`. *See also* future library directions.

locale-specific behavior[C89] Behavior that may be peculiar to a particular locale. Standard functions that have locale-specific behavior are: `atof`, `atoi`, `atol`, `atoll`, `isalnum`, `isalpha`, `isblank`, `isgraph`, `islower`, `isprint`, `ispunct`, `isspace`, `isupper`, `iswalpha`, `iswblank`, `iswctype`, `iswlower`, `isprint`, `iswpunct`, `iswspace`, `iswupper`, `strcoll`, `strftime`, `strftime`, `strtod`, `strtof`, `strtoimax`, `strtol`, `strtold`, `strtoll`, `strtouimax`, `strtoul`, `strtoull`, `strxfrm`, `tolower`, `toupper`, `towctrans`, `wcstod`, `wcstof`, `wcstol`, `wcstold`, `wcstoll`, `wcstoul`, and `wcstoull`. *See also* `wctrans_t`; `wctype_t`.

localization The process of adapting an internationalized program to a particular cultural environment. Known by its abbreviated name L10N. *See also* I18N

`localtime` A function that converts the calendar time pointed to by `timer` into a broken-down time, expressed as local time.

```
#include <time.h>
struct tm *localtime(const time_t *timer);
```

The value returned points to the broken-down time object.

`log[f|l]` A function that computes the natural logarithm of its argument `x`.

```
#include <math.h>
double log(double x);
float logf(float x);
long double logl(long double x);
```

If the argument is negative, a domain error is raised. If the argument is zero and the logarithm of zero cannot be represented (it could be represented as $-\infty$, perhaps), a range error occurs. Some implementations might generate a domain error instead.

The `float` and `long double` versions were an invention of C89, where they were optional; however, in C99, they are required.

`log10[f|l]` A function that computes the base-ten logarithm of its argument `x`.

```
#include <math.h>
double log10(double x);
float log10f(float x);
long double log10l(long double x);
```

If the argument is negative, a domain error is raised. If the argument is zero and the logarithm of zero cannot be represented (it could be represented as $-\infty$, perhaps), a range error occurs.

The `float` and `long double` versions were an invention of C89, where they were optional; however, in C99, they are required.

`log1p[f|l]`^{C99} A function that returns $log_e(1 + x)$.

```
#include <math.h>
double log1p(double x);
float log1pf(float x);
long double log1pl(long double x);
```

If the argument is less than -1 a domain error occurs. If the argument equals -1 a range error may occur.

`log2[f|l]`^{C99} A function that returns $log_2 x$.

```
#include <math.h>
double log2(double x);
float log2f(float x);
long double log2l(long double x);
```

If the argument is less than zero, a domain error occurs. If the argument equals zero, a range error may occur.

logarithmic and exponential functions The math.h functions `exp`, `exp2`, `expm1`, `frexp`, `ldexp`, `lgamma`, `log`, `log10`, `log1p`, `log2`, and `modf`, and their `float` and `long double` counterparts, both floating and complex.

`logb[f|l]`^{C99} A function that returns the signed exponent of `x`.

```
#include <math.h>
double logb(double x);
float logbf(float x);
long double logbl(long double x);
```

If the argument is zero, a domain error may occur.

logical AND **operator** *See* AND operator, logical.

logical negation operator A unary operator, `!`, that logically negates the value of its operand, which must have scalar type. The result has type `int`. If x is zero, `!`x is 1. If x is nonzero, `!`x is 0. This operator associates right to left.

logical OR **operator** *See* OR operator, logical.

logical source line *See* line, logical.

`long` A permitted abbreviation for `long int`. Also used in the type `long double`.

`long double`[C89] Keywords that are used to represent one of the three floating-point types. (The other two are `float` and `double`.) An object of this type must have at least the same range and precision as `double`. *See also* floating type.

`long double _Complex`[C99] *See* `complex`.

`long double _Imaginary`[C99] *See* `imaginary`.

`long double` **suffix**[C99] *See* constant, floating.

`long int` A standard integer type. Standard C requires it to be at least 32 bits. A plain `long int` is signed. *See also* integer type.

`long int` **suffix** *See* constant, integer.

`longjmp` A function that restores the program's context (or calling environment) that was saved by a previous call to `setjmp` in a user-defined object of type `jmp_buf`.

```
#include <setjmp.h>
void longjmp(jmp_buf env, int val);
```

`longjmp` does not return to its caller. Rather, it returns to the function that originally called `setjmp` to save the corresponding context. In doing so, it passes `val` back to `setjmp` so `setjmp` can return that value to its caller. If the value of `val` is zero, it is made `1` so that a call directly to setjmp (which returns 0) cannot be confused with longjmp's returning through setjmp with a value of 0.

The behavior is undefined if longjmp is invoked from a nested signal handler. Do not invoke longjmp from an exit handler, such as those registered by the atexit function.

long long[C99] A permitted abbreviation for long long int.

long long int[C99] A standard integer type. Standard C requires it to be at least 64 bits. A plain long long int is signed. *See also* integer type.

LONG_MAX[C89] A macro, defined in limits.h, that designates the maximum value for an object of type long int. It must be at least 2,147,483,647 (32 bits). This macro expands to an integer constant expression suitable for use with a #if directive.

LONG_MIN[C89] A macro, defined in limits.h, that designates the minimum value for an object of type long int. It must be at least −2,147,483,647 (32 bits). This macro expands to an integer constant expression suitable for use with an #if directive.

lrint[f|l][C99] A function that rounds its argument to the nearest integer value, according to the current rounding direction.

```
#include <math.h>
long long int llrint(double x);
long long int llrintf(float x);
long long int llrintl(long double x);
```

lround[f|l][C99] A function that returns the rounded integer value of its argument, rounding halfway cases away from zero, regardless of the current rounding direction.

```
#include <math.h>
long int lround(double x);
long int lroundf(float x);
long int lroundl(long double x);
```

A range error may occur.

L_tmpnam A macro, defined in stdio.h, that expands to an integer constant expression that is the size of a character array large enough to contain the temporary filename generated by tmpnam.

lvalue An expression that designates an object. The name comes from the fact that an lvalue is often found on the left-hand side of assignments. The most common forms of lvalue are the name of a variable and the expression *p where p is a pointer to an object. The operators [], unary *, and -> always produce an lvalue, and the dot operator usually produces one. No other operators produce lvalues. *See also* lvalue, modifiable; lvalue, non-modifiable; rvalue.

lvalue, modifiable[C89] An lvalue through which a value can be stored. Some operators require modifiable lvalues as operands. They are ++, --, and the left operand of all assignment operators. *See also* lvalue, non-modifiable.

lvalue, non-modifiable[C89] An lvalue through which a value cannot be stored. Examples include the name of an array and any expression designating a const object. *See also* lvalue, modifiable.

M

macro An identifier associated with a sequence of tokens (called its replacement list) by the preprocessor directive **#define**. During preprocessing, each occurrence of a macro name is replaced by its corresponding definition. As such, a macro is simply an abbreviation for its text value. Sometimes, a macro is referred to as a symbolic constant because its name is typically chosen to be symbolic of its underlying definition; for example,

```
#define PI 3.1415926
#define Max_Value 100
#define Clear_Screen() printf("\033[2J")
```

Note that a macro can be defined with no value; for example,

```
#define NAME
```

defines `NAME` to have no value, in which case all occurrences of that identifier are removed from the source during preprocessing.

Because one macro's definition can involve other, previously defined macros, subtle errors can occur that are difficult to debug. Most compilers provide a command-line option to allow you to save the output from the preprocessor so you can see exactly how the macros expanded.

See also macro, function-like; macro, object-like; macro, predefined; macro, replacement; **#undef**.

macro, function-like A macro defined with an argument list, which can be empty; for example,

```
#define Clear_Screen() printf("\033[2J")
#define INTSWAP(a,b) {int t = (a); (a) = (b); (b) = t;}
#define Isdigit(c) ((c) >= '0' && (c) <= '9')
```

The `(` token must immediately follow the name of the macro being defined. However, horizontal white space may be used to separate other preprocessing tokens in the definition; for example,

```
#define M( a ) ( a )
```

defines a function-like macro with one argument while:

```
#define M ( a ) ( a )
```

defines an object-like macro with the definition `( a ) ( a )`.

macro, object-like A macro defined without an argument list. This form of macro often is called a symbolic constant; for example,

```
#define PI 3.1415926
#define Max_Value 100
```

See also macro, function-like.

macro, predefined A macro automatically defined within the translator. C89 defined five such macros called `__FILE__`, `__LINE__`, `__DATE__`, `__TIME__`, and `__STDC__`. C95 added `__STDC_VERSION__`. C99 added `__STDC_HOSTED__` as well as the conditionally defined names `__STDC_IEC_559__`, `__STDC_IEC_559_COMPLEX__`, and `__STDC_ISO_10646__`. These macros cannot be the subject of `#undef` and they cannot be redefined. Implementations often have their own predefined macros as well. For example, a compiler running under the UNIX operating system might predefine the macros `UNIX` or `BSD`. A conforming implementation, however, must spell any extra predefined macros with a leading underscore followed by another underscore or an uppercase letter.

Many compilers support a translation-time option of defining macros before processing begins. This amounts to letting the user define a predefined macro. *See also* `__cplusplus`.

macro, redefinition of[C89] The redefining of a macro with another macro by the same name without an intervening `#undef`. A function-like macro may be redefined as a function-like macro provided all such definitions contain the same number and spelling of parameters and their replacement lists are identical. (Two replacement lists are identical if they contain the same set of tokens and the same number of sets of separating white space. The white space characters used may vary, however.) Similarly, an object-like macro may be redefined as an object-like macro provided all such definitions contain identical replacement lists. The following are valid redefinitions:

```
#define A 10  +tab5
#define A 10tab+ 5
#define A 10 + 5

#define B(a, b) a  +tabb
#define B(a, b) atab+ b
#define B(a, b) a + b
```

However, given the previous definitions, the following redefinitions are invalid:

```
#define A 10+tab5
#define A 10+ 5
#define A 10+5
#define A 15

#define B(a, b) a+tabb
#define B(a, b) a+b
#define B(x, y) x + y
```

This is because the absence of white space does not match the presence of white space.

macro replacement The process by which a macro is replaced by its definition. For object-like macros, the macro name at each call is simply replaced by the replacement list from its definition. For function-like macros, each call is replaced by the corresponding replacement list, however, each formal parameter is replaced by each actual argument in the process. If a macro expands to a set of tokens that includes the name of the macro originally being expanded, it is not further replaced. Standard C requires that macro expansion not be infinitely recursive. *See also* stringize operator; token-pasting operator.

macro, safe A function-like macro whose definition only evaluates each argument once. *See also* macro, unsafe.

macro, unsafe A function-like macro can be defined so that when it is expanded, the resulting text has one or more arguments appearing multiple times; for example,

```
#define Isdigit(c) ((c) >= '0' && (c) <= '9')
```

However, invoking this macro with an argument that contains a side effect can cause unexpected behavior. For example, `Isdigit(x++)`, where `x` contains the value `'9'`, tests false because `x` would be incremented before it is tested the second time. Also, `x` would be incremented twice. As such, this macro definition is said to be unsafe. Either it must be called with arguments that have no side effects or it must be scrapped and a function version used instead.

Except where explicitly exempted, Standard C permits all library functions to exist as macros also, provided they are safe macros.

`main` A function required within each hosted program, that marks the program's logical entry point. (Freestanding C programs do not need to have a function called `main`.) Although `main` has special semantics, it is just another function and therefore can have arguments passed to it. `main` can even be called recursively if you can find a good reason to do so. Standard C requires a conforming implementation to support `main` defined in both of the following ways:

```
int main(void) { /* ... */ }
int main(int argc, char *argv[]) { /* ... */ }
```

Other implementation-defined forms are permitted; for example, a common extension is to have a third argument of type `char *` called `envp`, which provides access to an array of environment variable strings much like `getenv`.

`malloc` A function that dynamically allocates contiguous memory of `size` bytes.

```
#include <stdlib.h>
void *malloc(size_t size);
```

The space allocated has no guaranteed initial value.

The value returned is of type `void *` and therefore is assignment compatible with any object or incomplete pointer type. Therefore, no explicit cast is needed. This value is the address of the beginning of the allocated memory and is guaranteed to be suitably aligned for use in storing any object.

If the memory cannot be allocated, `NULL` is returned.

If `size` is zero, it is implementation defined as to whether `NULL` or a unique pointer is returned.

By giving `realloc` a `NULL` first argument, `realloc` can be used to produce the same effect as `malloc` with the same size.

See also `calloc`; `free`.

manifest constant A synonym for object-like macro. Standard library examples are `NULL` and `EOF`.

`MATH_ERREXCEPT`[C99] A macro, defined in math.h, that expands to the integer constant 2. *See* `math_errhandling`.

`math_errhandling`[C99] A macro, defined in math.h, that expands to an expression that has type `int` and the value `MATH_ERRNO`, `MATH_ERREXCEPT` or the bitwise OR of both. The value of `math_errhandling` is constant for the duration of the program. It is unspecified whether `math_errhandling` is really a macro or an identifier with external linkage.

If the expression `math_errhandling & MATH_ERREXCEPT` can be nonzero, the implementation must define the macros `FE_DIVBYZERO`, `FE_INVALID`, and `FE_OVERFLOW` in fenv.h.

MATH_ERRNO[C99] A macro, defined in math.h, that expands to the integer constant 1. *See* math_errhandling.

math.h A header that contains support for the math library functions. (Other math-related names are declared in complex.h, fenv.h, and tgmath.h.) C89 requires a standard-conforming implementation to support only a double version of each function. However, if float or long double versions are also supported, the function names have a suffix of f or l, respectively (as indicated below by the optional suffix f or l). C99 requires all three versions. math.h contains definitions or declarations for the following identifiers:

Name	*Purpose*
acos[f|l]	Arc cosine
acosh[f|l][C99]	Arc hyperbolic cosine
asin[f|l]	Arc sine
asinh[f|l][C99]	Arc hyperbolic sine
atan[f|l]	Arc tan
atan2[f|l]	Principal arc tan
atanh[f|l][C99]	Arc hyperbolic tan
cbrt[f|l][C99]	Cube root
ceil[f|l]	Highest ceiling
copysign[f|l][C99]	Magnitude of x with sign of y
cos[f|l]	Cosine
cosh[f|l]	Hyperbolic cosine
double_t[C99]	Type-widening type
erf[f|l][C99]	Error function
erfc[f|l][C99]	Complementary error function
exp[f|l]	Exponential using base e
exp2[f|l][C99]	Exponential using base 2
expm1[f|l][C99]	Exponential using base e, minus 1
fabs[f|l]	Floating absolute
fdim[f|l][C99]	Positive difference
float_t[C99]	Type-widening type
floor[f|l]	Lowest floor
fma[f|l][C99]	Multiply-and-add
fmax[f|l][C99]	Maximum value
fmin[f|l][C99]	Minimum value
fmod[f|l]	Floating remainder
FP_FAST_FMA[C99]	Fma macro, double
FP_FAST_FMAF[C99]	Fma macro, float
FP_FAST_FMAL[C99]	Fma macro, long double
FP_ILOGB0[C99]	ilogb return value

<table>
<tr><th>Name</th><th>Purpose</th></tr>
<tr><td>FP_ILOGBNAN[C99]</td><td>ilogb return value</td></tr>
<tr><td>FP_INFINITE[C99]</td><td>Number classification macro</td></tr>
<tr><td>FP_NAN[C99]</td><td>Number classification macro</td></tr>
<tr><td>FP_NORMAL[C99]</td><td>Number classification macro</td></tr>
<tr><td>FP_SUBNORMAL[C99]</td><td>Number classification macro</td></tr>
<tr><td>FP_ZERO[C99]</td><td>Number classification macro</td></tr>
<tr><td>fpclassify[C99]</td><td>Classifies a value</td></tr>
<tr><td>frexp[f|l]</td><td>Breakdown floating number</td></tr>
<tr><td>HUGE_VAL</td><td>Huge floating value of type double</td></tr>
<tr><td>HUGE_VALF[C99]</td><td>Huge floating value of type float</td></tr>
<tr><td>HUGE_VALL[C99]</td><td>Huge floating value of type long double</td></tr>
<tr><td>hypot[f|l][C99]</td><td>Hypotenuse</td></tr>
<tr><td>ilogb[f|l][C99]</td><td>Extracts an exponent</td></tr>
<tr><td>INFINITY[C99]</td><td>Positive infinity of type float</td></tr>
<tr><td>isfinite[C99]</td><td>Test if finite</td></tr>
<tr><td>isgreater[C99]</td><td>Test if greater</td></tr>
<tr><td>isgreaterequal[C99]</td><td>Test if greater or equal</td></tr>
<tr><td>isinf[C99]</td><td>Test if infinite</td></tr>
<tr><td>isless[C99]</td><td>Test if less</td></tr>
<tr><td>islessequal[C99]</td><td>Test if less or equal</td></tr>
<tr><td>islessgreater[C99]</td><td>Test if less or greater</td></tr>
<tr><td>isnan[C99]</td><td>Test if Not-a-Number</td></tr>
<tr><td>isnormal[C99]</td><td>Test if normal</td></tr>
<tr><td>isunordered[C99]</td><td>Test if unordered</td></tr>
<tr><td>ldexp[f|l]</td><td>Load exponent</td></tr>
<tr><td>lgamma[f|l][C99]</td><td>Natural log of gamma</td></tr>
<tr><td>llrint[f|l][C99]</td><td>Rounding function</td></tr>
<tr><td>llround[f|l][C99]</td><td>Rounding function</td></tr>
<tr><td>log[f|l]</td><td>Base e logarithm</td></tr>
<tr><td>log10[f|l]</td><td>Base 10 logarithm</td></tr>
<tr><td>log1p[f|l][C99]</td><td>Base e logarithm of 1 plus arg</td></tr>
<tr><td>log2[f|l][C99]</td><td>Base 2 logarithm</td></tr>
<tr><td>logb[f|l][C99]</td><td>Extracts an exponent</td></tr>
<tr><td>lrint[f|l][C99]</td><td>Rounding function</td></tr>
<tr><td>lround[f|l][C99]</td><td>Rounding function</td></tr>
<tr><td>MATH_ERREXCEPT[C99]</td><td>math_errhandling flag</td></tr>
<tr><td>math_errhandling[C99]</td><td>Math error flags value</td></tr>
<tr><td>MATH_ERRNO[C99]</td><td>math_errhandling flag</td></tr>
<tr><td>modf[f|l]</td><td>Breakdown floating number</td></tr>
<tr><td>NAN[C99]</td><td>Not-a-Number of type float</td></tr>
<tr><td>nan[f|l][C99]</td><td>Generate a NaN value</td></tr>
<tr><td>nearbyint[f|l][C99]</td><td>Rounding function</td></tr>
<tr><td>nextafter[f|l][C99]</td><td>Manipulation function</td></tr>
<tr><td>nexttoward[f|l][C99]</td><td>Manipulation function</td></tr>
</table>

Name	*Purpose*
pow[f|l]	Power
remainder[f|l][C99]	IEEE remainder
remquo[f|l][C99]	Remainder function
rint[f|l][C99]	Rounding function
round[f|l][C99]	Rounding function
scalbln[f|l][C99]	Scale-by function
scalbn[f|l][C99]	Scale-by function
signbit[C99]	Tests sign bit
sin[f|l]	Sine
sinh[f|l]	Hyperbolic sine
sqrt[f|l]	Square root
tan[f|l]	Tan
tanh[f|l]	Hyperbolic tan
tgamma[f|l][C99]	Gamma function
trunc[f|l][C99]	Rounding function

See also future library directions.

`MB_CUR_MAX`[C89] A macro, defined in stdlib.h, that expands to a positive integer expression of type `size_t` whose value is the maximum number of bytes in a multibyte character for the extended character set specified by the current locale (category `LC_CTYPE`) and whose value is never greater than `MB_LEN_MAX` (defined in limits.h).

`mblen`[C89] A function that computes the number of bytes in the multibyte character pointed to by `s`.

```
#include <stdlib.h>
int mblen(const char *s, size_t n);
```

See also `mbtowc`.

`MB_LEN_MAX`[C89] A macro, defined in limits.h, that designates the maximum number of bytes in a multibyte character for any supported locale. (It must be at least 1.) This macro expands to an integer constant expression suitable for use with a `#if` directive. *See also* `MB_CUR_MAX`.

`mbrlen`[C95] A function that is equivalent to the call

```
mbrtowc(NULL, s, n, ps != NULL ? ps : &internal)
```

where `internal` is `mbrlen`'s `mbstate_t` object, except that the expression `ps` is evaluated only once.

```
#include <wchar.h>
size_t mbrlen(const char * restrict s, size_t n,
    mbstate_t * restrict ps);
```

The value returned is between zero and `n`, inclusive, `(size_t)(-2)`, or `(size_t)(-1)`.

`mbrtowc`C95 A function that is a restartable version of `mbtowc`.

```
#include <wchar.h>
size_t mbrtowc(wchar_t * restrict pwc,
    const char * restrict s, size_t n,
    mbstate_t * restrict ps);
```

`mbsinit`C95 A function that determines whether the pointed-to `mbstate_t` object describes an initial conversion state, if `ps` is non-null.

```
#include <wchar.h>
int mbsinit(const mbstate_t *ps);
```

The return value is nonzero if `ps` is null or if the pointed-to object describes an initial conversion state; otherwise, it is zero.

`mbsrtowcs`C95 A function that is a restartable version of `mbstowcs`.

```
#include <wchar.h>
size_t mbsrtowcs(wchar_t * restrict dst,
    const char ** restrict src,
    size_t len, mbstate_t * restrict ps);
```

`mbstate_t`C95 An object type, defined in wchar.h, other than an array type, that can hold the conversion state information necessary to convert between sequences of multibyte characters and wide characters.

`mbstowcs`C89 A function that converts a sequence of multibyte characters into a string of corresponding wide characters.

```
#include <stdlib.h>
int mbstowcs(wchar_t * restrict pwcs,
    const char * restrict s, size_t n);
```

`mbtowc`C89 A function that computes the number of bytes in the multibyte character pointed to by `s`. It then determines the code for a value of type `wchar_t` that corresponds to that multibyte character.

```
#include <stdlib.h>
int mbtowc(wchar_t * restrict pwc,
    const char * restrict s, size_t n);
```

`mem` **prefix** *See* future library directions.

member An identifier declared as part of a structure or union layout. Such members are referenced using the dot or arrow operator.

member selection operators *See* arrow operator; dot operator.

`memchr` A function that searches the first `n` characters of a string `s` for a character `c`.

```
#include <string.h>
void *memchr(const void *s, int c, size_t n);
```

If `c` is found, `memchr` returns a pointer to that location within `s`, otherwise, it returns `NULL`. `c` is converted to `unsigned char` before the search begins. *See also* `wmemchr`.

`memcmp` A function that compares `n` characters at the location pointed to by `s2` to the characters at the location pointed to by `s1`.

```
#include <string.h>
int memcmp(const void *s1, const void *s2, size_t n);
```

An integer less than, equal to, or greater than zero is returned to indicate whether the first `n` characters starting at `s1` have binary values less than, equal to, or greater than, respectively, those starting at `s2`. *See also* `wmemcmp`.

`memcpy` A function that copies `n` characters from the location pointed to by `s2` to the characters at the location pointed to by `s1`.

```
#include <string.h>
void *memcpy(void * restrict s1, const void * restrict s2,
    size_t n);
```

The value of `s1` is returned. If the objects located at `s1` and `s2` overlap, the behavior of `memcpy` is undefined. To copy overlapping objects, use `memmove` instead. *See also* `wmemcpy`.

`memmove`^{C89} A function that copies `n` characters from the location pointed to by `s2` to the characters at the location pointed to by `s1`.

```
#include <string.h>
void *memmove(void *s1, const void *s2, size_t n);
```

The value of `s1` is returned. `memmove` works correctly even if the objects located at `s1` and `s2` overlap. If the objects are known to not overlap, it may be more efficient to use `memcpy` instead. *See also* `wmemmove`.

memory management functions The stdlib.h functions `calloc`, `free`, `malloc`, and `realloc`.

`memset` A function that sets the first `n` characters of the object pointed to by `s` to the value `c`.

```
#include <string.h>
void *memset(void *s, int c, size_t n);
```

`c` is converted to an `unsigned char` before the copying begins. The value returned is `s`. *See also* `wmemset`.

minus operator, unary *See* unary minus operator.

`mktime` A function that converts a broken-down time (as defined in the type `struct tm` type), in the structure pointed to by `timeptr`, into a calendar time.

```
#include <time.h>
time_t mktime(struct tm *timeptr);
```

The value returned is the calendar time resulting from the conversion. If this time cannot be represented, the value returned is `(time_t)(-1)`. All the members required to be in the `tm` structure (except `tm_wday` and `tm_yday`) must be initialized. When `mktime` completes successfully, these two members have been filled in.

`modf[f|l]` A function that breaks a floating-point number into integer and fractional parts.

```
#include <math.h>
double modf(double value, double *iptr);
float modff(float value, float *iptr);
long double modfl(long double value, long double *iptr);
```

Each part has the same sign as the original number. The integer part is stored in the location pointed to by `iptr`, and the fractional part is the return value.

The `float` and `long double` versions were an invention of C89, where they were optional; however, in C99, they are required.

modifiable lvalue[C89] *See* lvalue; lvalue, modifiable; lvalue, non-modifiable.

modulus An often-used but incorrect name for the remainder when performing division. For integer remainder, *see* remainder operator; for floating-point remainder, *see* `modf`.

mon_decimal_point[C89] An lconv structure member that is a pointer to a string containing the decimal point used to format monetary quantities. If the string consists of "", the value is not available in the current locale or is of zero length. In the "C" locale this member must have the value "".

mon_grouping[C89] An lconv structure member that is a pointer to a string whose elements indicate the size of each group of digits in formatted monetary quantities. If the string consists of "", this indicates that the value is not available in the current locale or is of zero length. In the "C" locale this member must have the value "". The elements are interpreted as follows:

- CHAR_MAX No further grouping is to be performed.
- 0 The previous element is to be repeatedly used for the remainder of the digits.
- **other** The integer value is the number of digits that make up the current group. The next element is examined to determine the size of the next group of digits before the current group.

mon_thousands_sep[C89] An lconv structure member that is a pointer to a string containing the separator for groups of digits before the decimal point in formatted monetary quantities. If the string consists of "", the value is not available in the current locale or is of zero length. In the "C" locale this member must have the value ".".

multibyte character The result when a character from a writing system such as Chinese, Japanese, and Korean, whose characters cannot be represented in what C refers to as a byte, is encoded into one or more bytes. (Strictly speaking, since a multibyte character can have a single byte only, ASCII and EBCDIC are really multibyte character sets in which each character can be represented in a single byte.) The method of encoding the bytes is locale dependent; commonly used encoding schemes for Japanese text are EUC, JIS, and Shift-JIS. A multibyte character is stored as an array of one or more char, so a function taking a multibyte character argument by address or returning one by address, uses char * to describe that type. In fact, most library functions accepting or returning this type really traffic in multibyte characters. Multibyte characters must not be confused with wide characters. *See also* MB_CUR_MAX; MB_LEN_MAX; mblen; mbtowc; wctomb.

multibyte character functions The stdlib.h functions mblen, mbtowc, and wctomb, and the wchar.h functions mbrtowc and wcrtomb. The behavior of these functions is subject to the current locale, in particular, to the LC_CTYPE category.

multibyte string A string containing one or more multibyte characters. *See also* `mbstowcs`; `wcstombs`.

multibyte string functions The stdlib.h functions `mbstowcs` and `wcstombs`, and the wchar.h functions `mbsrtowcs` and `wcsrtombs`. The behavior of these functions is subject to the current locale, in particular, to the `LC_CTYPE` category.

multiplication assignment operator A binary operator, `*=`, that permits multiplication and assignment to be combined so that *exp1* `*=` *exp2* is equivalent to *exp1* `=` *exp1* `*` *exp2*, except that in the former, *exp1* is only evaluated once. The order of evaluation of the operands is unspecified. Both operands must have arithmetic type, and the left operand must be a modifiable lvalue. The type of the result is the type of *exp1*. This operator associates right to left. *See also* assignment operator, compound.

multiplication operator A binary operator, `*`, that causes the values of its operands to be multiplied together. The order of evaluation of the two operands is unspecified. Both operands must have arithmetic type. The usual arithmetic conversions are performed on the operands. This operator associates left to right.

`mutable` A C++ keyword that is not part of Standard C. If you think you might wish to move C code to a C++ environment in the future, you should refrain from using `mutable` as an identifier in new C code you write.

N

name space A collection of identifiers in which no two identifiers may have the same name. It is possible to use the same identifier for different purposes in the same scope (even though this might not be considered good style) provided each declaration of that identifier is in a different name space. Standard C defines the following name spaces for identifiers:

1. Formal parameter names in prototypes
2. Label names within a function
3. Structure, union, and enumeration tags
4. Each member set within a structure or union
5. All others—variables, functions, typedef names, and enumeration constants

Macro names are not included here because after preprocessing they no longer exist and, therefore, are not seen by the compiler. However, from a programmer's viewpoint, macro names should be thought of as sharing the same name space as all identifiers.

Each use of the identifier `x` in the following example is in a different name space. As such, the code fragment is valid.

```
void v(int x);
struct x {int x} s1;
struct y {int x} s2;

void f()
{
        int x;

        goto x;

x:      x = s1.x;
        x += s2.x;
}
```

`namespace` A C++ keyword that is not part of Standard C. If you think you might wish to move C code to a C++ environment in the future, you should refrain from using `namespace` as an identifier in new C code you write.

NAN[C99] A macro, defined in math.h, that is defined iff the implementation supports quiet NaNs for the `float` type. It expands to a constant expression of type `float` whose value represents a quiet NaN.

NaN An encoding for a floating-point value signifying Not-a-Number.

nan[f|l]C99 A function that returns a quiet NaN, if they are supported, otherwise it returns zero.

```
#include <math.h>
double nan(const char *tagp);
float nanf(const char *tagp);
long double nanl(const char *tagp);
```

In the case of nan, the argument tagp is interpreted as follows:
nan("*n-char-sequence*") ≡ strtod("NAN(*n-char-sequence*)", (char**) NULL),
nan("") ≡ strtod("NAN()", (char**) NULL),
nan(*any-other-string*) ≡ strtod("NAN", (char**) NULL).

Calls to nanf and nanl are equivalent to the corresponding calls to strtof and strtold.

NaN, quiet A kind of NaN that propagates through almost every arithmetic operation without raising a floating-point exception.

NaN, signaling A kind of NaN that generally raises a floating-point exception when used as an arithmetic operand.

narrow type *See* type, narrow.

NCEG The Numerical C Extensions Group. Convened early in 1989 by Rex Jaeschke, NCEG's mission was to define extensions to C89 to help numerical programmers. The main areas investigated were aliasing, variable dimensioned arrays, array syntax, vector support, complex arithmetic, IEEE-754 issues, and exception handling. Eventually, NCEG became committee X3J11.1, which, ultimately, was absorbed into X3J11 and what is now J11. The resulting Technical Report (TR) made up the bulk of J11's contribution to C99.

NCITS/J11 The formal name for the U.S. standards committee J11.

NCITS/J16 The formal name for the U.S. standards committee J16.

n_cs_precedesC89 An lconv structure member that is a nonnegative number set to 1 or 0 if the currency_symbol respectively precedes or succeeds the value for a negative formatted monetary quantity. A value of CHAR_MAX indicates that the value is not available in the current locale. In the "C" locale this member must have the value CHAR_MAX.

nearbyint[f|l]C99 A function that rounds its argument to an integer value in floating-point format, using the current rounding direction and without raising the "inexact" floating-point exception.

```
#include <math.h>
double nearbyint(double x);
float nearbyintf(float x);
long double nearbyintl(long double x);
```

nextafter[f|l][C99] A function that returns the next representable value after x in the direction of y, in the specified return type.

```
#include <math.h>
double nextafter(double x, double y);
float nextafterf(float x, float y);
long double nextafterl(long double x, long double y);
```

See also nexttoward.

nexttoward[f|l][C99] A function that is equivalent to the corresponding version of the nextafter function except that nexttoward's second parameter has type long double and that if x equals y, nexttoward returns y converted to the type of the function.

```
#include <math.h>
double nexttoward(double x, long double y);
float nexttowardf(float x, long double y);
long double nexttowardl(long double x, long double y);
```

See also nextafter.

not[C95] A macro, defined in iso646.h, that expands to the token !. It allows programmers using source character sets (such as ISO 646) that are missing certain characters necessary for writing C programs, to enter those characters using identifiers instead. Note that in C++, this name is a keyword.

not_eq[C95] A macro, defined in iso646.h, that expands to the token !=. It allows programmers using source character sets (such as ISO 646) that are missing certain characters necessary for writing C programs, to enter those characters using identifiers instead. Note that in C++, this name is a keyword.

NDEBUG An option user-defined macro. If a definition for this macro is present at the point where assert.h is included, the assert macro takes on the definition ((void)0). If NDEBUG is not defined at the point of this header inclusion, the assert macro is defined to produce an assertion (which may result in abnormal program termination).

nearest integer functions The math.h functions ceil, floor, lrint, lround, llround, nearbyint, rint, and round, and their float and long double counterparts.

`negative_sign`[C89] An `lconv` structure member that is a pointer to a string used to indicate a negative-valued formatted monetary quantity. If the string consists of `""`, the value is not available in the current locale or is of zero length. In the `"C"` locale this member must have the value `""`.

`new` A C++ keyword that is not part of Standard C. If you think you might wish to move C code to a C++ environment in the future, you should refrain from using `new` as an identifier in new C code you write.

new-line character One of the white space characters allowed in source text and as input to certain library functions. It is used to represent the logical end-of-line character, which is the effect generated when you type the ENTER or RETURN (or similar) key on a keyboard. On many systems, it is externally mapped into a carriage-return and line-feed pair, or just a line feed. However, internally, C always treats it as one character.

new-line escape sequence A new-line can be represented by the escape sequence `\n`.

`noalias` A type qualifier keyword invented by X3J11 and existed for a short while in a draft version of C89. The keyword was intended to provide the compiler with information about aliasing so that it could more aggressively optimize. While `noalias` is not part of Standard C, a subset of its properties was added in C99 via the keyword `restrict`.

nonlocal jumps header *See* setjmp.h.

not-equal-to operator *See* inequality operator.

`n_sep_by_space`[C89] An `lconv` structure member that is a nonnegative number set to 1 or 0 if the `currency_symbol` respectively is or is not separated by a space from the value for a negative formatted monetary quantity. A value of `CHAR_MAX` indicates that the value is not available in the current locale. In the `"C"` locale this member must have the value `CHAR_MAX`.

`n_sign_posn`[C89] An `lconv` structure member that is a nonnegative number set to a value indicating the positioning of the `negative_sign` for a negative formatted monetary quantity. The value is interpreted according to the following:

`0` Parentheses surround the quantity and `currency_symbol`.

`1` The sign string precedes the quantity and `currency_symbol`.

`2` The sign string succeeds the quantity and `currency_symbol`.

`3` The sign string immediately precedes the `currency_symbol`.

`4` The sign string immediately succeeds the `currency_symbol`.

`CHAR_MAX` indicates that the value is not available in the current locale.

In the "C" locale this member must have the value CHAR_MAX.

NULL A macro that expands to an implementation-defined null pointer constant. It typically has a value of 0, 0L, or ((void *)0) and is defined identically in each of the following headers: locale.h, stddef.h, stdio.h, stdlib.h, string.h, time.h, and wchar.h.

Standard C does not require the null pointer constant's value to have an internal representation of "all-bits-zero"—it can be any address guaranteed not to be used for an object or function.

NULL should never be used when a null character is meant because the definition of NULL is not always 0.

null character The character with value '\0' used to terminate character strings. A string literal token (having the form "ABCD") implicitly includes a trailing null character. Historically, many programmers used NULL in the context of a null character because they "knew" that NULL was defined as 0. This has always been bad style and, with Standard C, actually can fail because NULL can be defined otherwise.

null pointer The result when a null pointer constant is converted to a pointer type. A comparison between the null pointer and a pointer to any object or function is guaranteed to be unequal.

null pointer constant *See* constant, null pointer.

null preprocessing directive # A preprocessing directive that has the form:

```
#
```

and has no effect. It is an historic artifact.

null statement A statement consisting solely of a semicolon.

null wide character^{C89} A wide character with code value zero. It can be written as L'\0'.

number classification macro^{C99} One of FP_INFINITE, FP_NAN, FP_NORMAL, FP_SUBNORMAL, and FP_ZERO, or other implementation-defined macros having names beginning with FP_ and an uppercase letter, defined in math.h. These macros expand to integer constant expressions with distinct values.

Numerical C Extensions Group *See* NCEG.

numerical limits^{C89} *See* float.h; limits.h.

O

object A region of storage, the contents of which can represent values corresponding to a given type.

obsolescent A term applied to a practice or approach declaring it to be "out dated." Labelling something as obsolescent in a standard paves the way for it to be dropped from future versions of that standard. Some people use the term "deprecated" instead. *See also* future language directions; future library directions.

octal constant *See* constant, integer.

octal escape sequence A sequence of the form *ddd* that represents the character having a bit-pattern with value *ddd* octal. (*ddd* is a sequence of 1–3 octal digits.) The escape sequence `\0` is commonly used to represent the null character because it is required to have an internal representation of zero binary. The maximum number of octal digits is fixed at three. However, the maximum number for a hexadecimal escape sequence is not fixed.

`offsetof`[C89] A macro, defined in stddef.h, that allows you to find the offset (in bytes) of a member from the start of its parent structure. `offsetof` expands into an integer constant expression that has type `size_t`. If the member is a bit-field, the behavior is undefined because you cannot take the address of a bit-field. An example of its use is as follows:

```
#include <stddef.h>

struct tag {
        int i;
        double d;
};

size_t value = offsetof(struct tag, d);
```

Open Group Successor to X/Open.

operand The expression on which an operator acts. Unary operators have one operand, binary have two operands, and ternary have three operands. *See also* order of evaluation.

`operator` A C++ keyword that is not part of Standard C. If you plan to move C code to a C++ environment in the future, you should refrain from using `operator` as an identifier in new C code you write.

operator One or more tokens that, when taken together, specify an operation to be performed on one or more operands producing either a value, an object or function designator, a side effect, or a combination of these. (While most operators comprise a single token, a few do not. For example, `[ ]`, function call `()`, and `?:`.) The Standard C operators are

Symbol	*Meaning*
`!`	logical negation
`!=`	inequality
`%`	remainder
`&`	AND (bitwise) and address-of
`&&`	AND (logical)
`()`	cast and function call
`*`	multiplication and indirection
`+`	addition and unary plus
`++`	increment, prefix or postfix
`,`	comma
`-`	subtraction and unary minus
`--`	decrement, prefix or postfix
`->`	structure/union pointer (arrow)
`.`	structure/union member (dot)
`/`	division
`<`	less-than
`<<`	left-shift
`<=`	less-than-or-equal-to
`=`	assignment
`==`	equality
`>`	greater-than
`>=`	greater-than-or-equal-to
`>>`	right shift
`?:`	conditional
`[ ]`	subscript
`^`	OR (bitwise exclusive)
`|`	OR (bitwise inclusive)
`||`	OR (logical)
`~`	complement
op`=`	assignment, compound
`sizeof`	compute object size at translation-time

The unary plus operator was an invention of C89.

operator, binary An operator having two operands. Examples are `/`, `<<`, and `&&`.

operator precedence The order in which terms are grouped, as determined by a set of rules, written in the form of a precedence table. An operator in a higher row of the precedence table has higher precedence. The grouping of terms across operators having the same precedence is resolved by their associativity. Precedence and associativity are shown in the following table:

<table>
<tr><th>Operator</th><th>Associativity</th></tr>
<tr><td><code>() [] -> . ++ --</code></td><td>Left to Right</td></tr>
<tr><td><code>! ~ ++ -- + - * &</code> (type) <code>sizeof</code></td><td>Right to Left</td></tr>
<tr><td><code>* / %</code></td><td>Left to Right</td></tr>
<tr><td><code>+ -</code></td><td>Left to Right</td></tr>
<tr><td><code><< >></code></td><td>Left to Right</td></tr>
<tr><td><code>< <= > >=</code></td><td>Left to Right</td></tr>
<tr><td><code>== !=</code></td><td>Left to Right</td></tr>
<tr><td><code>&</code></td><td>Left to Right</td></tr>
<tr><td><code>^</code></td><td>Left to Right</td></tr>
<tr><td><code>|</code></td><td>Left to Right</td></tr>
<tr><td><code>&&</code></td><td>Left to Right</td></tr>
<tr><td><code>||</code></td><td>Left to Right</td></tr>
<tr><td><code>?:</code></td><td>Right to Left</td></tr>
<tr><td><code>= += -= *= /= %= >>= <<= &= ^= |=</code></td><td>Right to Left</td></tr>
<tr><td><code>,</code></td><td>Left to Right</td></tr>
</table>

Note that C89 promoted postfix versions of `++` and `--` to have higher precedence than their prefix counterparts. This breaks no old code; however, it did make some new expressions possible (such as `p++->m`).

Operator precedence is not related to the order of evaluation of individual terms. For example, in the expression `f() + g()` the precedence is clear—both functions are called before their return values are added together—but the order in which the functions are called is unspecified.

operator, ternary An operator having three operands. C has one of these, the conditional operator `?:`.

operator, unary An operator having only one operand. Examples are `++`, `!`, and `~`.

`or`[C95] A macro, defined in iso646.h, that expands to the token `||`. It allows programmers using source character sets (such as ISO 646) that are missing certain characters necessary for writing C programs, to enter those characters using identifiers instead. Note that in C++, this name is a keyword.

OR assignment operator, bitwise exclusive A binary operator, `^=`, that permits exclusive OR and assignment to be combined such that *exp1* `^=` *exp2* is equivalent to *exp1* `=` *exp1* `^` *exp2* except that in the former, *exp1* is only evaluated once. Both operands must have integer type. The left operand must be a modifiable lvalue. The order of evaluation of the operands is unspecified. The type of the result is the type of *exp1*. This operator associates right to left. *See also* assignment operator, compound.

OR **assignment operator, bitwise inclusive** A binary operator, `|=`, that permits OR and assignment to be combined such that *exp1* `|=` *exp2* is equivalent to *exp1* `=` *exp1* `|` *exp2* except that in the former, *exp1* is only evaluated once. Both operands must have integer type. The left operand must be a modifiable lvalue. The order of evaluation of the operands is unspecified. The type of the result is the type of *exp1*. This operator associates right to left. *See also* assignment operator, compound.

OR **operator, bitwise exclusive** A binary operator, `^`, that performs a bitwise exclusive-OR of its operands. Both operands must have integer type. The order of evaluation of the operands is unspecified. The usual arithmetic conversions are performed on the operands. This operator associates left to right.

OR **operator, bitwise inclusive** A binary operator, `|`, that performs a bitwise inclusive-OR of its operands. Both operands must have integer type. The order of evaluation of the operands is unspecified. The usual arithmetic conversions are performed on the operands. This operator associates left to right.

OR **operator, logical** A binary operator, `||`, that performs a logical OR of its operands. Both operands must have scalar type. The result has type `int` and value 0 (if false) or 1 (if true). There is a sequence point after the evaluation of the left operand. The left operand is evaluated first, and if it tests true, the right operand is not evaluated. This operator associates left to right.

order of evaluation The order in which terms in expressions are evaluated. Very few C operators specify the order of evaluation of their operands. Those that do are logical OR, logical AND, comma, and conditional. These four operators also contain sequence points. *See also* evaluation.

ordinary identifier name space The name space used for variables, functions, `typedef` names, and enumeration constants.

`or_eq`[C95] A macro, defined in iso646.h, that expands to the token `|=`. It allows programmers using source character sets (such as ISO 646) that are missing certain characters necessary for writing C programs, to enter those characters using identifiers instead. Note that in C++, this name is a keyword.

`overload` An archaic C++ keyword.

P

parameter *See* argument, formal.

parameter, ellipsis[C89] *See* ellipses.

parameter type list A comma-separated list of types (optionally containing identifiers) as used in a function prototype.

parentheses punctuator The tokens `()` that can be used as a grouping punctuator. Parentheses may be used in expressions to override operator precedence or to document the default precedence. For example, in `a + (b * c)` the grouping parentheses are redundant, whereas in `(a + b) * c` they are not. A parenthesized expression has the same type and value as the expression without the parentheses. For example, `(i) = (((6)))` is equivalent to `i = 6`. Note that grouping is not related to, and cannot be used to control, the order of evaluation of the individual terms.

parenthesized expression An expression surrounded by parentheses. *See also* expression, parenthesized; expression, primary.

`p_cs_precedes`[C89] An `lconv` structure member that is a nonnegative number set to 1 or 0 if the `currency_symbol` respectively precedes or succeeds the value for a nonnegative formatted monetary quantity. A value of `CHAR_MAX` indicates that the value is not available in the current locale. In the `"C"` locale this member must have the value `CHAR_MAX`.

`perror` A function that writes a message to `stderr` corresponding to the current value of `errno`. The message includes the user-supplied string pointed to by `s`.

```
#include <stdio.h>
void perror(const char *s);
```

The message output is prefixed with the string pointed to by `s` followed by a colon and a space, provided `s` is not `NULL` and doesn't point to an empty string. The contents and format of the message are implementation defined and are the same as those returned by the `strerror` function with argument `errno`.

phases of translation[C89] These are described by Standard C as follows:

"The precedence among the syntax rules of translation is specified by the following phases:[1]

[1]Implementations must behave as if these separate phases occur, even though many are typically folded together in practice.

1. Physical source file multibyte characters are mapped, in an implementation-defined manner, to the source character set (introducing new-line characters for end-of-line indicators) if necessary. Trigraph sequences are replaced by corresponding single-character internal representations.
2. Each instance of a backslash character (\) immediately followed by a new-line character is deleted, splicing physical source lines to form logical source lines. Only the last backslash on any physical source line shall be eligible for being part of such a splice. A source file that is not empty shall end in a new-line character, which shall not be immediately preceded by a backslash character before any such splicing takes place.
3. The source file is decomposed into preprocessing tokens[2] and sequences of white-space characters (including comments). A source file shall not end in a partial preprocessing token or in a partial comment. Each comment is replaced by one space character. New-line characters are retained. Whether each nonempty sequence of white-space characters other than new-line is retained or replaced by one space character is implementation defined.
4. Preprocessing directives are executed, macro invocations are expanded, and, in C99, `_Pragma` unary operator expressions are executed. Also in C99, if a character sequence that matches the syntax of a universal character name is produced by token concatenation, the behavior is undefined. A `#include` preprocessing directive causes the named header or source file to be processed from phase 1 through phase 4, recursively. All preprocessing directives are then deleted.
5. Each source character set member and escape sequence in character constants and string literals is converted to the corresponding member of the execution character set; if there is no corresponding member, it is converted to an implementation-defined member other than the null (wide) character.[3]
6. Adjacent character string literal tokens are concatenated and, in C99, adjacent wide string literal tokens are concatenated.
7. White-space characters separating tokens are no longer significant. Each preprocessing token is converted into a token. The resulting tokens are syntactically and semantically analyzed and translated.
8. All external object and function references are resolved. Library components are linked to satisfy external references to functions

[2]The process of dividing a source file's characters into preprocessing tokens is context-dependent. For example, see the handling of < within a `#include` preprocessing directive.

[3]An implementation need not convert all noncorresponding source characters to the same execution character.

and objects not defined in the current translation. All such translator output is collected into a program image which contains information needed for execution in its execution environment."

plain char *See* `char`, plain.

plain `int` bit-field *See* bit-field, plain `int`.

plus operator, unary^{C89} *See* unary plus operator.

pointer An object that contains the address of an object or function, or an expression that designates the address of an object or function. For example, given the following:

```
int i = 10;
int *pi = &i;
```

`pi` is a pointer object and `&i` is a pointer expression that does not involve a pointer object.

A pointer expression is dereferenced using the unary `*` operator or the subscript operator `[ ]`. Pointers to structures or unions are dereferenced using the arrow operator `->`. A pointer can be initialized by using the unary `&` operator, although this operator is redundant if the initializer is of some function type.

A function can be called by dereferencing a pointer to it.

pointer declarator A declarator involving the derived type "pointer to some type." *See also* declarator, punctuation in.

pointer, null *See* constant, null pointer.

pointer subtraction Two pointers can be subtracted, one from the other, provided both point to elements of the same array or one points to an element of an array and the other points to the (nonexistent) element immediately following the last element of that same array. The type of the result is `ptrdiff_t`, an integer type defined in stddef.h. Note that the difference between two such pointers is neither inclusive nor exclusive of the objects to which they point. For example, given the following:

```
int i[10];
int *p1 = &i[3];
int *p2 = &i[5];
```

the expression `p2 - p1` results in 2 while the expression `p1 - p2` results in −2. In both cases, the magnitude of the difference is 2, the number of elements between the start of `i[3]` and the start of `i[5]`. The sign indicates direction.

pointer to function An expression or variable used to represent the address of a function. Conceptually, a function pointer contains the address of the first byte or word of the executable code for that function. However, in some systems it contains the address of an object, which in turn points to the function. You cannot perform arithmetic operations on function pointers. *See also* jump table.

pointer to `void`[C89] *See* `void` pointer.

pointer type conversion *See* conversion, pointer.

portability The degree of ease with which a program can be moved from one computer system to another (somehow) dissimilar system. A primary obstacle in porting C code is that many aspects of C are implementation defined. *See also* program, strictly conforming.

`positive_sign`[C89] An `lconv` structure member that is a pointer to a string used to indicate a nonnegative-valued formatted monetary quantity. If the string consists of `""`, the value is not available in the current locale or is of zero length. In the `"C"` locale this member must have the value `""`.

POSIX A portable operating system definition based on UNIX, produced by IEEE committee P1003. POSIX defines many library functions over and above those defined by Standard C. The international counterpart to P1003 is WG15.

`pow[f|l]` A function that computes the power function x^y.

```
#include <math.h>
double pow(double x, double y);
float powf(float x, float y);
long double powl(long double x, long double y);
```

If `x` is negative and `y` is not a whole number, a domain error occurs. If `x` is 0 and `y` is less than or equal to 0, and the result cannot be represented, a domain error occurs. A range error may occur.

The `float` and `long double` versions were an invention of C89, where they were optional; however, in C99, they are required.

power functions The math.h functions `pow` and `sqrt`, and their `float` and `long double` counterparts, both floating and complex.

`_Pragma`[C99] A unary preprocessor operator that is used in expressions as follows:

```
_Pragma( string-literal )
```

Such an expression is processed as follows:

1. The string literal is destringized by deleting the L prefix, if present, deleting the leading and trailing double quotes, replacing each escape sequence \" by a double quote, and replacing each escape sequence \\ by a single backslash.
2. The resulting sequence of characters is processed through translation phase 3 to produce preprocessing tokens that are executed as if they were the tokens in a pragma directive.
3. The original four preprocessing tokens in the unary operator expression are removed.

Unlike **#pragma**, **_Pragma** can be used in a macro definition.

#pragma[C89] An implementation-defined preprocessor directive. If an implementation comes across a pragma it does not recognize, it ignores it. A pragma has the following general form:

#pragma [*preprocessor-tokens*]

Some compilers recognize a pragma that specifies how tightly adjacent members in a structure are packed; for example,

#pragma pack(*n*)

where *n* can be 1, 2, or 4 indicating byte, word, or double-word alignment, respectively. Other compilers define pragmas to change the way in which arguments are passed to functions and to help the compiler break the code into threads for a parallel processing environment.

Although an implementation is permitted to perform macro replacement in nonstandard pragmas, it not required to do so.

For information on standard pragmas, *see* **#pragma** STDC.

#pragma STDC[C99] A standard pragma, which must have one of the following forms:

#pragma STDC CX_LIMITED_RANGE *on-off-switch*
#pragma STDC FENV_ACCESS *on-off-switch*
#pragma STDC FP_CONTRACT *on-off-switch*

No macro replacement is performed on standard pragma directives. It is implementation defined whether macro replacement is performed on nonstandard pragma directives.

#pragma STDC CX_LIMITED_RANGE[C99] A standard pragma that can be used to indicate whether or not the usual mathematical formulas for complex multiply, divide, and absolute value are acceptable, based on their treatment of infinities and because of undue overflow and underflow. There are limits on where this pragma should be placed in a source file. The three forms of this pragma are:

```
#pragma STDC CX_LIMITED_RANGE ON
#pragma STDC CX_LIMITED_RANGE OFF
#pragma STDC CX_LIMITED_RANGE DEFAULT
```

where the default state is `OFF`.

`#pragma STDC FENV_ACCESS`$^{\text{C99}}$ A standard pragma that provides a means to inform the implementation when a program might access the floating-point environment to test floating-point status flags or run under nondefault floating-point control modes. There are limits on where in a source file this pragma should be placed. The three forms of this pragma are

```
#pragma STDC FENV_ACCESS ON
#pragma STDC FENV_ACCESS OFF
#pragma STDC FENV_ACCESS DEFAULT
```

where the default state is implementation defined.

`#pragma STDC FP_CONTRACT`$^{\text{C99}}$ A standard pragma that provides a way to allow or disallow the implementation to contract expressions. The three forms of this pragma are

```
#pragma STDC FP_CONTRACT ON
#pragma STDC FP_CONTRACT OFF
#pragma STDC FP_CONTRACT DEFAULT
```

where the default state is implementation defined.

precedence The hierarchy and associativity of operators. *See also* operator precedence.

predefined macro *See* macro, predefined.

preprocessing directives Source lines that have the following general format:

`#` [*directive-name*] [*preprocessing-tokens*]

Horizontal white space may exist before the `#`, between the `#` and *directive-name*, and before, after, or in between the preprocessing tokens. Unless continued by a backslash/new-line pair, a preprocessing source line terminates at the end of the current physical source line. The complete set of such directives is as follows:

Name	*Purpose*
`#define`	Define a macro
`#undef`	Remove a macro definition
`#include`	Include a header
`#if`	Compile based on truth of expression
`#ifdef`	Compile based on macro being defined
`#ifndef`	Compile based on macro not being defined
`#else`	Conditional compilation false path
`#elif`	Compound else/if
`#endif`	End conditional compilation group
`#line`	Override line number/source file name
`#error`	Generate a translation error
`#pragma`	Implementation-defined action
`#`	Null directive

preprocessing operator A number of operators are available only to the preprocessor. They are as follows:

Name	*Purpose*
`#`	Stringize
`##`	Token pasting
`defined`	Expression form of `#ifdef`
`_Pragma`^{C99}	Allows a pragma in a macro definition

preprocessing token A token in translation phases 3 through 6. The complete set of preprocessing tokens defined by C89 is character-constant, header-name, identifier, operator, preprocessing number, punctuator, string-literal, and each non-white-space character that cannot be one of the above. C99 dropped operator, moving such tokens into the punctuator category instead.

preprocessor A program that scans a C source file for lines beginning with a `#`, which it assumes to be directives that indicate some action to be taken before subsequent source code lines are handed off to the compiler. Typically, the preprocessor is actually integrated with the compiler proper.

`PRId`N^{C99} A macro, defined in inttypes.h, that expands to a character string literal containing a conversion specifier suitable for use with members of the `printf` and `wprintf` family when converting the type `int`N`_t`. For example,

```
int32_t x = 10;
printf("x = %2" PRId32 "\n", x);
```

PRIdLEASTN^{C99} A macro, defined in inttypes.h, that expands to a character string literal containing a conversion specifier suitable for use with members of the `printf` and `wprintf` family when converting the type `int_least`N`_t`.

PRIdFASTN^{C99} A macro, defined in inttypes.h, that expands to a character string literal containing a conversion specifier suitable for use with members of the `printf` and `wprintf` family when converting the type `int_fast`N`_t`.

PRIdMAX^{C99} A macro, defined in inttypes.h, that expands to a character string literal containing a conversion specifier suitable for use with members of the `printf` and `wprintf` family when converting the type `intmax_t`.

PRIdPTR^{C99} A macro, defined in inttypes.h, that expands to a character string literal containing a conversion specifier suitable for use with members of the `printf` and `wprintf` family when converting the type `intptr_t`.

printf A function that writes formatted output to `stdout` as specified by `format`.

```
#include <stdio.h>
int printf(const char * restrict format, ...);
```

Characters in `format` other than `%` and those specifying a particular conversion specifier are output verbatim. To output a `%` character, use `%%`.

`printf` returns the number of characters it transmitted. If an output error occurred, a negative value is returned.

A call to `printf` is equivalent to a call to `fprintf` using a stream of `stdout`.

The general format of a `printf` conversion specifier is as follows:

`%`[*flags*][*width*][*.precision*][*modifier*]*specifier*

where the values for *flags*, *modifier*, and *specifier* are as follows:

`printf` Flags

Symbol	*Meaning*
-	Left-justify
+	Leading sign
space	Leading space
#	Alternate output form
0	Leading zeros

printf Modifiers

Symbol	*Meaning*
h	short int
hh[C99]	char
j[C99]	[u]intmax_t
l	long int
L	long double
t[C99]	ptrdiff_t
z[C99]	size_t

printf Specifiers

Symbol	*Meaning*
a[C99]	Hex floating
A[C99]	Uppercase hex floating
c	Character
d	Signed decimal
e	Lowercase exponent
E	Uppercase exponent
f	Fractional (6 decimal places)
F[C99]	Uppercase NaN/Infinity
g	Shorter of e or f
G	Shorter of E or f
i	Signed decimal
n	Stores char count in int
o	Unsigned octal
p	Pointer to void
s	String
u	Unsigned decimal
x	Unsigned lowercase hex
X	Unsigned uppercase hex
%	Print % character

See also future library directions.

PRIoN[C99] A macro, defined in inttypes.h, that expands to a character string literal containing a conversion specifier suitable for use with members of the printf and wprintf family when converting the type uint$N$_t. For example,

```
uint32_t x = 10;
printf("x = %2" PRIo32 "\n", x);
```

PRIoLEASTN[C99] A macro, defined in inttypes.h, that expands to a character string literal containing a conversion specifier suitable for use with members of the **printf** and **wprintf** family when converting the type **uint_least**N**_t**.

PRIoFASTN C99 A macro, defined in inttypes.h, that expands to a character string literal containing a conversion specifier suitable for use with members of the **printf** and **wprintf** family when converting the type **uint_fast**N**_t**.

PRIoMAX C99 A macro, defined in inttypes.h, that expands to a character string literal containing a conversion specifier suitable for use with members of the **printf** and **wprintf** family when converting the type **uintmax_t**.

PRIoPTR C99 A macro, defined in inttypes.h, that expands to a character string literal containing a conversion specifier suitable for use with members of the **printf** and **wprintf** family when converting the type **uintptr_t**.

PRIuN C99 A macro, defined in inttypes.h, that expands to a character string literal containing a conversion specifier suitable for use with members of the **printf** and **wprintf** family when converting the type **uint**N**_t**. For example,

```
uint32_t x = 10;
printf("x = %2" PRIu32 "\n", x);
```

PRIuLEASTN C99 A macro, defined in inttypes.h, that expands to a character string literal containing a conversion specifier suitable for use with members of the **printf** and **wprintf** family when converting the type **uint_least**N**_t**.

PRIuMAX C99 A macro, defined in inttypes.h, that expands to a character string literal containing a conversion specifier suitable for use with members of the **printf** and **wprintf** family when converting the type **uintmax_t**.

PRIuFASTN C99 A macro, defined in inttypes.h, that expands to a character string literal containing a conversion specifier suitable for use with members of the **printf** and **wprintf** family when converting the type **uint_fast**N**_t**.

PRIuPTR C99 A macro, defined in inttypes.h, that expands to a character string literal containing a conversion specifier suitable for use with members of the **printf** and **wprintf** family when converting the type **uintptr_t**.

private A C++ keyword that is not part of Standard C. If you think you might wish to move C code to a C++ environment in the future, you should refrain from using **private** as an identifier in new C code you write.

`PRIX`N^{C99} A macro, defined in inttypes.h, that expands to a character string literal containing a conversion specifier suitable for use with members of the `printf` and `wprintf` family when converting the type `uint`N`_t`. For example,

```
uint32_t x = 10;
printf("x = %2" PRIX32 "\n", x);
```

`PRIx`N^{C99} A macro, defined in inttypes.h, that expands to a character string literal containing a conversion specifier suitable for use with members of the `printf` and `wprintf` family when converting the type `uint`N`_t`. For example,

```
uint32_t x = 10;
printf("x = %2" PRIx32 "\n", x);
```

`PRIXLEAST`N^{C99} A macro, defined in inttypes.h, that expands to a character string literal containing a conversion specifier suitable for use with members of the `printf` and `wprintf` family when converting the type `uint_least`N`_t`.

`PRIxLEAST`N^{C99} A macro, defined in inttypes.h, that expands to a character string literal containing a conversion specifier suitable for use with members of the `printf` and `wprintf` family when converting the type `uint_least`N`_t`.

`PRIXFAST`N^{C99} A macro, defined in inttypes.h, that expands to a character string literal containing a conversion specifier suitable for use with members of the `printf` and `wprintf` family when converting the type `uint_fast`N`_t`.

`PRIxFAST`N^{C99} A macro, defined in inttypes.h, that expands to a character string literal containing a conversion specifier suitable for use with members of the `printf` and `wprintf` family when converting the type `uint_fast`N`_t`.

`PRIXMAX`^{C99} A macro, defined in inttypes.h, that expands to a character string literal containing a conversion specifier suitable for use with members of the `printf` and `wprintf` family when converting the type `uintmax_t`.

`PRIxMAX`^{C99} A macro, defined in inttypes.h, that expands to a character string literal containing a conversion specifier suitable for use with members of the `printf` and `wprintf` family when converting the type `uintmax_t`.

`PRIXPTR`^{C99} A macro, defined in inttypes.h, that expands to a character string literal containing a conversion specifier suitable for use with members of the `printf` and `wprintf` family when converting the type `uintptr_t`.

`PRIxPTR`^{C99} A macro, defined in inttypes.h, that expands to a character string literal containing a conversion specifier suitable for use with members of the `printf` and `wprintf` family when converting the type `uintptr_t`.

program One or more (possibly separately compiled) functions of which one must be called `main`. These functions, along with any external data, make up an execution unit. A program may include functions from an external library.

program, conforming^{C89} A program that is acceptable to a conforming implementation. Note that a conforming program is not necessarily maximally portable, since it might use extensions particular to the conforming implementation that accepts it.

program name *See* `argv`.

program parameters *See* `argc`; `argv`; `envp`.

program startup That vendor-supplied code executed before control is passed to `main` in a host environment, or some implementation-defined function in a free-standing environment.

program, strictly conforming^{C89} A program that uses only those features of the language and library defined by Standard C. Its output must not depend on unspecified, undefined, or implementation-defined behavior. *See also* conforming implementation; program, conforming.

program termination The stopping of the execution of a program. A program may be terminated a number of ways: by dropping through the closing brace of `main`, by executing a `return` statement from `main`, by calling `abort` or `exit`, or by an interrupt occurring that caused program termination. *See also* exit code.

program termination, abnormal *See* `abort`.

program termination, normal *See* `exit`.

promotions, default argument *See* conversion, function arguments.

promotions, integer *See* conversion, integer type.

`protected` A C++ keyword that is not part of Standard C. If you think you might wish to move C code to a C++ environment in the future, you should refrain from using `protected` as an identifier in new C code you write.

prototype^{C89} *See* function prototype.

p_sep_by_space[C89] An lconv structure member that is a nonnegative number set to 1 or 0 if the currency_symbol respectively is or is not separated by a space from the value for a nonnegative formatted monetary quantity. A value of CHAR_MAX indicates that the value is not available in the current locale. In the "C" locale this member must have the value CHAR_MAX.

pseudo-random sequence functions The stdlib.h functions rand and srand.

p_sign_posn[C89] An lconv structure member that is a nonnegative number set to a value indicating the positioning of the positive_sign for a nonnegative formatted monetary quantity. The value is interpreted according to the following:

0 Parentheses surround the quantity and currency_symbol.

1 The sign string precedes the quantity and currency_symbol.

2 The sign string succeeds the quantity and currency_symbol.

3 The sign string immediately precedes the currency_symbol.

4 The sign string immediately succeeds the currency_symbol.

CHAR_MAX indicates that the value is not available in the current locale.

In the "C" locale this member must have the value CHAR_MAX.

PTRDIFF_MAX[C99] A macro, defined in stdint.h, that indicates the maximum value of the type ptrdiff_t. It expands to an integer constant expression suitable for use with a #if directive.

PTRDIFF_MIN[C99] A macro, defined in stdint.h, that indicates the minimum value of the type ptrdiff_t. It expands to an integer constant expression suitable for use with a #if directive.

ptrdiff_t[C89] The type of the difference between two pointers of the same type. This type is signed and integer. (In practice, both pointers must point to elements within the same array for the subtraction to be meaningful or, in fact, reliable.) ptrdiff_t is defined in stddef.h. *See also* pointer subtraction; printf conversion specifier %t; PTRDIFF_MAX; PTRDIFF_MIN.

public A C++ keyword that is not part of Standard C. If you think you might wish to move C code to a C++ environment in the future, you should refrain from using public as an identifier in new C code you write.

punctuator One of the following tokens: [,], (,), {, }, ., ->, ++, --, &, *, +, -, ~, !, /, %, <<, >>, <, >, <=, >=, ==, !=, ^, |, &&, ||, ?, ,, :, =, ;, ..., #, ##, =, *=, /=, %=, +=, -=, <<=, >>=, &=, ^=, |=, <:, :>, <%, %>, %:, %:%:. Many punctuators also serve as operators.

`putc` A function that writes the character specified by `c` (converted to `unsigned char`) to the file pointed to by `stream`.

```
#include <stdio.h>
int putc(int c, FILE *stream);
```

`putc` is equivalent to `fputc` except that `putc` is permitted to be an unsafe macro. *See also* `putwc`.

`putchar` A function that writes the character specified by `c` (converted to `unsigned char`) to `stdout`.

```
#include <stdio.h>
int putchar(int c);
```

`putchar` is equivalent to `putc` to `stdout`. Therefore, `putchar` may be implemented as an unsafe macro. *See also* `putwchar`.

`puts` A function that writes the string pointed to by `s`, followed by a new-line, to `stdout`.

```
#include <stdio.h>
int puts(const char *s);
```

The `'\0'` terminating the string is not written. Unlike `fputs`, `puts` appends a new-line to the output. `puts` returns `EOF` if an error occurs; otherwise, it returns a nonnegative value.

`putwc`^{C95} A function that is equivalent to `fputwc`, except that if it is implemented as a macro, it may evaluate `stream` more than once.

```
#include <stdio.h>
#include <wchar.h>
wint_t putwc(wchar_t c, FILE *stream);
```

The value returned is either the wide character written or `WEOF`.

`putwchar`^{C95} A function that writes the given wide character to standard output.

```
#include <wchar.h>
wint_t putwchar(wchar_t c);
```

The value returned is either the wide character written or `WEOF`.

Q

`qsort` A function that sorts an array of `nmemb` objects, the initial member of which is pointed to by `base`.

```
#include <stdlib.h>
void qsort(void *base, size_t nmemb, size_t size,
    int (*compar)(const void *, const void *));
```

`size` specifies the size of each member in the array. The members of the array are sorted in an ascending order corresponding to that expected by the comparison function pointed to by `compar`. This comparison function is passed two arguments that point to the objects being compared. Based on the comparison, a negative, zero, or positive value is returned by `compar`, which correspond to less than, equal to, and greater than, respectively. If two members compare as equal, it is unspecified as to their order in the array.

qualified type[C89] *See also* type, qualified; type, `const`-qualified; type, `restrict`-qualified; type, `volatile`-qualified.

Quality of Implementation A property of an implementation that allows it to meet the needs and demands of its customers, typically in areas unspecified by the standard. For example, when a diagnostic message is required, the implementation could simply issue the message, "Error somewhere in this program," and still claim conformance. However, a quality implementation also would identify the source line and possible reason for the error.

question mark escape sequence C89 added trigraphs of the form `??`x where x can be one of a number of characters. Trigraphs are recognized and replaced in the first phase of translation. Since `??(` is a trigraph for the character `[`, a string literal containing `"??(xxx)"` is interpreted as `"[xxx)"`. Such character sequences can exist in a string literal yet not be treated as trigraphs by using the question mark escape sequence `\?`. For example, `"?\?(xxx)"` is interpreted as `"??(xxx)"`. That is, the escaped question mark is treated as a single question mark character. Trigraphs allow for source to be written using character sets, such as ISO 646, that are missing characters essential for writing C source.

quiet change[C89] A change in semantics without a change in syntax. While the C committees tried to avoid any quiet changes in defining Standard C, some did occur. According to the Standard C rationale document, C89 introduced the following quiet changes:

- Programs with character sequences such as `??!` in string constants, character constants, or header names now will produce different results due to the addition of trigraphs.
- A program that depends upon internal identifiers matching only in the first eight characters may change to one with distinct objects for each variant spelling of the identifier.
- Unsuffixed integer constants may have different types. In K&R, unsuffixed decimal constants greater than `INT_MAX`, and unsuffixed octal or hexadecimal constants greater than `UINT_MAX` are of type `long`.
- A constant of the form `'\078'` is valid, but now has different meaning. It now denotes a character constant whose value is the (implementation-defined) combination of the values of the two characters `'\07'` and `'8'`. In some implementations, the old meaning is the character whose code is $078 \equiv 0100 \equiv 64$.
- A constant of the form `'\a'` or `'\x'` now may have different meaning. The old meaning, if any, was implementation dependent.
- A string of the form `"\078"` is valid, but now is interpreted as containing the two characters `\07` and `8`.
- A string of the form `"\a"` or `"\x"` now has different meaning.
- It is neither required nor forbidden that identical string literals be represented by a single copy of the string in memory; a program depending upon either scheme may behave differently.
- Expressions of the form `x=-3` and `x=+y` change meaning with the loss of the old-style assignment operators.
- A program that depends on unsigned preserving arithmetic conversions will behave differently, probably without complaint. This is considered the most serious semantic change made by X3J11 to a widespread current practice.
- Expressions with `float` operands now may be computed at lower precision. The Base Document specified that all floating point operations be done in `double`.
- Shifting by a `long` count no longer coerces the shifted operand to `long`.
- The empty declaration `struct x;` is no longer innocuous.
- Code that relies on a bottom-up parse of aggregate initializers with partially elided braces will not yield the expected initialized object.
- `long` expressions and constants in `switch` statements are no longer truncated to `int`.
- Functions that depend on `char` or `short` parameter types being widened to `int`, or `float` to `double`, may behave differently if called in the scope of a prototype containing narrow types.

- A macro that relies on formal parameter substitution within a string literal will produce different results.
- A program that relies on size zero memory allocation requests returning a nonnull pointer may behave differently.

C99 introduced the following quiet changes:

- Constructs such as `x //* ... */ y` are treated differently due to the addition of `//`-style comments.
- An integer constant whose value is greater than `LONG_MAX` that had type `unsigned long int` in C89, might have type `long long int` in C99.

`quot`^{C89} The name of one of the two members in the structure types `div_t`, `ldiv_t`, and `lldiv_t`. It is used to represent the quotient of an integer division and has type `int`, `long int`, and `long long int`, respectively, in these structures. *See also* `rem`.

R

radix point The point that separates the integer and fractional parts of a number. C always uses a period as the radix point character in floating point constants. In the standard "C" locale, a period is also used as the radix point in functions such as `printf`, `scanf`, and `strtod`. The standard routines using a radix point that is affected by the locale are: `atof`, `fprintf`, `fscanf`, `localeconv`, `printf`, `scanf`, `sprintf`, `sscanf`, `strtof`, `strtod`, `strtold`, `vfprintf`, `vprintf`, and `vsprintf`, and their wide-character counterparts.

`raise` A function that is used to send a signal `sig` to the program. It is useful for testing user-written signal handlers.

```
#include <signal.h>
int raise(int sig);
```

`raise` returns a value of zero if the raise was successful. Otherwise, it returns a nonzero value.

`rand` Repeated calls to this function generate a sequence of pseudo random integers in the range `0` to `RAND_MAX`. A single call generates a single number only.

```
#include <stdlib.h>
int rand(void);
```

See also `srand`.

`RAND_MAX` A macro, defined in stdlib.h, that expands to an integer constant expression representing the maximum value possible from `rand`. Standard C requires `RAND_MAX` to be at least 32,767. Its integer type is not specified, so use an explicit cast (or a prototype) when passing it as an argument.

range error An error that occurs if the result of the function cannot be represented in some specified type. If the result overflows, the function returns the value of `HUGE_VAL`, `HUGE_VALF`, or `HUGE_VALL`, as appropriate, with the same sign as the correct value would have. `errno` is set to the macro `ERANGE`. If the result underflows, the function returns 0 and `errno` may or may not be set to `ERANGE`, as the implementation defines. *See also* `math_errhandling`; `MATH_ERREXCEPT`; `MATH_ERRNO`.

`realloc` A function that changes the size of the dynamically allocated memory pointed to by `ptr` to size `size`. It returns the address of the (possibly) new location.

```
#include <stdlib.h>
void *realloc(void *ptr, size_t size);
```

If `ptr` is `NULL`, `realloc` behaves like `malloc`. Otherwise, if `ptr` is not a value previously returned by `calloc`, `malloc`, or `realloc`, the behavior is undefined. The same is true if `ptr` points to space that has been `freed`. `size` is absolute, not relative. If `size` is larger than the size of the existing space, new uninitialized contiguous space is allocated at the end; the previous contents of the space are preserved. If `size` is smaller, the excess space is freed; however, the contents of the retained space are preserved. If `realloc` cannot allocate the requested space, `NULL` is returned and the contents of the space pointed to by `ptr` remain intact. If `ptr` is non-`NULL` and `size` is 0, `realloc` acts like `free`.

Whenever the size of space is changed by `realloc`, the new space may begin at an address different from that given it, even when `realloc` is truncating. Therefore, if you use `realloc` in this manner, you must be aware of pointers that point into this possibly moved space. For example, if you build a linked list there and use `realloc` to allocate more (or less) space for the chain, it is possible that the space will be moved, in which case, the pointers now point to where successive links used to be, not where they are now. You should always use `realloc` as follows:

```
p2 = realloc(p1, new_size);
if (p2 != NULL)
        p1 = p2;
```

This way, you never care whether the object has been relocated because you always update `p1` with each successful call to point to the (possibly new) location.

recursion A recursive function is one that invokes itself directly or indirectly. For each invocation, a new set of automatic objects (if any) is created. *See also* recursion.

redefinition of macro *See* benign redefinition; macro, redefinition of.

redirection characters UNIX and MS-DOS/Windows (and other operating systems) allow `stdin` and `stdout` to be redirected using the command-line symbols `<`, `>`, and `>>`. They also might provide a way to redirect `stderr`.

`register` A storage class keyword used in the declaration of an object inside a function definition to designate automatic storage duration. `register` is a hint to the compiler to place the object in some "fast" location of memory, such as a machine register. If the compiler cannot or chooses not to do so, the keyword is treated as if it were `auto`. `register` also may be used in a prototype and in a function argument declaration.

An object with storage class `register` cannot have its address taken either explicitly (via the `&` operator) or implicitly (by passing an array to a function, for example). This helps an optimizer because it knows that object has no aliases.

`reinterpret_cast` A C++ keyword that is not part of Standard C. If you think you might wish to move C code to a C++ environment in the future, you should refrain from using `reinterpret_cast` as an identifier in new C code you write.

`rem`^{C89} The name of one of the two members in the structure types `div_t`, `ldiv_t`, and `lldiv_t`. It is used to represent the remainder of an integer division and has type `int`, `long int`, and `long long int`, respectively, in these structures. *See also* `quot`.

`remainder[f|l]`^{C99} A function that returns remainder x *REM* y, as required by IEC 60559.

```
#include <math.h>
double remainder(double x, double y);
float remainderf(float x, float y);
long double remainderl(long double x, long double y);
```

According to C99, "When $y \neq 0$, the remainder $r = x\ REM\ y$ is defined regardless of the rounding mode by the mathematical relation $r = x - ny$, where n is the integer nearest the exact value of x/y; whenever $| n - x/y | = 1/2$, then n is even. Thus, the remainder is always exact. If $r = 0$, its sign shall be that of x."

remainder assignment operator A binary operator, `%=`, that permits remainder and assignment to be combined such that *exp1* `%=` *exp2* is equivalent to *exp1* `=` *exp1* `%` *exp2*, except that in the former, *exp1* is only evaluated once. The order of evaluation of the operands is unspecified. The left operand must be a modifiable lvalue. The type of the result is the type of *exp1*. This operator associates right to left. *See also* assignment operator, compound.

remainder functions `fmod`, `remquo`, and `remainder`, declared in math.h.

remainder operator A binary operator, `%`, that computes the remainder when its left operand is divided by its right. Both operands must have integer type. (To compute a floating-point remainder, use the `fmod`, `remquo`, or `remainder` library functions.) The usual arithmetic conversions are performed on the operands. The order of evaluation of the operands is unspecified. This operator associates left to right. If either operand is negative, the sign of the remainder is implementation defined.

`remove` A function that causes the file whose name is pointed to by `filename` to be made inaccessible by that name.

```
#include <stdio.h>
int remove(const char *filename);
```

On many systems, the file is actually deleted. However, it may be that you are removing a synonym for a file's name, rather than deleting the file itself. In such cases, when the last synonym is being removed, the file is typically deleted. If `remove` succeeds, it returns a zero value; otherwise it returns a nonzero value.

`remquo[f|l]`[C99] A function that computes the remainder and quotient of x/y.

```
#include <math.h>
double remquo(double x, double y, int *quo);
float remquof(float x, float y, int *quo);
long double remquol(long double x, long double y,
    int *quo);
```

`rename` A function that causes a file, currently known by the name pointed to by `old`, to be known by the name pointed to by `new`.

```
#include <stdio.h>
int rename(const char *old, const char *new);
```

If a file called `new` already exists, the bchavior is implementation defined. If `rename` succeeds, it returns a zero value; otherwise it returns a nonzero value. On failure, the file still has the name `old`.

replacement list, macro *See* macro.

reserved identifier *See* identifier, reserved.

restore calling environment function *See* `longjmp`.

`restrict`[C99] A type qualifier that is intended to help generate optimal code by allowing the programmer to promise that all accesses to a given object are done through a particular pointer by making that pointer be `restrict`-qualified.

Consider the following declaration of `memcpy` in string.h:

```
void *memcpy(void * s1, const void * s2, size_t n);
```

By declaring both pointers to be `restrict`-qualified, we promise that the source and destination objects do not overlap, allowing a more efficient implementation.

Another good use of this keyword is in allocating memory; for example,

```
int * restrict p = malloc(100 * sizeof(int));
```

By declaring `p` to be `restrict`-qualified, the compiler can assume that no other pointers point to the same block of memory.

`restrict` may also be used inside any dimension of an array parameter (possibly along with `const` and/or `static`); for example,

```
void copy(int s[restrict], int d[restrict]);
```

This declaration specifies that the array arguments' do not overlap.

`return` A statement that causes control to be returned to the calling function. `return exp;` from `main` is equivalent to `exit(exp);`. A non-`void` function may return a value using the syntax `return exp;`. `return` is used as follows:

```
return [ expression ];
```

Falling through the end of the outermost closing brace in a function is an implied `return` without an expression. And if the function has a non-`void` return type, the value actually returned is undefined.

expression is a full expression.

`rewind` A function that sets the file's file position indicator to the start of the file.

```
#include <stdio.h>
void rewind(FILE *stream);
```

A call to `rewind` is identical to a call to `fseek` with `offset` `0L` and `whence` `SEEK_SET`. However, `rewind` also clears the error indicator as well.

right-shift assignment operator A binary operator, `>>=`, that permits right shift and assignment to be combined such that *exp1* `>>=` *exp2* is equivalent to *exp1* `=` *exp1* `>>` *exp2* except that in the former, *exp1* is only evaluated once. Both operands must have integer type, and the left operand must be a modifiable lvalue. The order of evaluation of the operands is unspecified. The type of the result is the type of *exp1*. This operator associates right to left. If the value of the right operand is negative, or equal to or greater than the number of bits in the promoted left operand, the behavior is undefined. If the left operand has a signed type and negative value, the result is implementation defined. *See also* assignment operator, compound.

right-shift operator A binary operator, `>>`, that causes the value of its left operand to be shifted right by the number of bits specified by its right operand. Both operands must have integer type. The order of evaluation of the operands is unspecified. This operator associates left to right. The usual arithmetic conversions are performed on the operands. If the value of the right operand is negative, or equal to or greater than the number of bits in the promoted left operand, the behavior is undefined. If the left operand has a signed type and negative value, the result is implementation defined.

`rint`[`f`|`l`][C99] A function that returns the rounded integer value for its argument, using the current rounding direction.

```
#include <math.h>
double rint(double x);
float rintf(float x);
long double rintl(long double x);
```

This function differs from `nearbyint` in the raising of the "inexact" floating-point exception.

Ritchie, Dennis M. A Distinguished Member of the Bell Labs Computer Science Research Center. He is the principal designer of the C language and a major contributor to the UNIX operating system. He is the "R" in K&R.

`round`[`f`|`l`][C99] A function that returns the rounded integer value of its argument.

```
#include <math.h>
double round(double x);
float roundf(float x);
long double roundl(long double x);
```

The argument is rounded to the nearest integer value in floating-point format, rounding halfway cases away from zero, regardless of the current rounding direction.

rounding direction[C99] An implementation may support one or more rounding directions by defining the macros `FE_DOWNWARD`, `FE_TONEAREST`,

FE_TOWARDZERO, and FE_UPWARD in fenv.h. They may also support other other rounding directions by providing macros whose names begin with FE_ and an uppercase letter. In any event, each defined rounding-direction macro must expand to an integer constant expression whose nonnegative value is distinct from all other such macros.

rounding mode *See* FLT_ROUNDS

rvalue The value of an expression. The name comes from the fact that an rvalue is often found on the right-hand side of assignments. *See also* lvalue.

S

save calling environment function *See* `setjmp`.

scalar An object having a simple type like `int`, `char`, `float`, or pointer. Nonscalar object types are unions and aggregates (structures and arrays).

SC22 The abbreviated name for a subcommittee within ISO/IEC JTC 1, that deals with standards for various programming languages and environments.

SC22/WG14 Working Group 14 (C Language) within ISO/IEC JTC 1 subcommittee SC22. *See also* WG14.

SC22/WG15 Working Group 15 (POSIX) within ISO/IEC JTC 1 subcommittee SC22. *See also* WG15.

SC22/WG21 Working Group 21 (C++ Language) within ISO/IEC JTC 1 subcommittee SC22. *See also* WG21.

`scalbln[f|l]`[C99] A function that computes $x \times$ `FLT_RADIX`^{n} efficiently.

```
#include <math.h>
double scalbln(double x, long int n);
float scalblnf(float x, long int n);
long double scalblnl(long double x, long int n);
```

A range error may occur. *See also* `scalbn[f|l]`.

`scalbn[f|l]`[C99] A function that computes $x \times$ `FLT_RADIX`^{n} efficiently.

```
#include <math.h>
double scalbn(double x, int n);
float scalbnf(float x, int n);
long double scalbnl(long double x, int n);
```

A range error may occur. *See also* `scalbln[f|l]`.

`scanf` A function that reads formatted input from `stdin` as specified by `format`.

```
#include <stdio.h>
int scanf(const char * restrict format, ...);
```

Characters in `format` other than white space and those specifying a particular conversion specifier are expected to appear in the input as written. %% matches a single %. An arbitrary amount of consecutive white space in the format causes white space on input to be skipped. When `scanf` completes its conversion, any white space left in the input buffer immediately following the last converted input field is left there.

The general format of a `scanf` conversion specifier is

%[*][*width*][*modifier*]*specifier*

where the values for *modifier* and *specifier* are as follows:

scanf Modifiers

Symbol	*Meaning*
h	Pointer to `short int`
hh[C99]	Pointer to `char`
j[C99]	Pointer to [u]`intmax_t`
l	Pointer to `long int` or `double`
ll[C99]	Pointer to `long long int`
L	Pointer to `long double`
t[C99]	Pointer to `ptrdiff_t`
z[C99]	Pointer to `size_t`

scanf Specifiers

Symbol	*Meaning*
a[C99]	Floating-point number
c	Character(s)
d	Signed decimal
e	Floating-point number
f	Floating-point number
g	Floating-point number
i	Signed decimal
n	Stores character count in `int`
o	Octal
p	Pointer to `void`
s	String
u	Decimal
x	Hexadecimal
[...]	String with pattern match
%	Read % character

`scanf` returns the number of input items assigned. This does not include items skipped using the assignment-suppression character (*) or input fields written that corresponded to `n` conversion characters. If an error occurred, `EOF` is returned.

All arguments must be passed to `scanf` by address.

A call to `scanf` is equivalent to a call to `fscanf` using a stream of `stdin`. *See also* future library directions; `wscanf`.

`SCHAR_MAX`[C89] A macro, defined in limits.h, that designates the maximum value for an object of type `signed char`. It must be at least 127 (8 bits). This macro expands to an integer constant expression suitable for use with a `#if` directive.

`SCHAR_MIN`[C89] A macro, defined in limits.h, that designates the minimum value for an object of type `signed char`. It must be at least −127 (8 bits). This macro expands to an integer constant expression suitable for use with a `#if` directive.

`SCNd`*N*[C99] A macro, defined in limits.h, that expands to a character string literal containing a conversion specifier suitable for use with members of the `scanf` and `wscanf` family when converting the type `int`*N*`_t`. For example

```
int32_t x;
int y;
scanf("%" SCNd32 " %d", &x, &y);
```

`SCNdLEAST`*N*[C99] A macro, defined in inttypes.h, that expands to a character string literal containing a conversion specifier suitable for use with members of the `scanf` and `wscanf` family when converting the type `int_least`*N*`_t`.

`SCNdFAST`*N*[C99] A macro, defined in inttypes.h, that expands to a character string literal containing a conversion specifier suitable for use with members of the `scanf` and `wscanf` family when converting the type `int_fast`*N*`_t`.

`SCNdMAX`[C99] A macro, defined in inttypes.h, that expands to a character string literal containing a conversion specifier suitable for use with members of the `scanf` and `wscanf` family when converting the type `intmax_t`.

`SCNdPTR`[C99] A macro, defined in inttypes.h, that expands to a character string literal containing a conversion specifier suitable for use with members of the `scanf` and `wscanf` family when converting the type `intptr_t`.

`SCNi`*N*[C99] A macro, defined in inttypes.h, that expands to a character string literal containing a conversion specifier suitable for use with members of the `scanf` and `wscanf` family when converting the type `int`*N*`_t`. For example

```
int32_t x;
int y;
scanf("%" SCNi32 " %d", &x, &y);
```

`SCNiLEAST`N^{C99} A macro, defined in inttypes.h, that expands to a character string literal containing a conversion specifier suitable for use with members of the `scanf` and `wscanf` family when converting the type `int_least`N`_t`.

`SCNiFAST`N^{C99} A macro, defined in inttypes.h, that expands to a character string literal containing a conversion specifier suitable for use with members of the `scanf` and `wscanf` family when converting the type `int_fast`N`_t`.

`SCNiMAX`^{C99} A macro, defined in inttypes.h, that expands to a character string literal containing a conversion specifier suitable for use with members of the `scanf` and `wscanf` family when converting the type `intmax_t`.

`SCNiPTR`^{C99} A macro, defined in inttypes.h, that expands to a character string literal containing a conversion specifier suitable for use with members of the `scanf` and `wscanf` family when converting the type `intptr_t`.

`SCNo`N^{C99} A macro, defined in inttypes.h, that expands to a character string literal containing a conversion specifier suitable for use with members of the `scanf` and `wscanf` family when converting the type `uint`N`_t`. For example

```
uint32_t x;
int y;
scanf("%" SCNo32 " %d", &x, &y);
```

`SCNoLEAST`N^{C99} A macro, defined in inttypes.h, that expands to a character string literal containing a conversion specifier suitable for use with members of the `scanf` and `wscanf` family when converting the type `uint_least`N`_t`.

`SCNoFAST`N^{C99} A macro, defined in inttypes.h, that expands to a character string literal containing a conversion specifier suitable for use with members of the `scanf` and `wscanf` family when converting the type `uint_fast`N`_t`.

`SCNoMAX`^{C99} A macro, defined in inttypes.h, that expands to a character string literal containing a conversion specifier suitable for use with members of the `scanf` and `wscanf` family when converting the type `uintmax_t`.

`SCNoPTR`^{C99} A macro, defined in inttypes.h, that expands to a character string literal containing a conversion specifier suitable for use with members of the `scanf` and `wscanf` family when converting the type `uintptr_t`.

`SCNu`N^{C99} A macro, defined in inttypes.h, that expands to a character string literal containing a conversion specifier suitable for use with members of the **scanf** and **wscanf** family when converting the type **uint**N**_t**. For example

```
uint32_t x;
int y;
scanf("%" SCNu32 " %d", &x, &y);
```

SCNuLEASTN^{C99} A macro, defined in inttypes.h, that expands to a character string literal containing a conversion specifier suitable for use with members of the **scanf** and **wscanf** family when converting the type **uint_least**N**_t**.

SCNuFASTN^{C99} A macro, defined in inttypes.h, that expands to a character string literal containing a conversion specifier suitable for use with members of the **scanf** and **wscanf** family when converting the type **uint_fast**N**_t**.

SCNuMAX^{C99} A macro, defined in inttypes.h, that expands to a character string literal containing a conversion specifier suitable for use with members of the **scanf** and **wscanf** family when converting the type **uintmax_t**.

SCNuPTR^{C99} A macro, defined in inttypes.h, that expands to a character string literal containing a conversion specifier suitable for use with members of the **scanf** and **wscanf** family when converting the type **uintptr_t**.

SCNxN^{C99} A macro, defined in inttypes.h, that expands to a character string literal containing a conversion specifier suitable for use with members of the **scanf** and **wscanf** family when converting the type **uint**N**_t**. For example

```
uint32_t x;
int y;
scanf("%" SCNx32 " %d", &x, &y);
```

SCNxLEASTN^{C99} A macro, defined in inttypes.h, that expands to a character string literal containing a conversion specifier suitable for use with members of the **scanf** and **wscanf** family when converting the type **uint_least**N**_t**.

SCNxFASTN^{C99} A macro, defined in inttypes.h, that expands to a character string literal containing a conversion specifier suitable for use with members of the **scanf** and **wscanf** family when converting the type **uint_fast**N**_t**.

SCNxMAX^{C99} A macro, defined in inttypes.h, that expands to a character string literal containing a conversion specifier suitable for use with members of the **scanf** and **wscanf** family when converting the type **uintmax_t**.

`SCNxPTR`[C99] A macro, defined in inttypes.h, that expands to a character string literal containing a conversion specifier suitable for use with members of the `scanf` and `wscanf` family when converting the type `uintptr_t`.

scope That region of a program within which an identifier is declared. The kinds of scope are block, file, function, and function prototype. *See also* linkage; storage duration.

scope, block A type of scope in which an identifier is declared inside a block or parameter list of a function definition. This scope ends at the } terminating that block (which, in the case of a parameter identifier, is at the end of the function body). All of the identifiers inside the following function `f` have block scope (although `f` itself has file scope):

```
void f(int j)
{
        int i, g(void);
        static int si;

        if (j > 5) {
                double d;
                int i;
        }
}
```

Note that while `g` has block scope, it has external linkage.

scope, file A type of scope in which an identifier is declared outside all blocks and parameter lists. This scope ends at the end of that translation unit. All of the identifiers in the following example have file scope:

```
int i;
static int si;
extern double ed;
void f(void);

void g()
{
}
```

scope, function The type of scope for user-defined labels. User-defined labels are the only identifiers that have function scope. That is, they are visible from anywhere in the function in which they are defined. As such, label names must be unique within a function.

scope, prototype[C89] The type of scope for an identifier declared inside a function prototype. This scope ends at the end of the function declarator. Although identifiers in prototypes are optional, if they exist, they must be unique within that prototype. For example, in

```
int f(int i, double d);
int g(int i, double d);
```

search functions The string.h functions `memchr`, `strchr`, `strcspn`, `strpbrk`, `strrchr`, `strspn`, `strstr`, and `strtok` and their wide counterparts.

`SEEK_CUR` A macro, defined in stdio.h, that expands to an integer constant expression that can be used as the third argument to `fseek`. It indicates a position relative to the current position. *See also* `SEEK_END`; `SEEK_SET`.

`SEEK_END` A macro, defined in stdio.h, that expands to an integer constant expression that can be used as the third argument to `fseek`. It indicates a position relative to the end of the file. *See also* `SEEK_CUR`; `SEEK_SET`.

`SEEK_SET` A macro, defined in stdio.h, that expands to an integer constant expression that can be used as the third argument to `fseek`. It indicates a position relative to the start of the file. *See also* `SEEK_CUR`; `SEEK_END`.

selection statements *See* `if/else`; `switch`.

semicolon punctuator A punctuator used as a statement or declaration terminator. It is also used to separate the three optional expressions in a `for` statement.

The null statement consists solely of a semicolon.

sequence point[C89] A point in a program at which all side effects of previous evaluations must be complete and no side effects of subsequent evaluations shall have taken place. There is a sequence point at the end of a full expression as well as at the end of a full declarator. The following operators also have sequence points: `&&` and `||`, after the left operand had been evaluated; `?:`, after the first operand has been evaluated; comma operator, after the left operand has been evaluated; and the function call operator, after all arguments and the function designator have been evaluated, but before the function is actually called.

`setbuf` A function that is equivalent to a specific invocation of `setvbuf`. That is, calling `setvbuf` with `mode` equal to `_IOFBF` and `size` equal to `BUFSIZ`, or with `buf` being `NULL` and `mode` being `_IONBF`, is the same as calling `setbuf`.

```
#include <stdio.h>
void setbuf(FILE * restrict stream, char * restrict buf);
```

`setbuf` returns no value. The responsibility is on the programmer to make sure `stream` points to an open file and that `buf` is either `NULL` or a pointer to a sufficiently large buffer.

setjmp A macro, defined in setjmp.h, that saves a program's current context (or calling environment) in a user-defined object of type `jmp_buf` so the program can be restored to that context by a subsequent call to `longjmp`.

```
#include <setjmp.h>
int setjmp(jmp_buf env);
```

Since `setjmp` can be a macro, its definition is restricted in certain ways. For example, it cannot be called via a pointer to function. See your library manual for details. When the programmer explicitly calls `setjmp`, it returns a zero value. When `setjmp` returns via an unconditional jump from `longjmp`, it returns a user-defined nonzero value.

Note that `setjmp` really saves its own context, not that of its caller. Therefore, when `longjmp` is called to restore a saved context, control is transferred back into `setjmp`, which then returns to its original caller.

setjmp.h A header that contains the type `jmp_buf` and declares the functions `setjmp` and `longjmp`, all of which are used to save and restore a program context. Together, these items provide a nonlocal goto facility—the ability to jump out of one function and into the middle of another, provided the destination function is further up the call hierarchy.

setjmp.h contains definitions or declarations for the identifiers in the following table:

Name	*Purpose*
`jmp_buf`	`setjmp` save buffer type
`longjmp`	Restore a saved environment
`setjmp`	Save a runtime environment

setlocale[C89] A function that allows the program to change either a complete locale or a category of the current locale, or to find the "name" of the current locale.

```
#include <locale.h>
char *setlocale(int category, char *locale);
```

`category` must be one of the standard or implementation-defined `LC_*` macros. `locale` is either the standard `"C"` locale or some other implementation-defined locale. At program startup, the locale is set to `"C"` automatically.

If a pointer to a locale string is given to `setlocale` and that locale is available, a locale string corresponding to the given category is returned. This string can be given back to `setlocale` in future calls. If the requested locale is not available or known, `NULL` is returned and the locale is not changed. A `NULL` locale pointer causes the string defining the current locale to be returned.

`setvbuf` A function that permits the type of buffering for a newly opened file to be changed. It also permits users to supply their own buffer for that file.

```
#include <stdio.h>
int setvbuf(FILE * restrict stream, char * restrict buf,
    int mode, size_t size);
```

`setvbuf` must be called before any reading or writing takes place on the newly opened stream. `mode` may be one of the following: `_IOFBF` (fully buffered), `_IOLBF` (line buffered), or `_IONBF` (no buffering). If `buf` is `NULL`, `setvbuf` uses its own internal buffer; otherwise, it uses that pointed to by `buf`, in which case, `size` should be at least as big as the array pointed to by `buf`. If `mode` equals `_IOFBF` and `size` equals `BUFSIZ`, `setbuf` can be used instead. The same is true if `buf` is `NULL` and `mode` is `_IONBF`.

`setvbuf` returns zero on success and nonzero on failure. A failure could result from an invalid value for `mode`.

shift state[C89] The context for a multibyte character set that has a state-dependent encoding. The value of a multibyte character may be encoded in a state-dependent way that involves switching between various shift states. A change in shift state is indicated by one or more characters with special values. When a change in shift state is found, subsequent characters are interpreted according to the current shift state until either the shift state changes again, or the sequence of characters ends. *See also* shift state, initial.

shift state, initial[C89] The default shift state in which the implementation starts out looking at multibyte characters. *See also* shift sequence.

shift sequence[C89] A sequence of one or more bytes that indicate a change in encoding. When a sequence of multibyte characters is being scanned, the detection of a shift sequence causes the characters following to be interpreted differently until the shift state is changed (possibly by restoring to the original state) or the end of the character sequence is reached. All comments, string literals, character constants, and header names are required to begin and end in their initial shift state. In the initial shift state, single-byte characters have their usual meaning; that is, they do not alter the shift state. A redundant shift sequence is one that is followed immediately by another shift sequence or is one that switches to the (already) current mode.

Shift-JIS A scheme commonly used to encode Japanese text in multibyte characters. *See also* EUC; JIS.

`short` A permitted abbreviation for `short int`.

`short int` An integer type. Standard C requires it to be at least 16 bits. A plain `short int` is signed. `short int` expressions traditionally were widened to `int` when used in expressions and as arguments to functions. However, Standard C allows them to be used without widening, provided the same result is obtained. *See also* conversion, function arguments; integer type.

`SHRT_MAX`^{C89} A macro, defined in limits.h, that designates the maximum value for an object of type `short int`. It must be at least 32,767 (16 bits). This macro expands to an integer constant expression suitable for use with a `#if` directive.

`SHRT_MIN`^{C89} A macro, defined in limits.h, that designates the minimum value for an object of type `short int`. It must be at least −32,767 (16 bits). This macro expands to an integer constant expression suitable for use with a `#if` directive.

side effect The act of accessing a volatile object, modifying an object, modifying a file, or calling a function that does any of these things, is known as a side effect. Essentially, a side effect results in a change in the state of the execution environment. Each of the following expressions contains side effects:

```
++i    j--    x = 4    j *= a    f()
```

In the call to function `f`, we assume the function body itself (or some function it calls) has one or more side effects.

Any statement other than `break`, `continue`, and `goto`, that does not directly or indirectly result in a side effect is a vacuous statement. *See also* sequence point.

`SIG*` Signal-type macros that can be used as the first argument to `signal`. This argument indicates the particular kind of signal the user wishes to process with the `signal` function. Standard C defines the following signal type macros: `SIGABRT`, `SIGFPE`, `SIGILL`, `SIGINT`, `SIGSEGV`, and `SIGTERM`. It also reserves names of the form `SIG*` (where * begins with an uppercase letter) for use as signal number macros. *See also* future library directions.

`SIG_*` Function pointer macros, the following three of which are defined by Standard C: `SIG_DFL`, `SIG_IGN`, and `SIG_ERR`. These macros expand to distinct constant expressions that have a type compatible with the second argument to, and the return value of, the function `signal`. Other, implementation-defined value macros are permitted so Standard C reserves names of the form `SIG_*` for that use, where * begins with an uppercase letter. *See also* future library directions.

`SIGABRT` A signal type macro, defined in signal.h, that indicates abnormal termination (such as a call to `abort`). *See also* `assert`.

`SIG_ATOMIC_MAX`[C99] A macro, defined in stdint.h, that is intended to indicate the maximum value which can be stored in an object of type `sig_atomic_t`. If that type is a signed integer, `SIG_ATOMIC_MAX` shall be no less than 127; if the type is an unsigned integer, `SIG_ATOMIC_MAX` shall be no less than 255.

This macro shall expand to a constant expression suitable for use in `#if` preprocessing directives.

`SIG_ATOMIC_MIN`[C99] A macro, defined in stdint.h, that is intended to indicate the minimum value that can be stored in an object of type `sig_atomic_t`. If that type is a signed integer, `SIG_ATOMIC_MIN` shall be no greater than -127; if the type is an unsigned integer, `SIG_ATOMIC_MIN` shall be 0.

This macro shall expand to a constant expression suitable for use in `#if` preprocessing directives.

`sig_atomic_t`[C89] The integer type, which is guaranteed to be accessed as an atomic entity, even in the presence of signals. That is, when a signal occurs, an object of this type cannot be partially updated—it has either been completely updated or not been updated at all. *See also* `SIG_ATOMIC_MAX`; `SIG_ATOMIC_MIN`.

`SIG_DFL` **macro** A macro, defined in signal.h, that expands to a constant expression suitable for use as the second argument to the `signal` function. Its value must not be equal to that of any declarable function, nor to that of `SIG_ERR` or `SIG_IGN`. It is used to tell `signal` to use the implementation-defined default handler for the given interrupt type.

`SIG_ERR` **macro** A macro, defined in signal.h, that expands to a constant expression suitable for use as the second argument to the `signal` function. Its value must not be equal to that of any declarable function, nor to that of `SIG_DFL` or `SIG_IGN`. It is returned by `signal` to indicate an error occurred when an attempt was made to specify handling for a particular interrupt type.

`SIGFPE` A signal type macro, defined in signal.h, that indicates an erroneous arithmetic operation, such as zero-divide or an operation resulting in overflow. (Its name comes from "Floating-Point Exception.")

SIG_IGN macro A macro, defined in signal.h, that expands to a constant expression suitable for use as the second argument to the `signal` function. Its value must not be equal to that of any declarable function, nor to that of `SIG_DFL` or `SIG_ERR`. It is used to tell `signal` to ignore the given interrupt type. In some implementations, while you can request certain signals to be ignored, they still will be trapped. For example, if a nonprivileged program requests to ignore all privileged attempts to kill it and this were to be permitted, a security hole would exist.

`SIGILL` A signal type macro, defined in signal.h, that indicates an invalid function image; possibly an illegal instruction was detected.

`SIGINT` A signal type macro, defined in signal.h, that indicates receipt of an interactive attention signal (such as CTRL/C or CTRL/D).

signal An asynchronous or synchronous event that interrupts a program. Some signals can be trapped or ignored. This is done using the machinery provided in signal.h. Standard C defines six specific signal types (named `SIG*`): abnormal termination; an erroneous arithmetic operation, such as zero-divide or an operation resulting in overflow; invalid function image (possibly an illegal instruction was detected); receipt of an interactive attention signal; an invalid access to storage; and a termination request sent to the program.

`signal` A function that is used to indicate the type of action to be taken when a signal of the specified type is encountered. A signal may be ignored, handled by the system in a default manner, or processed by a user-supplied handler.

```
#include <signal.h>
void (*signal(int sig, void (*func)(int)))(int);
```

`sig` is the signal type to be processed and is typically a macro name of the form `SIG*` (such as `SIGINT`). `func` is the signal-handling method to be used and is typically a macro name of the form `SIG_*` (such as `SIG_IGN`), or the address of a user-written signal handler function.

`signal` returns `SIG_ERR` if it cannot perform the requested operation. Otherwise, it returns the value given to `signal` (as its second argument) in the previous call for that signal number. That is, you can save the current signal-handling context, change it temporarily, and then restore it again using this return value.

The initial state of signal handling at program startup is implementation defined. *See also* `raise`.

signal handler A function that is given control when its associated signal type is detected. A signal-handling function must take one argument (of type `int`) and have `void` return type. A signal handler is registered via the `signal` function. Once a given signal type has been detected, the library behaves as if it calls `signal` with a second argument of `SIG_DFL` for that signal type, before it passes control to the user-written handler. That is, registering a signal handler lasts for only one signal detection. Each time the handler runs, it must reregister itself if you intend to catch further interrupts of that type.

signal.h A header that declares the type `sig_atomic_t` and declares several functions (`signal` and `raise`) and macros (`SIG*` and `SIG_*`) that are useful in handling signals. (Signals are often called exceptions or interrupts.)

signal.h contains definitions or declarations for the identifiers in the following table:

Name	*Purpose*
`raise`	Generate a signal synchronously
`sig_atomic_t`	Atomic operation type
`SIG_DFL`	Use default handler
`SIG_ERR`	`signal` return error value
`SIG_IGN`	Ignore a given signal type
`SIGABRT`	Abnormal termination
`SIGFPE`	Erroneous arithmetic operation
`SIGILL`	Invalid function image
`SIGINT`	Interactive attention signal
`signal`	Establish a signal handler
`SIGSEGV`	Invalid access to storage
`SIGTERM`	Termination request

See also future library directions.

`signed`[C89] A keyword used with integer data types to indicate they are signed. It may be applied to `char`, `short int`, `int`, `long int`, and `long long int`. It allows signed arithmetic to be performed. When used on its own, it implies signed int. The use of `signed` with `short`, `int`, `long`, and `long long` is redundant because these types are signed anyway. C89 invented this modifier to permit explicitly signed versions of `char` and `int` bit-fields. Prior to that, you had unsigned and plain `char`s only, and it was implementation defined as to the signedness of a plain `char` and a plain `int` bit-field. *See also* integer type.

`signed char` A `char` type that is explicitly signed. A plain `char` written without the modifier `signed` or `unsigned` might be signed or unsigned—that is implementation defined. *See also* `signed`.

`signed char` **type conversion** *See* conversion, integer type; unsigned preserving rule; value preserving rule.

signed integer types The types `signed char`, `signed short`, `short`, `int`, `signed int`, `long`, `signed long`, `long long`, and `signed long long`. *See also* bit-field, plain `int`; `char`, plain.

significand part, floating constant That part of a floating constant preceding the optional exponent and suffix parts.

`SIGSEGV` A signal type macro, defined in signal.h, that indicates an invalid access to storage (segment violation).

`SIGTERM` A signal type macro, defined in signal.h, that indicates that a termination request was sent to the program.

simple assignment operator *See* assignment operator, simple.

`sin`[`f`|`l`] A function that computes the sine of its argument `x` (measured in radians).

```
#include <math.h>
double sin(double x);
float sinf(float x);
long double sinl(long double x);
```

If the magnitude of the argument is large, `sin` may produce a result with little or no significance.

The `float` and `long double` versions were an invention of C89, where they were optional; however, in C99, they are required.

single quote escape sequence A single quote character `'` can be included in a character constant only in its escape sequence form `\'`. It can occur in a string literal in either form, however. That is, either as `"'"` or `"\'"`.

`sinh`[`f`|`l`] A function that computes the hyperbolic sine of its argument `x`.

```
#include <math.h>
double sinh(double x);
float sinhf(float x);
long double sinhl(long double x);
```

If the magnitude of the argument is too large, a range error occurs.

The `float` and `long double` versions were an invention of C89, where they were optional; however, in C99, they are required.

`SIZE_MAX`[C99] A macro, defined in stdint.h, that indicates the maximum value of the type `size_t`. It expands to an integer constant expression suitable for use with a `#if` directive.

`sizeof` A keyword used to represent an operator. It returns the size in bytes of its operand. It can be used with expressions or types, other than function and `void` type. It cannot be used with bit-fields. It does not evaluate its operand except to determine its type. The type of the result is `size_t`. `sizeof` can be used in either of the following ways:

```
sizeof( type )
sizeof expression
```

In the second case, the expression is often inside (redundant) grouping parentheses. Prior to C99, a `sizeof` expression was evaluated translation-time. However, with the addition of variable-length arrays in C99, `sizeof(`*vla_designator*`)` is actually computed at run time.

`size_t`[C89] The type of the result obtained from the `sizeof` operator. This type is an unsigned integer type. Many standard library functions (`strlen` and `calloc`, for example) expect arguments and/or return values of this type. Prior to C99, assuming an object's size could be represented in an `unsigned long`, the value of an expression of type `sizeof` could be displayed as follows:

```
printf("%lu", (unsigned long)sizeof(int));
```

however, with the addition of the `long long int` type in C99, as well as the possibility of implementations' supporting even larger extended integer types, C99 added the conversion specifier `%z` to the `printf` function family to allow values of type `size_t` to be printed in a portable fashion. `size_t` is defined in each of the following headers: stddef.h, stdio.h, stdlib.h, string.h, time.h, and wchar.h. *See also* `SIZE_MAX`.

`snprintf`[C99] A function that behaves like `fprintf`, except that it writes its output to an array instead of a stream.

```
#include <stdio.h>
int snprintf(char * restrict s, size_t n,
    const char * restrict format, ...);
```

If `n` is zero, no output is produced and `s` can be null. Otherwise, the first $n - 1$ characters are written to the array pointed to by `s`, and a null character is appended. The behavior is undefined if the source and destination arrays overlap.

sort function *See* `qsort`.

source file inclusion *See* `#include`.

Spirit of C A guiding principal used by X3J11 in determining just what changes and additions it should consider in producing C89. According to the Standard C Rationale document:

"There are many facets of the spirit of C, but the essence is a community sentiment of the underlying principles upon which the C language is based. Some of the facets of the spirit of C can be summarized in phrases like:

- Trust the programmer.
- Don't prevent the programmer from doing what needs to be done.
- Keep the language small and simple.
- Provide only one way to do an operation.

"One of the goals of the Committee was to avoid interfering with the ability of translators to generate compact, efficient code. In several cases, the Committee has introduced features to improve the possible efficiency of the generated code; for instance, floating point operations may be performed in single precision if both operands are `float` rather than `double`."

`sprintf` A function that writes formatted output to the string pointed to by `s` in a format specified by `format`.

```
#include <stdio.h>
int sprintf(char * restrict s,
    const char * restrict format, ...);
```

The value returned is the number of characters written to the string. It does not include the null character that is automatically appended. On error, a negative value is returned just as for `scanf` and `fprintf`. For details of `format` *see* `printf`. *See also* `wsprintf`.

`sqrt[f|l]` A function that computes the nonnegative square root of its argument `x`.

```
#include <math.h>
double sqrt(double x);
float sqrtf(float x);
long double sqrtl(long double x);
```

If the argument is negative, a domain error occurs. Note, however, that some implementations (for example, those based on the IEEE-754 standard) support signed zeros including a negative floating zero, in which case `sqrt(-0)` may be required to return `-0` with no domain error being produced. Standard C requires a domain error to be generated, but permits an implementation-defined value to be returned (thus permitting a result of `-0`).

The `float` and `long double` versions were an invention of C89, where they were optional; however, in C99, they are required.

`srand` A function that uses its argument `seed` as a seed for a new sequence of pseudo random numbers to be returned by subsequent calls to `rand`.

```
#include <stdlib.h>
void srand(unsigned int seed);
```

If `srand` has never been called, `rand` behaves as if `srand` had been called with a seed of 1. Identical seeds generate identical pseudo random number sequences.

`sscanf` A function that reads formatted input from the string specified by `s` using a format specified by `format`.

```
#include <stdio.h>
int sscanf(const char * restrict s,
    const char * restrict format, ...);
```

`sscanf` returns the number of input items assigned. If an error occurred, `EOF` is returned.

All arguments must be passed to `sscanf` by address. For a discussion of `format` *see* `scanf`. *See also* `wsscanf`.

stack An area of memory in which automatic objects and function argument lists often are stored depending on the machine's architecture. Depending on the amount of space required by these (and the existence of recursion), on some systems, you may need to specify a stack size when compiling or linking. It can be very difficult to estimate the amount of stack needed to run a program since that depends on how much is used for automatic variables, function call overhead, the depth of any recursive calls, and that used by library functions.

Standard C A generic term for the current formal definition of the C language, preprocessor, and runtime library. Although the original ANSI C standard preceded the first ISO C standard, once an ISO standard is adopted, the U.S. typically replaces its current ANSI standard with that from ISO. Because these two standards are expected to continue to be technically equivalent, the term "Standard C" is preferable to avoid the implication that these standards may differ. *See also* C89; C90; C95; C99; C9X.

standard header *See* header, standard.

standard streams *See* `stderr`; `stdin`; `stdout`.

state-dependent encoding[C89] *See* multibyte character; shift state.

statement A C statement consists of either one of the constructs defined by the language (such as `if/else`, `for`, and `while`), an expression statement, a block, or a null statement.

statement, compound *See* block.

`static` A storage class keyword used in the declaration of an object to designate static storage duration. A static object may have either no linkage or internal linkage. This keyword also can be used with functions. A static function is callable only from functions defined in the same source code file or in any headers included in that file.

C99 added the ability to use the keyword `static` inside any dimension of an array parameter (possibly along with `const` and/or `restrict`); for example,

```
void f(int table[static 5]);
```

This declaration specifies that the argument corresponding to `table` in any call to function `f` must be a nonnull pointer to the first of at least five `int`.

static storage duration *See* storage duration, static.

`static_cast` A C++ keyword that is not part of Standard C. If you think you might wish to move C code to a C++ environment in the future, you should refrain from using `static_cast` as an identifier in new C code you write.

stdarg.h[C89] A header that provides a way to access variable argument lists portably, such as those passed to the `printf` and `scanf` library families. It defines the type `va_list` and the macros `va_start`, `va_arg`, and `va_end`. The header stdarg.h was modeled closely on the UNIX varargs.h capability.

stdarg.h contains definitions or declarations for the identifiers in the following table:

Name	*Purpose*
`va_arg`	Get argument from list
`va_copy`[C99]	Copies a `va_list`
`va_end`	Terminate argument list processing
`va_list`	Argument list manipulation type
`va_start`	Prepare for argument list processing

stdbool.h[C99] A header that contains the following macro definitions pertaining to boolean type support:

Name	*Purpose*
`bool`	A synonym for the type `_Bool`
`__bool_true_false_are_defined`	Allow a test for boolean support
`false`	A value representing false
`true`	A value representing true

`STDC`[C99] A preprocessing token that immediately follows **`#pragma`** in a pragma directive to indicate the use of a standard pragma. *See also* **`#pragma`** `STDC`.

`__STDC_` **prefix**[C99] *See* future language directions.

`__STDC__`[C89] A predefined macro that is set to `1` for standard-conforming implementations.

`__STDC_CONSTANT_MACROS`[C99] The header stdint.h defines a family of function-like macros that describe minimum-width integer and greatest-width integer constants. These macros should only be defined by a C++ implementation if the macro `__STDC_CONSTANT_MACROS` is defined before that header is included.

`__STDC_FORMAT_MACROS`[C99] The header inttypes.h defines a family of object-like macros that expand to format specifiers. These macros should only be defined by a C++ implementation if the macro `__STDC_FORMAT_MACROS` is defined before that header is included.

`__STDC_HOSTED__`[C99] A predefined macro that expands to the integer constant 1 if the implementation is running in a hosted environment; otherwise it expands to the integer constant 0.

`__STDC_IEC_559__`[C99] A macro that is conditionally predefined to the integer constant 1 if the implementation conforms to the floating-point standard IEC 60559.

`__STDC_IEC_559_COMPLEX__`[C99] A macro that is conditionally predefined to the integer constant 1 if the implementation conforms to the floating-point standard IEC 60559-compatible complex arithmetic.

`__STDC_ISO_10646__`[C99] A macro that is conditionally predefined to an integer constant of the form *yyyymm*`L` if the implementation uses the ISO/IEC 10646 character set to represent values of type `wchar_t`. The date *yyyymm* indicates the version of that standard.

`__STDC_LIMIT_MACROS`^{C99} The header stdint.h defines a family of object-like macros that describe specified-width integer constants. These macros should only be defined by a C++ implementation if the macro `__STDC_LIMIT_MACROS` is defined before that header is included.

`__STDC_VERSION__`^{C95} Although not defined in C89, in C95, this macro expands to the integer constant 199409L while in C99, it expands to 199901L. It is the committee's intent to update this value with each new revision of the standard.

stddef.h^{C89} A header that contains several miscellaneous macro definitions and types. The macros are `NULL` and `offsetof`, and the types are `size_t`, `ptrdiff_t`, and `wchar_t`.

stddef.h contains definitions or declarations for the identifiers in the following table:

Name	*Purpose*
`NULL`	Null pointer constant
`offsetof`	Structure offset macro
`ptrdiff_t`	Pointer difference type
`size_t`	Size/count type
`wchar_t`	Wide character type

`stderr` A macro, defined in stdio.h, that expands to an expression of type `FILE *` that points to a file object corresponding to the standard error device. It is not necessarily a translation-time constant.

`stdin` A macro, defined in stdio.h, that expands to an expression of type `FILE *` that points to a file object corresponding to the standard input device. It is not necessarily a translation-time constant.

stdint.h^{C99} A header that declares sets of integer types having specified widths, and defines corresponding sets of macros. It also defines macros that specify limits of integer types corresponding to types defined in other standard headers. The identifiers defined in this header are as follows:

Name	*Purpose*
INT_FASTN_MAX	Maximum value of type int_fastN_t
INT_FASTN_MIN	Minimum value of type int_fastN_t
int_fastN_t	Fastest minimum-width integer type
INT_LEASTN_MAX	Maximum value of type int_leastN_t
INT_LEASTN_MIN	Minimum value of type int_leastN_t
int_leastN_t	Minimum-width integer type
INTMAX_C	Create a constant of type intmax_t
INTMAX_MAX	Maximum value of type intmax_t
INTMAX_MIN	Minimum value of type intmax_t
intmax_t	Largest signed integer type
INTN_C	Create a constant of type int_leastN_t
INTN_MAX	Maximum value of type intN_t
INTN_MIN	Minimum value of type intN_t
intN_t	Exact-width integer type
INTPTR_MAX	Maximum value of type intptr_t
INTPTR_MIN	Minimum value of type intptr_t
intptr_t	void pointer container
PTRDIFF_MAX	Maximum value of type ptrdiff_t
PTRDIFF_MIN	Minimum value of type ptrdiff_t
SIG_ATOMIC_MAX	Maximum value of type sig_atomic_t
SIG_ATOMIC_MIN	Minimum value of type sig_atomic_t
SIZE_MAX	Maximum value of type size_t
UINT_FASTN_MAX	Maximum value of type uint_fastN_t
uint_fastN_t	Fastest minimum-width integer type
UINT_LEASTN_MAX	Maximum value of type uint_leastN_t
uint_leastN_t	Minimum-width integer type
UINTMAX_C	Create a constant of type uintmax_t
UINTMAX_MAX	Maximum value of type uintmax_t
uintmax_t	Largest unsigned integer type
UINTN_C	Create a constant of type iunt_leastN_t
UINTN_MAX	Maximum value of type uintN_t
uintN_t	Exact-width integer type
UINTPTR_MAX	Maximum value of type uintptr_t
uintptr_t	void pointer container
WCHAR_MAX	Maximum value of type wchar_t
WCHAR_MIN	Minimum value of type wchar_t
WINT_MAX	Maximum value of type wint_t
WINT_MIN	Minimum value of type wint_t

In the names above, *N* represents an unsigned decimal integer with no leading zeros.

See future library directions.

stdio.h

stdio.h A header that defines several types and macros and declares numerous functions useful for performing file and terminal I/O. stdio.h contains definitions or declarations for the identifiers in the following table:

Name	*Purpose*
`BUFSIZ`	`setbuf` buffer size
`clearerr`	Clear error and end-of-file flags
`EOF`	End-of-file indicator
`fclose`	Close file
`feof`	Check for end-of-file
`ferror`	Check for file error
`fflush`	Force write to file
`fgetc`	Read character from file
`fgetpos`[C89]	Get file position
`fgets`	Read string from file
`FILE`	File context block type
`FILENAME_MAX`	Maximum length of a filename
`FOPEN_MAX`	Maximum number of open files
`fopen`	Open file
`fpos_t`	File position type
`fprintf`	Formatted write to file
`fputc`	Write character to file
`fputs`	Write string to file
`fread`	Binary read from file
`freopen`	Recycle `FILE` pointer
`fscanf`	Formatted read from file
`fseek`	Randomly position in file
`fsetpos`[C89]	Randomly position in file
`ftell`	Get file position
`fwrite`	Binary write to file
`getc`	Read character from `stdin`
`getchar`	Read character from `stdin`
`gets`	Read string from `stdin`
`_IOFBF`	Type of `setvbuf` buffering
`_IOLBF`	Type of `setvbuf` buffering
`_IONBF`	Type of `setvbuf` buffering
`L_tmpnam`	Maximum length of temporary file name
`NULL`	Null pointer constant
`perror`	Produce error message
`printf`	Formatted write to `stdout`
`putc`	Write character to `stdout`
`putchar`	Write character to `stdout`
`puts`	Write string to `stdout`
`remove`	Remove or delete file

Name	*Purpose*
`rename`	Rename file
`rewind`	Position to start of file
`scanf`	Formatted read from `stdin`
`SEEK_CUR`	`fseek` position argument
`SEEK_END`	`fseek` position argument
`SEEK_SET`	`fseek` position argument
`setbuf`	Set file buffer characteristics
`setvbuf`	Set file buffer characteristics
`size_t`	Size/count type
`snprintf`C99	Formatted write to an array
`sprintf`	Formatted write to string
`sscanf`	Formatted read from string
`stderr`	Pointer to standard error FILE
`stdin`	Pointer to standard input FILE
`stdout`	Pointer to standard output FILE
`TMP_MAX`	Minimum number of unique temporary files
`tmpfile`	Open scratch file
`tmpnam`	Create unique file name
`ungetc`	Pushback character to `stdin`
`vfprintf`	Formatted write to a file
`vfscanf`C99	Formatted read from a file
`vprintf`	Formatted write to `stdout`
`vscanf`C99	Formatted read from `stdin`
`vsnprintf`C99	Formatted read from an array
`vsprintf`	Formatted Write to a string
`vsscanf`C99	Formatted read from a string

See also future library directions.

stdlib.hC89 A header that contains definitions or declarations for the identifiers in the following table:

Name	*Purpose*
`abort`	Force abnormal termination
`abs`	Compute absolute value
`atexit`	Register exit processing function
`atof`	Convert string to floating
`atoi`	Convert string to integer
`atol`	Convert string to integer
`atoll`C99	Convert string to integer
`bsearch`	Do binary search
`calloc`	Allocate and initialize memory
`div`	Perform division
`div_t`	Type returned from `div`

Name	*Purpose*
exit	Force normal termination
_Exit C99	Force normal termination
EXIT_FAILURE	Failure value for exit
EXIT_SUCCESS	Success value for exit
free	Release allocated memory
getenv	Get environment variable
labs	Compute absolute value
ldiv	Perform division
ldiv_t	Type returned from ldiv
llabs C99	Compute absolute value
lldiv C99	Perform division
lldiv_t C99	Type returned from lldiv
malloc	Allocate memory
MB_CUR_MAX	Maximum size of a multibyte character
mblen	Length of multibyte character
mbstowcs	Convert multibyte string
mbtowc	Convert multibyte character
NULL	Null pointer constant
qsort	Quicksort
rand	Generate random number
RAND_MAX	Maximum value returned by rand
realloc	Expand/contract allocated memory
size_t	Size/count type
srand	Set random number seed
strtod	Convert string to floating
strtof C99	Convert string to floating
strtol	Convert string to integer
strtold C99	Convert string to floating
strtoll C99	Convert string to integer
strtoull C99	Convert string to integer
strtoul	Convert string to integer
system	Call out to system
wchar_t	Wide character type
wcstombs	Convert wide character string
wctomb	Convert wide character

See also future library directions.

`stdout` A macro, defined in stdio.h, that expands to an expression of type `FILE *` which points to a file object corresponding to the standard output device. It is not necessarily a translation-time constant.

storage class The characteristic of an object or function that indicates its scope and linkage. For objects, storage class also indicates their lifetime. Storage class is specified in a declaration by one of the keywords auto, static, extern, or register. Inside a function definition, an object declaration containing no class keyword has storage class auto. The particular storage class keyword used and the location of the declaration in a source file (relative to being inside or outside a function definition) dictate the identifier's storage duration and linkage. Technically, typedef is also a storage class keyword; however, it implies neither storage duration nor linkage. The storage class of a variable or function is not part of its type. A declaration cannot contain more than one storage class keyword. And because typedef is, technically, a storage class keyword, you cannot include a storage class keyword in a typedef. That is,

```
typedef static int si;
```

and

```
typedef auto int ai;
```

are both invalid.

storage-class keyword, position of The placement of a storage-class specifier other than at the beginning of the declaration specifiers in a declaration is obsolescent. For example, the declarations

```
long int static i;
struct {
        int i;
        double d;
} typedef stru;
```

are both valid; however, the keywords static and typedef should be placed at the beginning of their respective declarations.

storage duration The lifetime of an object. Storage duration refers to the time during which that object is guaranteed to actually exist. (An implementation may make it live longer.) There are three kinds of storage duration: allocated, automatic, and static. *See also* linkage; scope.

storage duration, allocated The storage duration of an object created by a call to calloc, malloc, or realloc. Such objects exist until their space is explicitly deallocated.

storage duration, automatic The storage duration of an object declared with the storage class keyword auto or register, or declared inside a function definition and having no storage class keyword. Conceptually, such objects are created each time their parent block is entered at run-time and are destroyed when that block is exited. Automatic variables typically are maintained on a stack, and their initial value, by default, is undefined.

storage duration, static The storage duration of an object declared inside a function definition with the storage class keyword `static`, or outside a function definition, either with or without a storage class keyword. Such objects are created and initialized prior to `main` beginning execution. They retain their values across function calls. Their initial value (if none is provided) is zero, cast to their type. A `static` function also has static storage duration. This means it only can be called by name from within the source file in which it is defined.

storage unit The implementation-defined object into which bit-fields are packed. The order in which bit-fields are packed and whether or not they may span storage unit boundaries, is also implementation defined.

`str` prefix *See* future library directions.

`strcat` A function that copies the string pointed to by `s2` to the end of the string pointed to by `s1`. In the process, the trailing null of `s1` is overwritten by the first character of the string pointed to by `s2`. The destination string is nullterminated.

```
#include <string.h>
char *strcat(char * restrict s1, const char * restrict s2);
```

The value of `s1` is returned. If the strings located at `s1` and `s2` overlap, the behavior of `strcat` is undefined. *See also* `wcscat`.

`strchr` A function that searches the string `s` for a character `c`.

```
#include <string.h>
char *strchr(const char *s, int c);
```

If `c` is found, `strchr` returns a pointer to that location within `s`; otherwise it returns `NULL`. `c` is converted to `char` before the search begins. The null terminating `s` is included in the search. Therefore, `strchr` can be used to locate the trailing null as well. *See also* `wcschr`.

`strcmp` A function that compares a string at the location pointed to by `s2` to a string at the location pointed to by `s1`.

```
#include <string.h>
int strcmp(const char *s1, const char *s2);
```

An integer less than, equal to, or greater than zero is returned to indicate whether s1 is less than, equal to, or greater than s2, respectively. *See also* wcscmp.

strcoll[C89] A function that compares a string at the location pointed to by s2 to a string at the location pointed to by s1.

```
#include <string.h>
int strcoll(const char *s1, const char *s2);
```

An integer less than, equal to, or greater than zero is returned to indicate whether s1 is less than, equal to, or greater than s2, respectively. The comparison is locale specific and, therefore, permits any arbitrary collation sequence to be used, as long as that sequence is provided by the implementation as a locale. The sequence can include non-English letters and characters. In the "C" locale, strcoll should give the same result as strcmp. *See also* wcscoll.

strcpy A function that copies the string pointed to by s2 to the location pointed to by s1. The destination string is null terminated.

```
#include <string.h>
char *strcpy(char * restrict s1, const char * restrict s2);
```

The value of s1 is returned. If the strings located at s1 and s2 overlap, the behavior of strcpy is undefined. To copy overlapping objects, use memmove instead. *See also* wcscpy.

strcspn A function that finds the longest string starting at the location pointed to by s1 such that it does not contain any of the characters in the string pointed to by s2. Alternatively, it could be viewed that strcspn locates the first character in the string pointed to by s1 that is present in the string pointed to by s2.

```
#include <string.h>
size_t strcspn(const char *s1, const char *s2);
```

The return value indicates the length of the nonmatching string found at s1 (which is the same as the subscript of the first matching character in s1). *See also* wcscspn.

stream The logical channel on which I/O is performed. The three standard streams stdin, stdout and stderr refer to standard input, standard output and standard error, respectively. They are opened for you at the start of each program and are closed when the program terminates. A file is associated with a stream by `fopen`. *See also* `FILE`; `FOPEN_MAX`; stream, binary; stream, text.

stream, binary An ordered sequence of characters that can transparently record internal data. Once written, such data can be retrieved exactly as written, by the same implementation. (The differences of byte ordering within words and words within longwords, etc., might prohibit it from being read correctly by other implementations.) There may be some implementation-defined number of null characters appended to the end of a binary stream. When a stream is opened in binary mode (using the `b` mode with `fopen`), no logical translation is performed. For example, if a carriage-return/line-feed pair normally is converted to a new-line on input, in binary mode it would be read as those two separate characters. *See also* stream, text.

stream, fully buffered A stream in which it is intended that characters be read or written when a block or buffer is empty, or full, respectively. *See also* `_IOFBF`; `setvbuf`; stream, line buffered; stream, unbuffered.

stream, line buffered A stream in which it is intended that characters be read or written when a new-line is encountered. *See also* `_IOLBF`; `setvbuf`; stream, fully buffered; stream, unbuffered.

stream, standard error *See* `stderr`.

stream, standard input *See* `stdin`.

stream, standard output *See* `stdout`.

stream, text A stream in which the characters are organized into lines, each of which is terminated by a new-line. When data is written out to and read in from a text stream, there may be some kind of logical-to-physical or physical-to-logical translation. For example, on input, a carriage-return/line-feed pair may be translated to a new-line. An implementation does not have to distinguish between text and binary streams. *See also* the mode argument to `fopen`; stream, binary.

stream, unbuffered A stream in which characters should be read or written as soon as practical; that is, they should not be buffered. *See also* `_IONBF`; `setvbuf`; stream, fully buffered; stream, line buffered.

`strerror` A function that returns the address of a string containing a message corresponding to the message code used as the argument.

```
#include <string.h>
char *strerror(int errnum);
```

`strerror` is similar in capability to `perror` in that it is designed for use with `errno`. However, `perror` writes the message directly to `stderr` along with the user-supplied text, while `strerror` returns a pointer to the message allowing the programmer to process it as desired.

`strftime`[C89] A function that constructs a date and time string by putting characters into the array pointed to by `s` according to the controlling format specified by `format`. No more than `maxsize` characters are written to the array. `timeptr` points to a structure whose contents are used to determine the appropriate characters for the array.

```
#include <time.h>
size_t strftime(char * restrict s, size_t maxsize,
    const char * restrict format,
    const struct tm * restrict timeptr);
```

This function provides a locale-specific way of generating date and time strings. For example,

```
#include <stdio.h>
#include <time.h>

int main()
{
        char string[100];
        time_t cur_time;
        struct tm *ptime;

        cur_time = time(NULL);
        if ((ptime = gmtime(&cur_time)) != NULL) {
                strftime(string, sizeof(string)-1,
                        "%Y %B %A %c",ptime);
                printf("%s\n", string);
        }
        else {
                printf("UTC time not available\n");
        }

        return 0;
}
```

```
1991 April Monday Mon Apr 08 15:10:37 1991
```

Refer to your library documentation for specific details of the controlling format conversion specifiers. *See also* `wcsftime`.

strictly conforming program[C89] *See* program, strictly conforming.

string An array of `char` terminated by a null character. *See also* string literal; string literal, wide; wide string.

string conversion functions The string.h functions `atof`, `atoi`, `atol`, `strtod`, `strtof`, `strtol`, `strtold`, and `strtoul`.

string functions *See* string.h; wchar.h.

string literal A source token having the form `"..."` where `...` can be zero or more characters from the source character set except the double-quote, backslash, or new-line characters. A string literal is stored by the compiler as a `static` array of `char` with a trailing null character appended. It is implementation defined as to whether strings are stored in a writable memory location and whether identical strings are distinct.

string literal, wide[C89] A source token having the form `L"..."` where `...` can be zero or more characters from the source character set except the double-quote, backslash, or new-line characters. A wide string literal is stored by the compiler as a `static` array of `wchar_t` with a trailing null wide character appended. It is implementation defined as to whether strings are stored in a writable memory location and whether identical strings are distinct.

string.h A header that contains definitions or declarations for the identifiers in the following table:

Name	*Purpose*
`memchr`	Search memory for character
`memcmp`	Compare memory blocks
`memcpy`	Copy memory blocks
`memmove`	Safe copy of memory blocks
`memset`	Initialize memory block
`NULL`	Null pointer constant
`size_t`	Size/count type
`strcat`	Concatenate strings
`strchr`	Search string for character
`strcmp`	Compare strings
`strcoll`	Collate strings
`strcpy`	Copy a string
`strcspn`	Compute initial length match
`strerror`	Produce error message
`strlen`	Compute string length
`strncat`	Concatenate strings
`strncmp`	Compare leading part of strings
`strncpy`	Copy leading part of string

Name	*Purpose*
strpbrk	Locate character in string
strrchr	Reverse search for character
strspn	Compute initial length match
strstr	Search string for string
strtok	Break string into tokens
strxfrm	Transform string

See also future library directions; wchar.h.

stringize operator[C89] A unary preprocessor operator, #, that is defined only for function-like macros. If a parameter in the macro's replacement list is preceded by this operator, both are replaced by a single character string literal token that contains the text of the corresponding argument. If the argument contains " characters, they are escaped with a \ in the string created. Leading and trailing white-space characters in the argument are ignored, and each occurrence of contiguous white space is replaced by a single space character. For example, given the following macro definition:

```
#define M(a) f(#a)
```

the macro call:

```
M( 5  "10 \n"  )
```

expands to:

```
f("5 \"10 \\n\"")
```

The precedence and associativity of the # and ## preprocessor operators are unspecified.

`strlen` A function that returns the number of characters in the string (excluding the trailing null) pointed to by `s`.

```
#include <string.h>
size_t strlen(const char *s);
```

`strncat` A function that copies, at most, the first `n` characters from the string pointed to by `s2` to the end of the string pointed to by `s1`. The destination string is null terminated.

```
#include <string.h>
char *strncat(char * restrict s1,
    const char * restrict s2, size_t n);
```

The value of `s1` is returned. If a null is not found in the first `n` characters of `s2`, `n` characters will be copied followed by a null. If a null is found, it is copied to `s1` and the copy is terminated. If the strings located at `s1` and `s2` overlap, the behavior of `strncat` is undefined. *See also* `wcsncat`.

`strncmp` A function that compares no more than `n` characters from a string at the location pointed to by `s2` to a string at the location pointed to by `s1`. If a null is seen in the first `n` characters, the comparison is terminated.

```
#include <string.h>
int strncmp(const char *s1, const char *s2, size_t n);
```

An integer less than, equal to, or greater than zero is returned to indicate whether `s1` is less than, equal to, or greater than `s2`, respectively. *See also* `wcsncmp`.

`strncpy` A function that copies, at most, the first `n` characters from the string pointed to by `s2` to the location pointed to by `s1`. The destination string is null terminated.

```
#include <string.h>
char *strncpy(char * restrict s1,
    const char * restrict s2, size_t n);
```

The value of `s1` is returned. If a null is not found in the first `n` characters of `s2`, the string pointed to by `s1` will not be null terminated. If a null is found, it is copied to `s1`. If there are less than `n` characters in the string pointed to by `s1`, extra null characters are appended to the end of the string pointed to by `s1` such that `n` characters are actually copied there. If the strings located at `s1` and `s2` overlap, the behavior of `strncpy` is undefined. To copy overlapping objects, use `memmove` instead. *See also* `wcsncpy`.

`strpbrk` A function that searches the string pointed to by `s1` for the first of any one of the characters in the string pointed to by `s2`.

```
#include <string.h>
char *strpbrk(const char *s1, const char *s2);
```

The return value is a pointer to the character found in `s1` or `NULL` if no match was found. *See also* `wcspbrk`.

`strrchr` A function that searches the string `s` for the last occurrence of the character `c`.

```
#include <string.h>
char *strrchr(const char *s, int c);
```

If `c` is found, `strrchr` returns a pointer to that location within `s`; otherwise it returns `NULL`. `c` is converted to `char` before the search begins. The null-terminating `s` is included in the search. Therefore, `strrchr` can be used to locate the trailing null as well. *See also* `wcsrchr`.

`strspn` A function that finds the longest string starting at the location pointed to by `s1` such that it contains only those characters in the string at the location pointed to by `s2`. Alternatively, it could be viewed that `strspn` locates the first character in the string pointed to by `s1` that is not present in the string pointed to by `s2`.

```
#include <string.h>
size_t strspn(const char *s1, const char *s2);
```

The return value indicates the length of the matching string found at `s1` (which is the same as the subscript of the first nonmatching character in `s1`). *See also* `wcsspn`.

`strstr` A function that searches the string pointed to by `s1` for the substring pointed to by `s2`.

```
#include <string.h>
char *strstr(const char *s1, const char *s2);
```

The return value represents the location of the substring `s2` within the string `s1`. If the substring is not found, `NULL` is returned. By definition, the null string is always found at the beginning of any string, including a null string. *See also* `wcsstr`.

`strtod` A function that converts the leading part of the string pointed to by `nptr` to a `double` value.

```
#include <stdlib.h>
double strtod(const char * restrict nptr,
    char ** restrict endptr);
```

Leading white space is ignored. The floating-point constant is terminated by any character not permissible in such a constant (including the null that terminates the input string). A leading sign character is permitted as is a (possibly signed) exponent using either 'e' or 'E'. A floating-point suffix of 'f' (or 'F') or 'l' (or 'L') is not recognized as such. If no exponent or decimal point appears, a decimal point is assumed to be at the end of the number. The format of the floating-point number is locale specific. If the input contains all white space, is empty, or contains no convertible characters, no conversion occurs, nptr is stored in *endptr (provided endptr is not NULL), and a zero value is returned. If the converted value causes overflow, plus or minus HUGE_VAL is returned (according to the sign of the value) and errno is set to ERANGE. On underflow, zero is returned, and errno is set to ERANGE. strtod is a superset of atof and is recommended over it.

C99 extended this function to allow it to recognize the following input: hexadecimal floating-point values, infinity, and NaN.

strtof[C99] A function that converts the leading part of the string pointed to by nptr to a float value.

```
#include <stdlib.h>
float strtof(const char * restrict nptr,
    char ** restrict endptr);
```

Leading white space is ignored. The floating-point constant is terminated by any character not permissible in such a constant (including the null that terminates the input string). A leading sign character is permitted as is a (possibly signed) exponent using either 'e' or 'E'. A floating-point suffix of 'f' (or 'F') or 'l' (or 'L') is not recognized as such. If no exponent or decimal point appears, a decimal point is assumed to be at the end of the number. The format of the floating-point number is locale specific. If the input contains all white space, is empty, or contains no convertible characters, no conversion occurs, nptr is stored in *endptr (provided endptr is not NULL), and a zero value is returned. If the converted value causes overflow, plus or minus HUGE_VALF is returned (according to the sign of the value) and errno is set to ERANGE. On underflow, zero is returned, and errno is set to ERANGE.

The following input is recognized as such: hexadecimal floating-point values, infinity, and NaN.

strtoimax[C99] A function that is equivalent to the strtol and strtoll functions, except that the initial portion of the string is converted to type intmax_t.

```
#include <inttypes.h>
intmax_t strtoimax(const char * restrict nptr,
    char ** restrict endptr, int base);
```

If no conversion could be performed, zero is returned. If the correct value is outside the range of representable values, INTMAX_MAX or INTMAX_MIN is returned (depending on the sign of the value), and errno is set to ERANGE.

strtok A function in which successive calls can be used to break a string, pointed to by s1, into a series of null-terminated tokens using the token terminator characters specified by the string pointed to by s2.

```
#include <string.h>
char *strtok(char * restrict s1, const char * restrict s2);
```

The value returned is either a pointer to the token found or NULL if no token was found. *See also* wcstok.

strtol A function that converts the leading part of the string pointed to by nptr to a long int value.

```
#include <stdlib.h>
long int strtol(const char * restrict nptr,
    char ** restrict endptr, int base);
```

Leading white space is ignored. The integer constant is terminated by any character not permissible in such a constant (including the null that terminates the input string). A leading sign character is permitted, but the suffixes 'u' (or 'U') or 'l' (or 'L') are not. The integer value is interpreted using radix base. If base is 0, the radix will be determined based on the presence or absence of a leading 0 or 0x (or 0X). Otherwise, base may be between 2 and 36. The format of the integer value is locale specific. If the input contains all white space, is empty, or contains no convertible characters, no conversion occurs, nptr is stored in *endptr (provided endptr is not NULL), and a zero value is returned. If the converted value causes overflow, either LONG_MAX or LONG_MIN is returned (depending on the sign of the value) and errno is set to ERANGE. strtol is a superset of atol and atoi and is recommended over them. *See also* wcstol.

strtold^{C99} A function that converts the leading part of the string pointed to by nptr to a long double value.

```
#include <stdlib.h>
long double strtold(const char * restrict nptr,
    char ** restrict endptr);
```

Leading white space is ignored. The floating-point constant is terminated by any character not permissible in such a constant (including the null that terminates the input string). A leading sign character is permitted as is a (possibly signed) exponent using either 'e' or 'E'. A floating-point suffix of 'f' (or 'F') or 'l' (or 'L') is not recognized as such. If no exponent or decimal point appears, a decimal point is assumed to be at the end of the number. The format of the floating-point number is locale specific. If the input contains all white space, is empty, or contains no convertible characters, no conversion occurs, nptr is stored in *endptr (provided endptr is not NULL), and a zero value is returned. If the converted value causes overflow, plus or minus HUGE_VALL is returned (according to the sign of the value) and errno is set to ERANGE. On underflow, zero is returned, and errno is set to ERANGE.

The following input is recognized as such: hexadecimal floating-point values, infinity, and NaN.

strtoll[C99] A function that converts the leading part of the string pointed to by nptr to a long long int value.

```
#include <stdlib.h>
long long int strtoll(const char * restrict
    nptr, char ** restrict endptr, int base);
```

Leading white space is ignored. The integer constant is terminated by any character not permissible in such a constant (including the null that terminates the input string). A leading sign character is permitted, but the suffixes 'u' (or 'U') or 'l' (or 'L') are not. The integer value is interpreted using radix base. If base is 0, the radix will be determined based on the presence or absence of a leading 0 or 0x (or 0X). Otherwise, base may be between 2 and 36. The format of the integer value is locale specific. If the input contains all white space, is empty, or contains no convertible characters, no conversion occurs, nptr is stored in *endptr (provided endptr is not NULL), and a zero value is returned. If the converted value causes overflow, either LLONG_MAX or LLONG_MIN is returned (depending on the sign of the value) and errno is set to ERANGE. *See also* wcstoll.

strtoul A function that converts the leading part of the string pointed to by nptr to an unsigned long int value.

```
#include <stdlib.h>
unsigned long int strtoul(const char * restrict nptr,
    char ** restrict endptr, int base);
```

Leading white space is ignored. The integer constant is terminated by any character not permissible in such a constant (including the null that terminates the input string). A leading sign character is permitted, but the suffixes 'u' (or 'U') or 'l' (or 'L') are not. The integer value is interpreted using radix base. If base is 0, the radix will be determined based on the presence or absence of a leading 0 or 0x (or 0X). Otherwise, base may be between 2 and 36. The format of the integer value is locale specific. If the input contains all white space, is empty, or contains no convertible characters, no conversion occurs, nptr is stored in *endptr (provided endptr is not NULL), and a 0 value is returned. If the converted value causes overflow, ULONG_MAX is returned, and errno is set to ERANGE. *See also* wcstoul.

strtoull^C99 A function that converts the leading part of the string pointed to by nptr to an unsigned long long int value.

```
#include <stdlib.h>
unsigned long long int strtoull(const char * restrict nptr,
    char ** restrict endptr, int base);
```

Leading white space is ignored. The integer constant is terminated by any character not permissible in such a constant (including the null that terminates the input string). A leading sign character is permitted, but the suffixes 'u' (or 'U') or 'l' (or 'L') are not. The integer value is interpreted using radix base. If base is 0, the radix will be determined based on the presence or absence of a leading 0 or 0x (or 0X). Otherwise, base may be between 2 and 36. The format of the integer value is locale-specific. If the input contains all white space, is empty, or contains no convertible characters, no conversion occurs, nptr is stored in *endptr (provided endptr is not NULL), and a 0 value is returned. If the converted value causes overflow, ULLONG_MAX is returned, and errno is set to ERANGE. *See also* wcstoull.

strtoumax^C99 A function that is equivalent to the strtoul and strtoull functions, except that the initial portion of the string is converted to type uintmax_t.

```
#include <inttypes.h>
uintmax_t strtoumax(const char * restrict nptr,
    char ** restrict endptr, int base);
```

If no conversion could be performed, zero is returned. If the correct value is outside the range of representable values, UINTMAX_MAX is returned, and errno is set to ERANGE.

struct The keyword used to define a structure type and to declare identifiers of that type.

structure An aggregate type that contains one or more members that typically are related. Sufficient storage is allocated for a structure so that at any time, one occurrence of each member can be stored simultaneously. It is declared as follows:

```
struct [ tag ] {
        member-1 ;
        member-2 ;
            ...
        member-n ;
};
```

The size of a structure is at least the sum of the sizes of its members. Holes may exist between adjacent members or after the last member to accommodate hardware alignment requirements. Such holes are included in the structure and in the size produced by `sizeof`.

Although a union is syntactically very similar to a structure, it is subtly different. *See also* arrow operator; bit-field; dot operator.

structure tag *See* tag.

structure/union arrow operator *See* arrow operator.

structure/union dot operator *See* dot operator.

structure/union member name space *See* name space.

`strxfrm`[C89] A function that transforms the string pointed to by `s2` into another string pointed to by `s1`. The transformation is locale specific.

```
#include <string.h>
size_t strxfrm(char * restrict s1,
    const char * restrict s2, size_t n);
```

If two strings are transformed, and the resultant strings are compared using `strcmp`, the same result should be obtained as if the original two strings had been compared using `strcoll`. No more than `n` transformed characters are to be written into `s1`. If the transformed string is bigger than `n`, only `n` characters are copied to `s1`, and the function returns the total number needed to hold the whole transformed string. Normally, `n` is large enough and the return value is the number of characters actually used in `s1` (excluding the null). If `s1` and `s2` designate strings that overlap, the result is undefined. *See also* `wcsxfrm`.

subnormal A nonzero floating-point value whose absolute value is smaller than the smallest nonzero normalized value.

subscript operator A primary operator, `[ ]`, is used to subscript an array designator or data pointer. One of the two operands must have an object pointer type, and the other must have an integer type. The order of evaluation of the operands is unspecified. This operator is commutative. That is, `a[i]` is equivalent to and completely interchangeable with `i[a]`, although the latter is not recommended as a coding style. This operator always produces an lvalue. It associates left to right. The type of the result is the type of the object to which the pointer operand points.

subtraction assignment operator A binary operator, `-=`, that permits subtraction and assignment to be combined such that *exp1* `-=` *exp2* is equivalent to *exp1* `=` *exp1* `-` *exp2* except that in the former, *exp1* is only evaluated once. The order of evaluation of the operands is unspecified. Both operands must have arithmetic type, or the right may have integer type if the left is a pointer to an object. The left operand must be a modifiable lvalue. The type of the result is the type of *exp1*. This operator associates right to left. *See also* assignment operator, compound.

subtraction operator A binary operator, `-`, that causes the value of its right operand to be subtracted from the value of its left. The order of evaluation of the two operands is unspecified. Both operands must have arithmetic type, or the right may have integer type if the left is a pointer to an object or both point to elements in the same array. The usual arithmetic conversions are performed on the operands. This operator associates left to right.

`switch` A keyword that introduces a construct allowing control to be passed to one of a given set of labels based on the value of a controlling integer expression. It is used as follows:

```
switch ( expression ) {

case 1:
        statement(s)

case 2:
        statement(s)

        ...

case n:
        statement(s)

[ default:
        statement(s) ]
}
```

If a `case` label with the value of *expression* exists, control is transferred to that label. If no such label exists and a `default` label exists, control transfers to the `default` label. Otherwise, control is transferred to the statement following the `switch`. When control is transferred to a `case` or `default` label, execution continues from that point on, possibly until the end of the `switch`. To interrupt this flow (to make each case mutually exclusive, for example) use something like `break` or `return`. The order in which the `case` and `default` labels are written, can be arbitrary although control can be made to flow through from one case to the next. *expression* is a full expression.

See also label, `case`; label, `default`; `break`.

switch case label *See* label, `case`.

switch default label *See* label, `default`.

symbolic constant *See* macro, object-like.

`swprintf`[C95] The wide character analog of `sprintf`.

```
#include <wchar.h>
int swprintf(wchar_t * restrict s, size_t n,
    const wchar_t * restrict format, ...);
```

`swscanf`[C95] The wide character analog of `sscanf`.

```
#include <wchar.h>
int swscanf(const wchar_t * restrict s,
    const wchar_t * restrict format, ...);
```

`system` A function that passes off the string pointed to by `string` to the host environment command-line processor.

```
#include <stdlib.h>
int system(const char *string);
```

Standard C does not require that a command-line processor (or its equivalent) exists, in which case an implementation-defined value is returned. To ascertain whether such an environment exists, call `system` with a `NULL` argument; if a nonzero value is returned, a command-line processor is available. The format of the string passed is implementation defined.

T

tag The identifier that may optionally follow the keyword **struct**, **union**, or **enum** in a structure, union, or enumerated type definition, respectively. The tag is used later to refer to that particular type; for example, in a function prototype or object definition. Structure, union, and enumeration type tags have their own name space. If the tag is omitted, all identifiers having the resultant unknown structure, union, or enumerated type must be declared at that time because that same unknown type cannot be referenced later; for example,

```
struct {
        int i;
        double d;
} sa, sb;

struct {
        int i;
        double d;
} s1, s2;
```

By definition, `sa` and `sb` have the same unknown structure type. Likewise, `s1` and `s2` have the same unknown structure type. However, the two unknown structure types are different; they are also not assignment compatible. Objects (and pointers to such objects) of such tagless types cannot be passed to nor returned from functions because there is no way to declare the unknown type in a prototype. (One exception is that a pointer to such an unknown type is assignment compatible with a `void *`.)

tag compatibility The compiler can assume that if two different parameters to a function definition are pointers to objects having different structure types, then those pointers cannot be aliases to the same object.

`tan`[`f`|`l`] A function that computes the tangent of its argument `x` (measured in radians).

```
#include <math.h>
double tan(double x);
float tanf(float x);
long double tanl(long double x);
```

If the magnitude of the argument is large, `tan` may produce a result with little or no significance.

The `float` and `long double` versions were an invention of C89, where they were optional; however, in C99, they are required.

`tanh`[`f`|`l`] A function that computes the hyperbolic tangent of its argument.

```
#include <math.h>
double tanh(double x);
float tanhf(float x);
long double tanhl(long double x);
```

The `float` and `long double` versions were an invention of C89, where they were optional; however, in C99, they are required.

`template` A C++ keyword that is not part of Standard C. If you think you might wish to move C code to a C++ environment in the future, you should refrain from using `template` as an identifier in new C code you write.

tentative definition[C89] *See* definition, tentative.

termination, abnormal *See* `abort`.

termination, normal *See* `exit`.

termination, program *See* program termination.

ternary operator *See* operator, ternary.

text stream *See* stream, text.

`tgamma`[`f`|`l`][C99] A function that computes the gamma function of `x`.

```
#include <math.h>
double tgamma(double x);
float tgammaf(float x);
long double tgammal(long double x);
```

If `x` is a negative integer or if the result cannot be represented when `x` is zero, a domain error occurs. A range error might occur if the magnitude of `x` is too large or too small. The value returned is $\Gamma(x)$.

tgmath.h[C99] A header that includes the standard headers math.h and complex.h; it also defines a number of type-generic macros.

Except for `modf`, the functions without the suffix `f` or `l` declared in math.h and complex.h have a corresponding type-generic macro defined in this header. For example, the math function `sin` and complex function `csin` have a corresponding generic macro called `sin`. When the macro is used, it expands to a function whose argument types are determined by those passed to the macro.

The complete set of type-generic macro names is: acos, acosh, asin, asinh, atan, atan2, atanh, carg, cbrt, ceil, cimag, conj, copysign, cos, cosh, cproj, creal, erf, erfc, exp, exp2, expm1, fabs, fdim, floor, fma, fmax, fmin, fmod, frexp, hypot, ilogb, ldexp, lgamma, llrint, llround, log, log10, log1p, log2, logb, lrint, lround, nearbyint, nextafter, nexttoward, pow, remainder, remquo, rint, round, scalbln, scalbn, sin, sinh, sqrt, tan, tanh, tgamma, and trunc.

this A C++ keyword that is not part of Standard C. If you think you might wish to move C code to a C++ environment in the future, you should refrain from using this as an identifier in new C code you write.

thousands_sep[C89] An lconv structure member that is a pointer to a string containing the character used to separate groups of digits before the decimal-point character in formatted nonmonetary quantities. If the string consists of "", this indicates that the value is not available in the current locale or is of zero length. In the "C" locale this member must have the value "".

throw A C++ keyword that is not part of Standard C. If you think you might wish to move C code to a C++ environment in the future, you should refrain from using throw as an identifier in new C code you write.

time A function that determines the current calendar time.

```
#include <time.h>
time_t time(time_t *timer);
```

The encoding of the type time_t is not specified by Standard C. The returned value is an approximation of the current calendar time. If this time is not available, (time_t)(-1) is returned. If timer is not NULL, the return value is also assigned to the object pointed to by timer.

__TIME__ A predefined macro that expands to a string containing the time of compilation in the form "hh:mm:ss". This macro can be used in any context where a string literal is permitted or required; for example,

```
char time[] = __TIME__;

printf("%s", __TIME__);
```

Because adjacent string literals are concatenated, the following is also permitted:

```
printf(">%s<\n", "---" __TIME__ "---");
```

Note that there is no wide string version of this macro, so it was difficult to get the time string concatenated with wide strings; however, C99 allows wide and single-byte strings to be concatenated directly, so that operation becomes trivial.

This macro cannot be the subject of `#undef`.

time components *See* broken-down time; `tm`.

time conversion functions The time.h functions `asctime`, `ctime`, `gmtime`, `localtime`, and `strftime`.

time manipulation functions The time.h functions `clock`, `difftime`, `mktime`, and `time`.

time.h A header that defines several macros and types and declares functions that manipulate time information.

time.h contains definitions or declarations for the identifiers in the following table:

Name	*Purpose*
`asctime`	Convert time
`clock`	Get processor time
`clock_t`	Time type
`CLOCKS_PER_SEC`	Number/second from `clock`
`ctime`	Convert time
`difftime`	Get difference between times
`gmtime`	Convert to UTC (GMT) time
`localtime`	Convert calendar time to local time
`mktime`	Construct a time from components
`NULL`	Null pointer constant
`size_t`	Size/count type
`strftime`	Format a time into a string
`time`	Get calendar time
`time_t`	Time type
`struct tm`	A calendar time type

`time_t`[C89] A type, defined in time.h, that is an implementation-defined arithmetic type capable of representing times.

`tm` A structure type, defined in time.h and wchar.h, that contains the individual components of a calendar time. Collectively, they are known as the broken-down time. The following members must be present in the structure, in any order. Other implementation-defined members also may be present.

```
struct tm {
    int tm_sec;    seconds after the minute
    int tm_min;    minutes after the hour
    int tm_hour;   hours since midnight
    int tm_mday;   day of the month
    int tm_mon;    months since January
    int tm_year;   years since 1900
    int tm_wday;   days since Sunday
    int tm_yday;   days since January 1
    int tm_isdst;  daylight saving time flag
};
```

where

```
tm_isdst >  0   daylight savings in effect
         == 0   daylight savings not in effect
         <  0   information not available
```

`tm_*` *See* `tm`.

`tmpfile` A function that creates a temporary binary file that is removed when it is closed or at normal program termination.

```
#include <stdio.h>
FILE *tmpfile(void);
```

`tmpfile` opens the file for update as if it had been opened by `fopen` using the mode `"wb+"`. If this mode is inappropriate, use `setvbuf` or `setbuf` to change it. Alternatively, you can get a unique filename from `tmpnam` and `fopen` it yourself.

If a temporary file cannot be created, `NULL` is returned; otherwise a `FILE` pointer is returned. *See also* `FOPEN_MAX`.

`TMP_MAX` A macro, defined in stdio.h, that expands to an integer constant expression representing the maximum number of unique filenames that can be generated by `tmpnam`. Standard C requires `TMP_MAX` to be at least 25.

`tmpnam` A function that generates and returns a filename that is guaranteed not to be that of any existing file. A file by that name then can be opened using `fopen`.

```
#include <stdio.h>
char *tmpnam(char *s);
```

If `s` is `NULL`, `tmpnam` leaves its result in its own area and returns a pointer to that area. Subsequent calls to `tmpnam` may modify that area. If `s` is not NULL, it is assumed to be a pointer to an array of at least L_tmpnam characters; tmpnam puts the result in that array and returns the address of the first character in that array. tmpnam has no way to communicate an error, so if you give it a non-NULL address that points to an area smaller than L_tmpnam characters, the behavior is undefined. *See also* TMP_MAX.

to prefix *See* future library directions.

token The fundamental unit of source code in a program. C89 defines six token types: keywords, identifiers, constants, string literals, punctuators, and operators. C99 dropped operator, moving such tokens into the punctuator category instead. A token cannot contain another token. Adjacent tokens may be separated by an arbitrary amount of white space. A token is sometimes referred to by the name "lexical element."

token-pasting operator[C89] A binary preprocessor operator, ##, that is defined only for function-like macros. It allows two preprocessing tokens to be concatenated to form a new preprocessing token. For example, given the following macro definition:

```
#define M(value) name ## value
```

the macro call M(4) expands to name4. The precedence and associativity of the # and ## preprocessor operators are unspecified.

tolower A locale-specific function that returns the lowercase equivalent of its argument c, provided it is an uppercase character. Otherwise, the argument is returned unchanged.

```
#include <ctype.h>
int tolower(int c);
```

In the "C" locale, only those characters testing true for isupper are converted to their corresponding lowercase equivalent. *See also* towlower.

In non-"C" locales, the mapping from uppercase to lowercase does not need to be one for one. For example, an uppercase letter might be represented as two lowercase letters taken together, or, perhaps, it may not even have a lowercase equivalent. If the mapping is one to many (i.e., two different results could be produced), it is implementation defined as to which alternative is returned. If, in the human language, more than one character at a time is translated to a single output character, these functions will fail to produce the human language correct results since the decision as to the character to return is based on processing a single input character at a time.

`toupper` A locale-specific function that returns the uppercase equivalent of its argument `c`, provided it is a lowercase character. Otherwise, the argument is returned unchanged.

```
#include <ctype.h>
int toupper(int c);
```

In the `"C"` locale, only those characters testing true for `islower` are converted to their uppercase equivalent. In non-`"C"` locales, the mapping from lowercase to uppercase does not need to be one for one. For example, a lowercase letter might be represented as two uppercase letters taken together, or, perhaps, it may not even have an uppercase equivalent. *See also* `tolower`; `towupper`.

`towctrans`C95 A function that maps the wide character `wc` using the mapping described by `desc`.

```
#include <wctype.h>
wint_t towctrans(wint_t wc, wctrans_t desc);
```

The setting of the `LC_CTYPE` category must be the same as that during the call to `wctrans` that produced `desc`.

`towlower`C95 A locale-specific function that returns the lowercase equivalent of its wide character argument `wc`, provided it is an uppercase character. Otherwise, the argument is returned unchanged.

```
#include <wctype.h>
wint_t towlower(wint_t wc);
```

In the `"C"` locale, only those characters testing true for `isupper` are converted to their corresponding lowercase equivalent. In non-`"C"` locales, the mapping from uppercase to lowercase does not need to be one for one. If more than one candidate exists, this function returns one of the corresponding wide characters; however, for a given locale, it always returns the same one. *See also* `tolower`.

`towupper`C95 A locale-specific function that returns the uppercase equivalent of its wide character argument `wc`, provided it is a lowercase character. Otherwise, the argument is returned unchanged.

```
#include <wctype.h>
wint_t towupper(wint_t wc);
```

In the `"C"` locale, only those characters testing true for `islower` are converted to their uppercase equivalent. In non-`"C"` locales, the mapping from lowercase to uppercase does not need to be one-for-one. If more than one candidate exists, this function returns one of the corresponding wide characters; however, for a given locale, it always returns the same one. *See also* `toupper`.

translation, phases of[C89] *See* phases of translation.

translation limits *See* environmental limits.

translation unit The set of source lines resulting after a source file is processed, all referenced headers have been included, conditional preprocessing directives have been executed, and all macros have been expanded.

trap representation The bit pattern contained within an object that does not correspond to a value of the object's type.

trigonometric functions The math.h functions `acos`, `asin`, `atan`, `atan2`, `cos`, `sin`, and `tan`, and their `float` and `long double` counterparts.

trigraph[C89] A three-character sequence beginning with `??` that permits certain punctuation characters to have an alternative representation. Trigraphs were invented by X3J11 to allow C source to be mechanically converted to and from machines supporting the ISO-646 character set (which is missing certain characters needed to write C source). Trigraphs are processed in translation phase 1. The complete set of trigraphs and their meanings are as follows:

<table>
<tr><th>Sequence</th><th>Meaning</th></tr>
<tr><td>??!</td><td>|</td></tr>
<tr><td>??'</td><td>^</td></tr>
<tr><td>??(</td><td>[</td></tr>
<tr><td>??)</td><td>]</td></tr>
<tr><td>??-</td><td>~</td></tr>
<tr><td>??/</td><td>\</td></tr>
<tr><td>??<</td><td>{</td></tr>
<tr><td>??=</td><td>#</td></tr>
<tr><td>??></td><td>}</td></tr>
</table>

Following is a program written without trigraphs.

```
#include <stdio.h>

int main()
{
        static int i[10][20] =
                {{1, 2, 4}};
        int j;

        j = ~(i[0][0]
                | i[0][1]
                ^ i[0][2]);
        printf("j = %d\n", j);

        return 0;
}
```

The equivalent program with trigraphs is as follows:

```
??=include <stdio.h>

int main()
??<
        static int i??(10??)??(20??)
                = ??<??<1, 2, 4??>??>;
        int j;

        j = ??-(i??(0??)??(0??)
                ??! i??(0??)??(1??)
                ??' i??(0??)??(2??));
        printf("j = %d??/n", j);

        return 0;
??>
```

true One of the two possible truth values, true and false. In C, an expression tests true if its value is nonzero; otherwise it tests false. Logical tests, such as `if (x)`, are equivalent to and treated as `if (x != 0)`. As such, logical tests may be performed on pointer expressions as well as arithmetic expressions because a zero valued pointer expression represents the null pointer constant.

By definition, logical, relation, and equality expressions have type `int` and value 0 (false) or 1 (true).

true[C99] A macro, defined in stdbool.h, that expands to the integer constant 1. It is intended for use in contexts involving the `bool` macro (or its underlying type, `_Bool`.) *See also* `false`.

trunc[f|l][C99] A function that rounds its argument to the integer value, in floating format, nearest to but no larger in magnitude than the argument.

```
#include <math.h>
double trunc(double x);
float truncf(float x);
long double truncl(long double x);
```

try A C++ keyword that is not part of Standard C. If you think you might wish to move C code to a C++ environment in the future, you should refrain from using `try` as an identifier in new C code you write.

type Describes the meaning of a value stored in an object or returned by a function. *See also* type, function; type, incomplete; type, object.

type, compatible Two types are compatible if they are the same. Two structure, union, or enumeration types declared in separate translation units are compatible if they have the same number of members, the same member names, and compatible member types; for two structures, the members shall be in the same order. For two structures or unions, the bit-fields shall have the same widths; for two enumerations, the members shall have the same values.

Two pointer types are compatible if they are identically qualified and they point to compatible types.

Two qualified types are compatible if they are identically qualified versions of compatible types.

Two array types are compatible if they are compatible element types and, if both size specifiers are present, they are equal.

Two function types are compatible if they return compatible types. If both parameter lists are present, they must have the same number of parameters and the corresponding parameters in each must be compatible.

C99 added the following requirements: "[T]wo structure, union, or enumerated types declared in separate translation units are compatible if their tags and members satisfy the following requirements: If one is declared with a tag, the other shall be declared with the same tag. If both are complete types, then the following additional requirements apply: there shall be a one-to-one correspondence between their members such that each pair of corresponding members are declared with compatible types, and such that if one member of a corresponding pair is declared with a name, the other member is declared with the same name. For two structures, corresponding members shall be declared in the same order. For two structures or unions, corresponding bit-fields shall have the same widths. For two enumerations, corresponding members shall have the same values."

type, compositeC89 A composite type can be constructed from two types that are compatible; it is a type that is compatible with both of the two types and satisfies the following conditions:

- If one type is an array of known constant size, the composite type is an array of that size; otherwise, if one type is a variable length array, the composite type is that type.
- If only one type is a function type with a parameter type list (a function prototype), the composite type is a function prototype with the parameter type list.
- If both types are function types with parameter type lists, the type of each parameter in the composite parameter type list is the composite type of the corresponding parameters.
- These rules apply recursively to the types from which the two types are derived.
- For an identifier with external or internal linkage declared in the same scope as another declaration for that identifier, the type of the identifier becomes the composite type.

In the following declarations:

```
int i[];
int i[5];

void f();
void f(int);

int j;
char c;
short s;
```

the composite type of `i` is "array of 5 `int`s," the composite type of `f` is "function taking one argument of type `int` and returning no value," and the composite type of `j ? c : s` is "`int`."

type, `const`-qualifiedC89 A type that includes the `const` type qualifier.

type conversion *See* conversion *and its subentries.*

type definition A type synonym created via the `typedef` keyword.

type, derived *See* derived type.

type, effective Ordinarily, the type with which an object is declared. Objects can only be accessed by lvalues having the appropriate type, which is referred to as the effective type. Although objects that are allocated at run time do not have a declared type, they still have a type. This term was invented to help describe the rules for aliasing.

type, function A type that describes a function. It includes the return type and also the argument list type information if present. For example,

```
int f();
int g(void);
```

The type of `f` is "function returning an `int` and having an unknown number and type of arguments." The type of `g` is "function returning an `int` and having no arguments."

type, incomplete[C89] A type that describes an object but contains insufficient information for the object's size to be computed. In the case of `int (*p)[];` `p` is a "pointer to array of unknown size." This type could be completed by a future (re)declaration of `p`. Other examples of incomplete types are `extern double d[];` and `struct tag;`. The `void` type is a special incomplete type in that it can never be completed.

type, narrow The signed and unsigned versions of `char` and `short`, and `float` are often referred to as narrow types because they are converted to wide types in certain contexts. *See also* conversion, function arguments; UP rule; VP rule.

type, object A type that completely describes the value of an object. *See also* type, incomplete.

type, qualified[C89] A type that includes the `const`, `restrict`, or `volatile` qualifier. *See also* type, unqualified.

type qualifier[C89,C99] A keyword used to somehow qualify an object type. C89 invented: `const` and `volatile`, while C99 added `restrict`.

C99 allows the same qualifier to be used multiple types in the same declarator, without ill effect, as in `const const int i = 10;`

type, `restrict`-qualified[C89] A type that includes the `restrict` qualifier.

type specifier One of the following:

```
void
char
short
int
long
float
double
signed
unsigned
```
struct-or-union-specifier
enum-specifier
typedef-name

type, unqualifiedC89 A type that does not include the `const`, `restrict`, or `volatile` qualifier. *See also* type, qualified.

type, `volatile`-qualifiedC89 A type that includes the `volatile` qualifier.

type, wide *See* conversion, function arguments.

`typedef` A keyword used to create a synonym for a type. Examples of its use are as follows:

```
typedef int counter;

typedef struct {
        int key;
        double data;
'} Node;
```

Technically, `typedef` is a storage class keyword, although it has nothing to do with storage classes.

typedef name The identifier defined using `typedef` to be a synonym for a type. Typedef names share the same name space as enumeration constants, functions, and variables.

`typeid` A C++ keyword that is not part of Standard C. If you think you might wish to move C code to a C++ environment in the future, you should refrain from using `typeid` as an identifier in new C code you write.

`typename` A C++ keyword that is not part of Standard C. If you think you might wish to move C code to a C++ environment in the future, you should refrain from using `typename` as an identifier in new C code you write.

U

U suffix *See* constant, integer.

u suffix *See* constant, integer.

UCHAR_MAX[C89] A macro, defined in limits.h, that designates the maximum value for an object of type `unsigned char`. It must be at least 255 (8 bits). This macro expands to an integer constant expression suitable for use with a `#if` directive. C99 requires `UCHAR_MAX` to be $2^{CHAR\_BIT} - 1$.

UCN *See* universal character name.

uint_fast8_t[C99] *See* uint_fast*N*_t.

uint_fast16_t[C99] *See* uint_fast*N*_t.

uint_fast32_t[C99] *See* uint_fast*N*_t.

uint_fast64_t[C99] *See* uint_fast*N*_t.

UINT_FAST*N*_MAX[C99] A macro, defined in stdint.h, that indicates the maximum value of the corresponding fastest minimum-width unsigned integer type, uint_fast*N*_t. It expands to an integer constant expression suitable for use with a `#if` directive.

uint_fast*N*_t[C99] A type, defined in stdint.h, that is the fastest signed integer type with a width of at least *N* bits. For example, `uint_fast32_t` denotes a signed integer type with a width of at least 32 bits. The following types must be defined: `uint_fast8_t`, `uint_fast16_t`, `uint_fast32_t`, and `uint_fast64_t`. Other types of this form are optional. *See also* int_fast*N*_t; UINT_FAST*N*_MAX.

uint_least8_t[C99] *See* uint_least*N*_t.

uint_least16_t[C99] *See* uint_least*N*_t.

uint_least32_t[C99] *See* uint_least*N*_t.

uint_least64_t[C99] *See* uint_least*N*_t.

UINT_LEAST*N*_MAX[C99] A macro, defined in stdint.h, that indicates the maximum value of the corresponding minimum-width unsigned integer type, uint_least*N*_t. It expands to an integer constant expression suitable for use with a `#if` directive.

uint_least*N*_t[C99] A macro, defined in stdint.h, that expands to a signed integer type with a width of at least *N* bits, such that no signed integer type of lesser size has at least the specified width. For example, `uint_least32_t` denotes a signed integer type with a width of at least 32 bits. The following types must be defined: `uint_least8_t`, `uint_least16_t`, `uint_least32_t`, and `uint_least64_t`. Other types of this form are optional.

See also `int_least`*N*`_t`; `UINT_LEAST`*N*`_MAX`.

`UINT_MAX`[C89] A macro, defined in limits.h, that designates the maximum value for an object of type `unsigned int`. It must be at least 65,535 (16 bits). This macro expands to an integer constant expression suitable for use with a `#if` directive.

`UINTMAX_C`[C99] A function-like macro, defined in stdint.h, that has the form `UINTMAX_C(`*value*`)` and expands to an integer constant with the specified value and type `uintmax_t`. `value` is a decimal, octal, or hexadecimal constant whose value does not exceed the limits for the corresponding type..

`UINTMAX_MAX`[C99] A macro, defined in stdint.h, that indicates the maximum value of `uintmax_t`, the corresponding greatest-width unsigned integer type. It expands to an integer constant expression suitable for use with a `#if` directive.

`uintmax_t`[C99] A type, defined in stdint.h, that is an unsigned integer type capable of representing any value of any unsigned integer type, including extended types. Preprocessor arithmetic is done using this type. *See also* `intmax_t`; `UINTMAX_MAX`.

`UINT`*N*`_C`[C99] A function-like macro, defined in stdint.h, that has the form `UINT`*N*`_C(`*value*`)` and expands to an unsigned integer constant with the specified value and type `uint_least`*N*`_t`. `value` is a decimal, octal, or hexadecimal constant whose value does not exceed the limits for the corresponding type..

`UINT`*N*`_MAX`[C99] A macro, defined in stdint.h, that indicates the maximum value of the corresponding exact-width unsigned integer type, `uint`*N*`_t`. It expands to an integer constant expression suitable for use with a `#if` directive.

`uint`*N*`_t`[C99] A type, defined in stdint.h, that designates an unsigned integer type having width *N*. For example, `uint32_t` denotes an unsigned integer type with a width of exactly 32 bits.

Such types are optional, but if an implementation provides integer types with widths of 8, 16, 32, or 64 bits, it must define the corresponding typedef names. *See also* `UINT`*N*`_MAX`; `int`*N*`_t`.

`UINTPTR_MAX`[C99] A macro, defined in stdint.h, that indicates the maximum value of `uintptr_t`, the corresponding pointer-holding unsigned integer type. It expands to an integer constant expression suitable for use with a `#if` directive.

uintptr_t[C99] An optional type, defined in stdint.h, that designates an unsigned integer type such that any valid pointer to `void` can be converted to this type and back again, with the result comparing equal to the original pointer. *See also* `intptr_t`; `UINTPTR_MAX`.

`ULLONG_MAX`[C99] A macro, defined in limits.h, that designates the maximum value for an object of type `unsigned long long int`. Its value must be at least 18,446,744,073,709,551,615 (64 bits). This macro expands to an integer constant expression suitable for use with a `#if` directive.

`ULONG_MAX`[C89] A macro, defined in limits.h, that designates the maximum value for an object of type `unsigned long int`. It must be at least 4,294,967,295 (32 bits). This macro expands to an integer constant expression suitable for use with a `#if` directive.

unary arithmetic operators The unary operators `+`, `-`, `~`, and `!`.

unary minus operator A unary operator, `-`, that negates the value of its operand. The operand must have arithmetic type. Note there is no such thing as a negative constant in C. The expression `-32768` consists of two tokens—the unary minus and the constant 32768. (Note that on a 16-bit, twos-complement machine, although -32,768 is the smallest negative value one can store in an `int` object, the constant `-32768` actually has type `long int`. *See also* constant, type of.) The usual arithmetic conversions are performed on the operand, and the result has the promoted type. This operator associates right to left.

unary operator *See* operator, unary.

unary plus operator[C89] A unary operator, `+`, that has no effect on the value of its operand. The operand must have arithmetic type. The usual arithmetic conversions are performed on the operand, and the result has the promoted type. This operator associates right to left.

`#undef` A preprocessor directive used to remove a macro definition. It is not an error to `#undef` a non-existent macro. It is used as follows:

```
#undef identifier
```

One reason to use this directive is to remove a macro to get at an underlying function version; for example,

```
#include <ctype.h>
#undef isalpha

int (*fp)(int) = isalpha;
```

Because library functions such as **isalpha** also can be implemented as macros, it is necessary to remove any such macro definition before taking the address of the underlying function. Unless this is done, a compilation error may result because if a macro version exists, it almost certainly won't be able to have its address taken.

It is not possible to **#undef** a predefined macro or the preprocessor operator **defined**.

undefined behavior Behavior for an erroneous or nonportable program construct or erroneous data for which the standard imposes no requirements. Examples include the passing of an argument of the incorrect type to a function and using the value of a function that does not return one.

underscore A character allowed in identifier names. Certain identifier names with leading underscores are reserved for use by implementers and future versions of Standard C. To avoid conflicts with private names invented by implementers in standard headers, never invent an identifier name that begins with an underscore. Some environments do not have the underscore character in their external character set. In such cases, it is typically mapped to some other character. The underscore is neither a punctuator nor an operator.

ungetc A function that pushes the character specified by **c** (after converting it to **unsigned char**) back into the input stream pointed to by **stream**.

```
#include <stdio.h>
int ungetc(int c, FILE *stream);
```

Characters pushed back can be gotten (in the reverse order of which they were pushed back) with subsequent reads from that stream. If you call **rewind**, **fseek**, or **fsetpos**, any unread, pushed-back characters are discarded. Standard C guarantees only one character of pushback. If more characters are pushed back than can be handled, an error is returned.

If **ungetc** is successful, it returns **c**, and the end-of-file indicator for that stream is cleared; otherwise, it returns **EOF**. *See also* **ungetwc**.

ungetwc[C95] A function that pushes the wide character specified by **c** (after converting it to **wint_t**) back into the input stream pointed to by **stream**.

```
#include <stdio.h>
#include <wchar.h>
wint_t ungetwc(wint_t c, FILE *stream);
```

Characters pushed back can be gotten (in the reverse order of which they were pushed back) with subsequent reads from that stream. If you call `rewind`, `fseek`, or `fsetpos`, any unread, pushed-back characters are discarded. Standard C guarantees only one character of pushback. If more characters are pushed back than can be handled, an error is returned.

If `ungetwc` is successful, it returns `c`, and the end-of-file indicator for that stream is cleared; otherwise, it returns `WEOF`. *See also* `ungetc`.

Unicode A 16-bit character set developed by the Unicode Consortium. It was adopted as standard ISO/IEC 10646. New operating systems, new releases of some older systems, and some languages (most notably Java) are adopting Unicode as their basic character set. *See also* ISO/IEC 10646.UCS-2; `__STDC_ISO_10646__`; `wchar_t`; wide character.

union A union contains one or more members. Sufficient storage is allocated to a union so that, at any time, one occurrence of only one member can be stored. The size of a union is at least the size of its largest member. Although a union is syntactically very similar to a structure, it is subtly different. A union is defined using the keyword `union`. A union is neither a scalar nor an aggregate; it is in a category by itself.

If a union contains two or more structures that share a common initial sequence, and if an object of that type currently contains one of these structures, the common initial parts of those structures overlap directly, so they can be accessed via any of the structures.

`union` The keyword used to define a union type and to declare identifiers of that type; for example,

```
union tag {
        int i;
        double d;
        char *pc;
} u1;

union tag u2, *pu;
```

It is the programmer's responsibility to keep track of which member a union was last stored through. If a union is stored through one member and its value is retrieved through a member of different type, the result is undefined.

union initialization The use of an initializer in a union declaration. Prior to C89, unions could not have initializers. Standard C now permits this and uses an initializer format like that for structures. That is, the initializer is a brace-delimited list where the list contains one expression unless the member of the element being initialized is an aggregate. The initializer is interpreted according to the first member of the union, which means that for the purpose of initialization only, it is significant which member is defined first. For example,

```
union {
        int i;
        double d;
} u = {1.2};
```

results in `u.i` being initialized with the integer value 1. If, however, the two members' order was swapped, `u.d` would be initialized with the floating-point value 1.2.

With the addition of designated initializers in C99, a union can be initialized using any of its members; for example,

```
union {
        // order of members i and j is irrelevant
} u = {.d = 1.2};
```

causes the union to be initialized through the `double` member `d`.

union tag *See* tag.

universal character name (UCN) A sequence of characters that can be used in identifiers, character constants, and string literals to represent characters not found in the basic character set. There are two forms: \u*nnnn* and \U*nnnnnnnn*, where *n* is a hexadecimal digit, allowing for the use of both 16- and 32-bit character sets. The coding scheme used is ISO 10646; therefore, for example, `\u03A0` and `\u03C0` represent the Greek letters Π and π, respectively, while `\u2020` and `\u2021` represent † and ‡, respectively.

It is system and locale dependent whether an implementation will be able to convert any given UCN to a character in the execution character set.

Universal Time Coordinated The international standard name for what was previously known as Greenwich Mean Time (GMT). It is often abbreviated as UTC.

unordered A situation in which two floating-point numbers are not equal and neither number is greater than the other. A NaN is unordered when compared to any numeric value or to another NaN. *See* `isunordered`.

unqualified type[C89] *See* type, unqualified.

`unsigned` A keyword used as an unsigned integer data type prefix. It may be applied to `char`, `short int`, `int`, `long int`, and `long long int`. It allows unsigned arithmetic to be performed. When used on its own, it implies `unsigned int`. *See also* integer type.

`unsigned int` **suffix** *See* constant, integer.

unsigned integer types The types `unsigned char`, `unsigned short`, `unsigned int`, `unsigned long`, and `unsigned long long`. *See also* bit-field, plain `int`; `char`, plain.

`unsigned long` A permitted abbreviation for `unsigned long int`.

`unsigned long int` A standard integer type. Standard C requires it to be at least 32 bits. *See also* integer type.

`unsigned long long`[C99] A permitted abbreviation for `unsigned long long int`.

`unsigned long long int`[C99] A standard integer type. Standard C requires it to be at least 62 bits. Note that an unsuffixed decimal constant cannot have this type. *See also* integer type.

unsigned preserving rule The rule by which expressions having type `unsigned int` bit-field, `unsigned char`, or `unsigned short`, are converted to `unsigned int` when these "narrow" types are widened. This rule was widely followed prior to the advent of Standard C, which now requires following the value preserving rule instead. *See also* conversion, integer type; value-preserving rule.

`unsigned` **type conversion** *See* conversion, integer type.

unspecified behavior Behavior for a correct program construct and correct data for which the standard imposes no requirements. For example, the order of evaluation of expressions (except those involving `&&`, `||`, `?:` and the comma operator) is unspecified.

unspecified value A valid value of the appropriate type where the C standard imposes no requirements on which value is used.

UP rule *See* unsigned preserving rule.

`USHRT_MAX`[C89] A macro, defined in limits.h, that designates the maximum value for an object of type `unsigned short int`. It must be at least 65,535. This macro expands to an integer constant expression suitable for use with a `#if` directive.

`using` A C++ keyword that is not part of Standard C. If you think you might wish to move C code to a C++ environment in the future, you should refrain from using `using` as an identifier in new C code you write.

usual arithmetic conversion *See* conversion, usual arithmetic.

UTC *See* Universal Time Coordinated.

V

va_arg A macro, defined in stdarg.h, that causes the next function argument, of the type *type*, to be retrieved from the variable argument list and returned as the value of the whole expression.

```
#include <stdarg.h>
type va_arg(va_list ap, type);
```

The ap argument must be the same as that passed to the corresponding va_start or va_copy. If there are no more arguments, or *type* is not the type of the next argument, the result is undefined.

__VA_ARGS__[C99] An identifier that can appear only in the replacement list of a function-like macro that contains an ellipsis. It is replaced by the variable argument list to which it corresponds.

Here is an example of its use:

```
#define trace(...) printf(__VA_ARGS__)

trace("value = %d\n", value);
trace("x = %d, y = %d\n", x, y);
```

va_copy[C99] A macro, defined in stdarg.h, that allows a va_list to be copied.

```
#include <stdarg.h>
void va_copy(va_list dest, va_list src);
```

va_end A macro, defined in stdarg.h, that performs any necessary cleanup of variable argument list processing.

```
#include <stdarg.h>
void va_end(va_list ap);
```

The ap argument must be the same as that passed to the corresponding va_start. Once you have called va_end, you must call va_start before attempting to reprocess the argument list; otherwise, the behavior is undefined. va_end must be invoked from the same function in which the corresponding va_start was invoked. *See also* va_copy.

validation The process whereby a compiler that claims conformance to a standard is actually tested for such conformance. This process is usually performed by an accredited agency of a government, a national standards body, or a recognized professional association.

va_list A type, defined in stdarg.h, that is suitable for holding information needed by the stdarg.h macros `va_start`, `va_arg`, `va_copy`, and `va_end`. It is defined in stdarg.h.

value preserving rule The rule by which expressions having type `unsigned int` bit-field, `unsigned char`, or `unsigned short` are converted to `int` (if their value can be represented); otherwise, they are converted to `unsigned int` when these "narrow" types are widened. This rule was not widely followed prior to the advent of Standard C, which now requires it to be used. *See also* conversion, integer type; unsigned preserving rule.

varargs.h A common nonstandard version of, and predecessor to, stdarg.h.

variable argument list *See* argument list, variable; ellipsis.

variable-length array[C99] *See* array, variable-length.

variable name The name used to designate a named-object. Such names are called identifiers, which, in the case of variables, share the same name space as enumeration constants, functions, and typedef names.

va_start A macro, defined in stdarg.h, that prepares for processing of a variable argument list by initializing the `ap` (argument pointer) argument using the address of the last fixed parameter. `parmN` is the last of the list of fixed arguments.

```
#include <stdarg.h>
void va_start(va_list ap, parmN);
```

`va_start` must be called before `va_arg` or `va_end` are used for a given variable argument list. If `register` is used with `parmN`, or `parmN` has type function or array, or `parmN` is a narrow type, the behavior is undefined. *See also* `va_copy`.

vertical-tab character One of the white space characters allowed in source text.

vertical-tab escape sequence An escape sequence, \v, which allows the vertical tab character to be represented in a string literal or character constant.

vfprintf[C89] A function that is equivalent to `fprintf`, except that the argument list has been replaced by a variable argument list identified by `arg`, which has been initialized by the `va_start` macro (and possibly subsequent `va_arg` calls).

```
#include <stdio.h>
int vfprintf(FILE * restrict stream,
    const char * restrict format, va_list arg);
```

The return value is the number of characters transmitted or a negative value on error. *See also* stdarg.h.

vfscanf[C99] A function that is like **fscanf**, except that the variable argument list is replaced by a **va_list**.

```
#include <stdarg.h>
#include <stdio.h>
int vfscanf(FILE * restrict stream,
    const char * restrict format, va_list arg);
```

The **va_list** must have already been initialized by **va_start**. This function does not call **va_end**.

vfwprintf[C95] A function that is like **fwprintf**, except that the variable argument list is replaced by a **va_list**.

```
#include <stdarg.h>
#include <stdio.h>
#include <wchar.h>
int vfwprintf(FILE * restrict stream,
    const wchar_t * restrict format, va_list arg);
```

The **va_list** must have already been initialized by **va_start**. This function does not call **va_end**.

vfwscanf[C95] A function that is like **fwscanf**, except that the variable argument list is replaced by a **va_list**.

```
#include <stdarg.h>
#include <stdio.h>
#include <wchar.h>
int vfwscanf(FILE * restrict stream,
    const wchar_t * restrict format, va_list arg);
```

The **va_list** must have already been initialized by **va_start**. This function does not call **va_end**.

virtual A C++ keyword that is not part of Standard C. If you think you might wish to move C code to a C++ environment in the future you should refrain from using **virtual** as an identifier in new C code you write.

visibility of identifiers *See* linkage; scope.

VLA[C99] *See* array, variable-length.

`void` The type of an expression that has no value. Obtained by calling a `void` function or by casting an expression to type `void`.

The keyword also may be used in two other unrelated contexts: as the only token inside a function prototype to indicate there are no arguments, or as part of the generic pointer type `void *`.

`void *` **type**[C89] *See* `void` pointer.

`void` **cast** An explicit conversion of an expression to type `void`. Such a cast results in the value of that expression's being discarded. An expression of type `void` can be cast to type `void`, even though such a cast is vacuous.

The need for an explicit `void` cast is rare because failing to use the value of an expression results in that value being discarded anyway. However, there is one valuable application. If you are writing a macro that mimics what might otherwise be a `void` function, you should explicitly cast the macro definition to `void` to prohibit its value being incorrectly used; for example,

```
void swap(int, int);

#define swap(a, b) ((a) ^= (b), \
        (b) ^= (a), (void) ((a) ^= (b)))
```

See also conversion, `void` type.

void expression An expression that has no value. It results from either having a function returning `void` or from having explicitly cast an expression to type `void`.

`void` **in prototypes** Two distinct and unrelated uses of the `void` keyword in a prototype. Consider the following example:

```
void f(void);
```

The first use of `void` indicates that function `f` is a `void` function and, as such, does not return a value. The second use of `void` (as introduced by C89) indicates that the function expects no arguments. If the second `void` were omitted, the declaration would indicate that the function expected an unknown number of arguments and the compiler could do no checking.

`void` **pointer**[C89] A pointer type adopted from C++ to help implementers on systems where pointers are not all the same size and/or representation (such as with word architectures) and to provide a generic pointer type. All standard library routines that previously used `char *` for such pointers now use `void *` (for example, `malloc`, `calloc`, and `memcpy`). A `void` pointer cannot be dereferenced directly or have arithmetic performed on it.

`void` **type conversion** *See* conversion, `void` type.

`volatile`[C89] A keyword used as a type qualifier. It indicates that the object to which it applies is not owned entirely by this program. That is, it might be read or written asynchronously by some other program (or by an interrupt handler in the same program) or hardware device as well, and the optimizer had better not eliminate various accesses to this object. The `volatile` qualifier also may be applied to the underlying object in a pointer declaration. Consider the following cases:

```
char *nvpnvc;
char * volatile vpnvc;
volatile char *nvpvc;
volatile char * volatile vpvc;
```

`nvpnvc` is a non-`volatile` pointer to a non-`volatile char`. `vpnvc` is a `volatile` pointer to a non-`volatile char`. `nvpvc` is a non-`volatile` pointer to a `volatile char`. `vpvc` is a `volatile` pointer to a `volatile char`.

Declarations containing the `volatile` qualifier also may contain the `const` and `restrict` qualifiers.

VP rule *See* value preserving rule.

`vprintf`[C89] A function that is equivalent to `printf`, except that the argument list has been replaced by a variable argument list identified by `arg`, which has been initialized by the `va_start` macro (and possibly subsequent `va_arg` calls).

```
#include <stdio.h>
int vprintf(const char * restrict format, va_list arg);
```

The return value is the number of characters transmitted or a negative value on error. *See also* stdarg.h.

`vscanf`[C99] A function that is like `scanf`, except that the variable argument list is replaced by a `va_list`.

```
#include <stdarg.h>
#include <stdio.h>
int vscanf(const char * restrict format, va_list arg);
```

The `va_list` must have already been initialized by `va_start`. This function does not call `va_end`.

`vsnprintf`C99 A function that is like `snprintf`, except that the variable argument list is replaced by a `va_list`.

```
#include <stdarg.h>
#include <stdio.h>
int vsnprintf(char * restrict s, size_t n,
    const char * restrict format, va_list arg);
```

The `va_list` must have already been initialized by `va_start`. This function does not call `va_end`.

`vsprintf`C89 A function that is equivalent to `sprintf`, except that the argument list has been replaced by a variable argument list identified by `arg`, which has been initialized by the `va_start` macro (and possibly subsequent `va_arg` calls).

`vsscanf`C99 A function that is like `sscanf`, except that the variable argument list is replaced by a `va_list`.

```
#include <stdarg.h>
#include <stdio.h>
int vsscanf(const char * restrict s,
    const char * restrict format, va_list arg);
```

The `va_list` must have already been initialized by `va_start`. This function does not call `va_end`.

`vswprintf`C95 A function that is like `swprintf`, except that the variable argument list is replaced by a `va_list`.

```
#include <stdarg.h>
#include <wchar.h>
int vswprintf(wchar_t * restrict s, size_t n,
    const wchar_t * restrict format, va_list arg);
```

The `va_list` must have already been initialized by `va_start`. This function does not call `va_end`.

`vswscanf`C95 A function that is like `swscanf`, except that the variable argument list is replaced by a `va_list`.

```
#include <stdarg.h>
#include <wchar.h>
int vswscanf(const wchar_t * restrict s,
    const wchar_t * restrict format, va_list arg);
```

The `va_list` must have already been initialized by `va_start`. This function does not call `va_end`.

`vwprintf`[C95] A function that is like `wprintf`, except that the variable argument list is replaced by a `va_list`.

```
#include <stdarg.h>
#include <wchar.h>
int vwprintf(const wchar_t * restrict format, va_list arg);
```

The `va_list` must have already been initialized by `va_start`. This function does not call `va_end`.

`vwscanf`[C95] A function that is like `wscanf`, except that the variable argument list is replaced by a `va_list`.

```
#include <stdarg.h>
#include <wchar.h>
int vwscanf(const wchar_t * restrict format, va_list arg);
```

The `va_list` must have already been initialized by `va_start`. This function does not call `va_end`.

W

wchar.h[C95] A header that declares machinery supporting multibyte and wide character processing. It contains definitions or declarations for the identifiers in the following table:

Name	*Purpose*
`btowc`	Test for valid character
`fgetwc`	Read wide character from file
`fgetws`	Read wide string from file
`fputwc`	Write wide character to file
`fputws`	Write wide string to file
`fwide`	Determine orientation of stream
`fwprintf`	Formatted write to file
`fwscanf`	Formatted read from file
`getwc`	Read wide character from `stdin`
`getwchar`	Read wide character from `stdin`
`mbrlen`	Find length of multibyte string
`mbrtowc`	Convert multibyte character to wide character
`mbsinit`	Check for initial conversion state
`mbsrtowcs`	Convert multibyte string to wide character
`mbstate_t`	Conversion state object type
`NULL`	Null pointer constant
`putwc`	Write wide character to `stdout`
`putwchar`	Write wide character to `stdout`
`size_t`	Size/count type
`swprintf`	Formatted write to wide string
`swscanf`	Formatted read from wide string
`tm`	A calendar time type
`ungetwc`	Pushback wide character to `stdin`
`vfwprintf`	Formatted write to a file
`vfwscanf`	Formatted read from a file
`vswprintf`	Formatted write to a wide string
`vswscanf`	Formatted read from a wide string
`vwprintf`	Formatted write to `stdout`
`vwscanf`	Formatted read from `stdin`
`WCHAR_MAX`	Max value of type `wchar_t`
`WCHAR_MIN`	Min value of type `wchar_t`
`wchar_t`	Wide character type
`wcrtomb`	Convert wide character to multibyte character
`wcsrtombs`	Convert wide string to multibyte string

Name	*Purpose*
wcscat	Concatenate wide strings
wcschr	Search wide string for wide character
wcscmp	Compare wide strings
wcscoll	Collate wide strings
wcscpy	Copy a wide string
wcscspn	Compute initial length match
wcserror	Produce error message
wcsftime	Format a time into a wide string
wcslen	Compute wide string length
wcsncat	Concatenate wide strings
wcsncmp	Compare leading part of wide strings
wcsncpy	Copy leading part of wide string
wcspbrk	Locate wide character in wide string
wcsrchr	Reverse search for wide character
wcsspn	Compute initial length match
wcsstr	Search wide string for wide string
wcstod	Convert wide string to double
wcstof	Convert wide string to float
wcstok	Break wide string into tokens
wcstol	Convert wide string to long
wcstold	Convert wide string to long double
wcstoll	Convert wide string to long long
wcstoul	Convert wide string to unsigned long
wcstoull	Convert wide string to unsigned long long
wcsxfrm	Transform wide string
wctob	Test if multibyte character
WEOF	Wide end-of-file
wint_t	Type to hold any character
wmemchr	Search memory for wide character
wmemcmp	Compare memory blocks
wmemcpy	Copy memory blocks
wmemmove	Safe copy of memory blocks
wmemset	Initialize memory block
wprintf	Formatted write to stdout
wscanf	Formatted read from stdin

See future library directions.

WCHAR_MAX[C95,C99] A macro, defined in stdint.h, that indicates the maximum value of the type wchar_t. It expands to an integer constant expression suitable for use with a #if directive. C95 defined it in wchar.h, and C99 added it to stdint.h as well. If that type is a signed integer, WCHAR_MAX shall be no less than 127; if the type is an unsigned integer, WCHAR_MAX shall be no less than 255.

WCHAR_MIN[C95,C99] A macro, defined in stdint.h, that indicates the minimum value of the type wchar_t. It expands to an integer constant expression suitable for use with a #if directive. C95 defined it in wchar.h, and C99 added it to stdint.h as well. If that type is an unsigned integer, WCHAR_MIN shall be no greater than -127; if the type is an unsigned integer, WCHAR_MIN shall be zero.

wchar_t[C89] An integer type that has a range of values capable of representing distinct codes for all members of the largest extended character set specified among the supported locales. wchar_t is needed when declaring or referencing wide characters and wide strings. It is defined in stddef.h, stdlib.h, and wchar.h. Note that in C++, this name is a keyword. *See also* Unicode; WCHAR_MAX; WCHAR_MIN

wcrtomb[C95] A function that is a restartable version of wctomb.

```
#include <wchar.h>
size_t wcrtomb(char * restrict s,
    wchar_t wc, mbstate_t * restrict ps);
```

wcs **prefix** *See* future library directions.

wcscat[C95] A function that copies the wide string pointed to by s2 to the end of the wide string pointed to by s1. In the process, the trailing wide null of s1 is overwritten by the first wide character of the wide string pointed to by s2. The destination wide string is terminated with a wide null.

```
#include <wchar.h>
wchar_t *wcscat(wchar_t * restrict s1,
    const wchar_t * restrict s2);
```

The value of s1 is returned. If the wide strings located at s1 and s2 overlap, the behavior of wcscat is undefined. *See also* strcat.

wcschr[C95] A function that searches the wide string s for a wide character c.

```
#include <wchar.h>
wchar_t *wcschr(const wchar_t *s, wchar_t c);
```

If c is found, wcschr returns a pointer to that location within s; otherwise it returns NULL. The wide null that terminates s is included in the search; so wcschr can be used to locate the trailing null as well. *See also* strchr.

wcscmp[C95] A function that compares a wide string at the location pointed to by s2 to a wide string at the location pointed to by s1.

```
#include <wchar.h>
int wcscmp(const wchar_t *s1, const wchar_t *s2);
```

An integer less than, equal to, or greater than zero is returned to indicate whether `s1` is less than, equal to, or greater than `s2`, respectively. *See also* `strcmp`.

`wcscoll`C95 A function that compares a wide string at the location pointed to by `s2` to a wide string at the location pointed to by `s1`.

```
#include <wchar.h>
int wcscoll(const wchar_t *s1, const wchar_t *s2);
```

An integer less than, equal to, or greater than zero is returned to indicate whether `s1` is less than, equal to, or greater than `s2`, respectively. The comparison is locale specific (based on the value of `LC_COLLATE`). In the `"C"` locale, `wcscoll` should give the same result as `wcscmp`. *See also* `strcoll`.

`wcscpy`C95 A function that copies the wide string pointed to by `s2` to the location pointed to by `s1`. The destination wide string is terminated with a wide null.

```
#include <wchar.h>
wchar_t *wcscpy(wchar_t * restrict s1,
    const wchar_t * restrict s2);
```

The value of `s1` is returned. If the wide strings located at `s1` and `s2` overlap, the behavior of `wcscpy` is undefined. To copy overlapping objects, use `wmemmove` instead. *See also* `strcpy`.

`wcscspn`C95 A function that finds the longest wide string starting at the location pointed to by `s1`, such that it does not contain any of the wide characters in the wide string pointed to by `s2`. Alternatively, it could be viewed that `wcscspn` locates the first wide character in the string pointed to by `s1` that is present in the wide string pointed to by `s2`.

```
#include <wchar.h>
size_t wcscspn(const wchar_t *s1, const wchar_t *s2);
```

The return value indicates the length of the nonmatching wide string found at `s1` (which is the same as the subscript of the first matching wide character in `s1`). *See also* `strcspn`.

`wcsftime`C95 A function that constructs a date and time wide string by putting wide characters into the array pointed to by `s` according to the controlling format specified by `format`. No more than `maxsize` wide characters are written to the array. `timeptr` points to a structure whose contents are used to determine the appropriate wide characters for the array.

```
#include <time.h>
#include <wchar.h>
size_t wcsftime(wchar_t * restrict s, size_t maxsize,
    const wchar_t * restrict format,
    const struct tm * restrict timeptr);
```

This function provides a locale-specific way of generating date and time wide strings. Refer to your library documentation for specific details of the controlling format conversion specifiers. *See also* `strftime`.

`wcslen`^{C95} A function that returns the number of wide characters in the wide string (excluding the trailing wide null) pointed to by `s`.

```
#include <wchar.h>
size_t wcslen(const wchar_t *s);
```

`wcsncat`^{C95} A function that copies, at most, the first `n` wide characters from the wide string pointed to by `s2` to the end of the wide string pointed to by `s1`. The destination wide string is terminated with a wide null.

```
#include <wchar.h>
wchar_t *wcsncat(wchar_t * restrict s1,
    const wchar_t * restrict s2, size_t n);
```

The value of `s1` is returned. If a wide null is not found in the first `n` wide characters of `s2`, `n` wide characters will be copied followed by a wide null. If a wide null is found, it is copied to `s1` and the copy is terminated. If the wide strings located at `s1` and `s2` overlap, the behavior of `wcsncat` is undefined. *See also* `strncat`.

`wcsncmp`^{C95} A function that compares no more than `n` wide characters from a wide string at the location pointed to by `s2` to a wide string at the location pointed to by `s1`. If a wide null is seen in the first `n` wide characters, the comparison is terminated.

```
#include <wchar.h>
int wcsncmp(const wchar_t *s1, const wchar_t *s2, size_t n);
```

An integer less than, equal to, or greater than zero is returned to indicate whether `s1` is less than, equal to, or greater than `s2`, respectively. *See also* `strncmp`.

`wcsncpy`C95 A function that copies, at most, the first `n` wide characters from the wide string pointed to by `s2` to the location pointed to by `s1`. The destination string is terminated with a wide null character.

```
#include <wchar.h>
wchar_t *wcsncpy(wchar_t * restrict s1,
    const wchar_t * restrict s2, size_t n);
```

The value of `s1` is returned. If a wide null is not found in the first `n` wide characters of `s2`, the wide string pointed to by `s1` will not be null terminated. If a wide null is found, it is copied to `s1`. If there are less than `n` wide characters in the string pointed to by `s1`, extra null wide characters are appended to the end of the string pointed to by `s1` such that `n` wide characters are actually copied there. If the wide strings located at `s1` and `s2` overlap, the behavior of `wcsncpy` is undefined. To copy overlapping objects, use `wmemmove` instead. *See also* `strncpy`.

`wcspbrk`C95 A function that searches the wide string pointed to by `s1` for the first of any one of the wide characters in the wide string pointed to by `s2`.

```
#include <wchar.h>
wchar_t *wcspbrk(const wchar_t *s1, const wchar_t *s2);
```

The return value is a pointer to the wide character found in `s1` or `NULL` if no match was found. *See also* `strpbrk`.

`wcsrchr`C95 A function that searches the wide string `s` for the last occurrence of the wide character `c`.

```
#include <wchar.h>
wchar_t *wcsrchr(const wchar_t *s, wchar_t c);
```

If `c` is found, `wcsrchr` returns a pointer to that location within `s`; otherwise it returns `NULL`. The wide null terminating `s` is included in the search, so `wcsrchr` can be used to locate the trailing wide null as well. *See also* `strrchr`.

`wcsrtombs`C95 A function that is a restartable version of `wcstomb`.

```
#include <wchar.h>
size_t wcsrtombs(char * restrict dst,
    const wchar_t ** restrict src,
    size_t len, mbstate_t * restrict ps);
```

`wcsspn`C95 A function that finds the longest wide string starting at the location pointed to by `s1` such that it contains only those wide characters in the wide string at the location pointed to by s2. Alternatively, it could be viewed that wcsspn locates the first wide character in the string pointed to by s1 that is not present in the wide string pointed to by s2.

```
#include <wchar.h>
size_t wcsspn(const wchar_t *s1, const wchar_t *s2);
```

The return value indicates the length of the matching wide string found at s1 (which is the same as the subscript of the first nonmatching wide character in s1). *See also* strspn.

wcsstr[C99] A function that searches the wide string pointed to by s1 for the wide substring pointed to by s2.

```
#include <wchar.h>
wchar_t *wcsstr(const wchar_t *s1, const wchar_t *s2);
```

The return value represents the location of the wide substring s2 within the wide string s1. If the substring is not found, NULL is returned. By definition, the null wide string is always found at the beginning of any wide string, including a null string. *See also* strstr.

wcstod[C95] A function that is the wide character equivalent to strtod.

```
#include <wchar.h>
double wcstod(const wchar_t * restrict nptr,
    wchar_t ** restrict endptr);
```

wcstof[C99] A function that is the wide character equivalent to strtof.

```
#include <wchar.h>
float wcstof(const wchar_t * restrict nptr,
    wchar_t ** restrict endptr);
```

wcstoimax[C99] A function that is equivalent to the wcstol and wcstoll functions, except that the initial portion of the string is converted to type intmax_t.

```
#include <stddef.h>
#include <inttypes.h>
intmax_t wcstoimax(const wchar_t * restrict nptr,
    wchar_t ** restrict endptr, int base);
```

If no conversion could be performed, zero is returned. If the correct value is outside the range of representable values, INTMAX_MAX or INTMAX_MIN is returned (depending on the sign of the value), and errno is set to ERANGE.

`wcstok`^C95 Successive calls to this function can be used to break a wide string, pointed to by `s1`, into a series of wide null-terminated tokens using the token terminator wide characters specified by the wide string pointed to by `s2`.

```
#include <wchar.h>
wchar_t *wcstok(wchar_t * restrict s1,
    const wchar_t * restrict s2, wchar_t ** restrict ptr);
```

The value returned is either a pointer to the token found or `NULL` if no token was found.

Unlike `strtok`, `wcstok` has a third argument, which points to a user-provided `wchar_t` pointer into which the `wcstok` function stores information necessary for it to continue scanning the same wide string in a future call.

`wcstol`^C95 A function that is the wide character equivalent to `strtol`.

```
long int wcstol(const wchar_t * restrict nptr,
    wchar_t ** restrict endptr, int base);
```

`wcstold`^C99 A function that is the wide character equivalent to `strtold`.

```
#include <wchar.h>
long double wcstold(const wchar_t * restrict nptr,
    wchar_t ** restrict endptr);
```

`wcstoll`^C99 A function that is the wide character equivalent to `strtoll`.

```
long long int wcstoll(const wchar_t * restrict nptr,
    wchar_t ** restrict endptr, int base);
```

`wcstombs`^C89 A function that converts a sequence of wide characters in `pwcs` to a sequence of multibyte characters pointed to by `s`.

```
#include <stdlib.h>
int wcstombs(char * restrict s, wchar_t * restrict pwcs,
    size_t n);
```

See also `wcsrtombs`.

`wctomb`^C89 A function that determines the number of bytes needed to represent the multibyte character corresponding to the code whose value is `wchar`. It also converts that wide character `wchar` to a multibyte character which it stores at `s`.

```
#include <stdlib.h>
int wctomb(char *s, wchar_t wchar);
```

See also wcrtomb.

wcstoul[C95] A function that is the wide character equivalent to strtoul.

```
unsigned long int wcstoul(const wchar_t * restrict nptr,
    wchar_t ** restrict endptr, int base);
```

wcstoull[C99] A function that is the wide character equivalent to strtoull.

```
unsigned long long int wcstoull(const wchar_t * restrict
    nptr, wchar_t ** restrict endptr, int base);
```

wcstoumax[C99] A function that is equivalent to the wcstoul and wcstoull functions, except that the initial portion of the string is converted to type uintmax_t.

```
#include <stddef.h>
#include <inttypes.h>
uintmax_t wcstoumax(const wchar_t * restrict nptr,
    wchar_t ** restrict endptr, int base);
```

If no conversion could be performed, zero is returned. If the correct value is outside the range of representable values, UINTMAX_MAX is returned, and errno is set to ERANGE.

wcsxfrm[C95] A function that transforms the wide string pointed to by s2 into another wide string pointed to by s1. The transformation is locale specific.

```
#include <wchar.h>
size_t wcsxfrm(wchar_t * restrict s1,
    const wchar_t * restrict s2, size_t n);
```

If two wide strings are transformed, and the resultant wide strings are compared using wcscmp, the same result should be obtained as if the original two strings had been compared using wcscoll. No more than n transformed wide characters are to be written into s1. If the transformed wide string is bigger than n, only n wide characters are copied to s1, and the function returns the total number needed to hold the whole transformed string. Normally, n is large enough and the return value is the number of wide characters actually used in s1 (excluding the wide null). If s1 and s2 designate wide strings that overlap, the result is undefined. *See also* strxfrm.

`wctob`[C95] A function that indicates whether its argument `c` corresponds to a member of the extended character set whose multibyte character representation is a single byte when in the initial shift state. If there is such a correspondence, the wide character is converted.

```
#include <stdio.h>
#include <wchar.h>
int wctob(wint_t c);
```

If `c` does not correspond to a multibyte character with length one in the initial shift state, `EOF` is returned; otherwise, the single-byte representation of that character as an `unsigned char` converted to an `int` is returned.

`wctrans`[C95] A function that constructs a value of type `wctrans_t` which describes a mapping between wide characters identified by `property`.

```
#include <wctype.h>
wctrans_t wctrans(const char *property);
```

The strings recognized by this function and their corresponding meaning are as follows:

String	*Class*
`"tolower"`	`towlower`
`"toupper"`	`towupper`

These strings are valid in all locales.

If `property` represents a valid mapping of wide characters according to the `LC_CTYPE` category of the current locale, the nonzero value returned is valid as the second argument to `towctrans`; otherwise, zero is returned.

`wctrans_t`[C95] A scalar type, defined in wctype.h, that is capable of holding values that represent locale-specific character mappings. *See also* `towctrans`; `wctrans`.

`wctype`[C95] A function that constructs a value of type `wctype_t` which describes a class of wide characters identified by the string argument `property`.

```
#include <wctype.h>
wctype_t wctype(const char *property);
```

The strings recognized by this function and their corresponding meaning are as follows:

String	*Class*
"alnum"	iswalnum
"alpha"	iswalpha
"blank"	iswblank
"cntrl"	iswcntrl
"digit"	iswdigit
"graph"	iswgraph
"lower"	iswlower
"print"	iswprint
"punct"	iswpunct
"space"	iswspace
"upper"	iswupper
"xdigit"	iswxdigit

These strings are valid in all locales.

If `property` identifies a valid class of wide characters according to the `LC_CTYPE` category of the current locale, this function returns a nonzero value that is valid as the second argument to the function `iswctype`; otherwise, it returns zero.

wctype.h[C95] A header that contains various character testing and conversion functions, some type definitions, and a macro. The `isw*` family members return a zero or nonzero value based on the truth of their operation while the `tow*` family members return a possibly case-converted value of their character argument.

All functions take one `wint_t` argument. However, the `wint_t` argument must be either representable in a `wchar_t` or it must be the macro `WEOF`. If the argument has any other value, the behavior is undefined.

The behavior of some functions is locale specific.

This header contains definitions or declarations for the following identifiers:

Name	*Purpose*
iswalnum	Test if wide character is alphanumeric
iswalpha	Test if wide character is alphabetic
iswblank[C99]	Test if wide character is blank
iswcntrl	Test if wide character is control
iswctype	Test if some character classification
iswdigit	Test if wide character is digit (0–9)
iswgraph	Test if wide character is graphic
iswlower	Test if wide character is lowercase
iswprint	Test if wide character is printable
iswpunct	Test if wide character is punctuation

Name	*Purpose*
`iswspace`	Test if wide character is space
`iswupper`	Test if wide character is uppercase
`iswxdigit`	Test if wide character is hex digit
`towctrans`	Map a character
`towlower`	Produce lowercase version
`towupper`	Produce uppercase version
`wint_t`	Type to hold any character
`wctrans`	Convert mapping name to value
`wctrans_t`	Character mapping value
`wctype`	Convert classification name to value
`wctype_t`	Character classification value
`WEOF`	Wide character end-of-file indicator

See also ctype.h; future library directions.

`wctype_t`^{C95} A scalar type, defined in wctype.h, that is capable of holding values that represent locale-specific character classifications. *See also* `iswctype`; `wctype`.

`WEOF`^{C95} A macro, defined in wchar.h and wctype.h, that is a constant expression of type `wint_t` which is returned by numerous functions to indicate an end-of-file condition. *See also* `EOF`.

WG14 Known formally as ISO/IEC JTC 1 SC22/WG14, this standards committee is responsible for the production and maintenance of what is generally known as the ISO C standard. Its U.S. counterpart is J11.

WG15 Known formally as ISO/IEC JTC 1 SC22/WG15, this standards committee is responsible for the production and maintenance of POSIX, the Portable Operating System Interface for Computer Environments. Its U.S. counterpart is IEEE P1003.

WG21 Known formally as ISO/IEC JTC 1 SC22/WG21, this standards committee is responsible for the production and maintenance of what is generally known as the ISO C++ standard. Its U.S. counterpart is J16.

`while` A looping construct that evaluates its controlling expression before each iteration of the loop, like `for` and unlike `do/while`, which always executes at least once. A `while` construct can always be rewritten as a `for` construct and vice versa. It is used as follows:

```
while ( expression )
        statement
```

expression is evaluated. If it tests false, the body of the `while` statement is bypassed. If it tests true, *statement* is executed. The process is then repeated. The equivalent `for` construct is

```
for ( ; expression ; )
        statement
```

expression is a full expression.

white space One or more adjacent space, horizontal tab, vertical tab, form-feed, and new-line characters that separate adjacent source tokens. A comment may occur any place white space is permitted and is replaced by a single space character.

wide character[C89] *See* character, wide.

wide character constant[C89] *See* constant, character, wide.

wide string[C89] An array of `wchar_t` terminated by a null wide character. *See also* string; string literal; string literal, wide.

wide string literal[C89] *See* string literal, wide.

wide type *See* type, wide.

widening The conversion of an expression from a narrower to a wider type. For example, `char` and `short` expressions typically are promoted to type `int`, and `float` is promoted to `double`, when used in expressions such as function call arguments. (Standard C permits narrow types to be kept as such via the appropriate use of prototypes, although an implementation is not obliged to do so.)

`WINT_MAX`[C99] A macro, defined in stdint.h, that indicates the maximum value of the type `wint_t`. It expands to an integer constant expression suitable for use with a `#if` directive. If that type is a signed integer, `WINT_MAX` shall be no less than 32767; if the type is an unsigned integer, `WINT_MAX` shall be no less than 65535.

`WINT_MIN`[C99] A macro, defined in stdint.h, that indicates the minimum value of the type `wint_t`. It expands to an integer constant expression suitable for use with a `#if` directive. If that type is an unsigned integer, `WINT_MIN` shall be no greater than -32767; if the type is an unsigned integer, `WINT_MIN` shall be zero.

`wint_t`[C95] An integer type, defined in wchar.h and wctype.h, that is capable of holding any character from the extended character set, as well as at least one value that does not correspond to any member of the extended character set (where one such value is reserved for `WEOF`). *See also* `WINT_MAX`; `WINT_MIN`.

wmemchr[C95] A function that searches the first **n** wide characters of a wide string **s** for a wide character **c**.

```
#include <wchar.h>
wchar_t *wmemchr(const wchar_t *s, wchar_t c, size_t n);
```

If **c** is found, **wmemchr** returns a pointer to that location within **s**, otherwise, it returns **NULL**. *See also* **memchr**.

wmemcmp[C95] A function that compares **n** wide characters at the location pointed to by **s2** to the wide characters at the location pointed to by **s1**.

```
#include <wchar.h>
int wmemcmp(const wchar_t * s1, const wchar_t * s2,
    size_t n);
```

An integer less than, equal to, or greater than zero is returned to indicate whether the first **n** characters starting at **s1** have binary values less than, equal to, or greater than, respectively, those starting at **s2**. *See also* **memcmp**.

wmemcpy[C95] A function that copies **n** wide characters from the location pointed to by **s2** to the wide characters at the location pointed to by **s1**.

```
#include <wchar.h>
wchar_t *wmemcpy(wchar_t * restrict s1,
    const wchar_t * restrict s2, size_t n);
```

The value of **s1** is returned. If the objects located at **s1** and **s2** overlap, the behavior of **wmemcpy** is undefined. To copy overlapping objects, use **wmemmove** instead. *See also* **memcpy**.

wmemmove[C95] A function that copies **n** wide characters from the location pointed to by **s2** to the wide characters at the location pointed to by **s1**.

```
#include <wchar.h>
wchar_t *wmemmove(wchar_t *s1, const wchar_t *s2, size_t n);
```

The value of **s1** is returned. **wmemmove** works correctly even if the objects located at **s1** and **s2** overlap. If the objects are known to not overlap, it may be more efficient to use **wmemcpy** instead. *See also* **memmove**.

wmemset[C95] A function that sets the first **n** wide characters of the object pointed to by **s** to the value **c**.

```
#include <wchar.h>
wchar_t *wmemset(wchar_t *s, wchar_t c, size_t n);
```

The value returned is `s`. *See also* `memset`.

`wprintf`[C95] The wide character analog of `printf`.

```
#include <wchar.h>
int wprintf(const wchar_t * restrict format, ...);
```

`wscanf`[C95] The wide character analog of `scanf`.

```
#include <wchar.h>
int wscanf(const wchar_t * restrict format, ...);
```

◇ ◇ ◇

X

X3J11 *See* J11.

X3J11.1 A working group within X3J11 that defined a number of numerical extensions to C89. *See also* NCEG; J11.

X3J16 *See* J16.

X/Open A hardware and software consortium involved in operating system, language, and applications development tool standardization. This group became known as the Open Group.

`xor`^{C95} A macro, defined in iso646.h, that expands to the token `^`. It allows programmers using source character sets (such as ISO 646) that are missing certain characters necessary for writing C programs, to enter those characters using identifiers instead. Note that in C++, this name is a keyword.

`xor_eq`^{C95} A macro, defined in iso646.h, that expands to the token `^=`. It allows programmers using source character sets (such as ISO 646) that are missing certain characters necessary for writing C programs, to enter those characters using identifiers instead. Note that in C++, this name is a keyword.